W9-CNN-386

Mergers, Managers, and the Economy

Mergers, Managers, and the Economy

Samuel Richardson Reid
College of Business Administration
University of Illinois   Chicago Circle

McGraw-Hill Book Company
New York   St. Louis   San Francisco
Toronto   London   Sydney

Mergers, Managers, and the Economy

Library of Congress Catalog Card Number 68-25661

1234567890MAMM7543210698

To Helen and Our Children,
Rich, Peter, Meg, Lucy, and Joe

Preface

Art Buchwald is credited with having remarked that the whole country is in the process of merging itself into one giant firm. No doubt he was exaggerating his concern about the merger phenomenon, and yet in his usual perceptive way, he touched on a major problem which the United States has yet to solve.

As a measure of magnitude, it is estimated that during 1967, well over one thousand industrial firms, with assets valued at close to $12 billion, were absorbed into other firms, mostly the existing industrial giants in the economy. While power groups are forming and exerting pressures in all aspects of American life, the largest private power centers developing in big business are virtually ignored. This is a striking development, and one that has not been sufficiently recognized by government, the academic community, or the other groups one would expect to demonstrate legitimate concern about blocs of power of any type. Perhaps the main reason for this apathy is the lack of information, adequate theories, and empirical testing related to the merger phenomenon.

This book represents an attempt to correct the existing deficiencies in this important area of economics and business, which affects so many individuals and groups in society. The first part of the book is devoted to an examination of various facets of merger activity, the objective being to determine the relative role of each during the major merger waves in American economic history. The isolation of the various homogeneous and heterogeneous facets of merger serves as a frame of reference for the discussion in Chapter 6, "A Merger Mosaic."

The second part of the book contains some important and interesting economic and behavioral hypotheses concerning mergers and presents the results of the most extensive series of empirical tests conducted to date concerning the problem. Large samples of industrial and commercial banking firms were studied to determine whether the interests of managers and stockholders of merging firms are aligned, independent, or in conflict. In addition, the results of the first extensive tests designed to determine the relative performance of firms following the conglomerate strategy, as well as the other alternative growth methods, are presented. The results of other tests, which were formulated to isolate the effects of bank mergers and branching and which indicate the need for improved regulatory and legislative concern, are discussed.

The final two chapters, which make up Part 3 of the book, contain a number of public policy suggestions and recommendations formulated to revitalize and improve the market for capital assets and raise the level of managerial talent. The current free enterprise system in the United States needs renewal, and the proposals presented are designed to improve its structure and performance.

I owe a heavy debt to a multitude of scholars, most of whom are acknowledged in the text or the footnotes. The style of the book was dictated by my desire to present the thoughts of the many individuals who have contributed in various ways to the construction of the "merger mosaic" I present. It would be easy to paraphrase others' contributions, but I abhor this technique of presentation. I ask the reader to have patience with my eccentricities in this matter.

My personal debt of gratitude to numerous individuals and institutions is large. Among those who have helped to make this work possible and who deserve special mention are Dean Richard M. Cyert and Prof. Kalman J. Cohen of the Graduate School of Industrial Administration of Carnegie-Mellon University (formerly Carnegie Institute of Technology). The year I spent as a Ford Faculty Research Fellow at Carnegie provided me with the financial and intellectual support necessary to complete this work. In addition, Profs. William W. Tongue and Robert W. French of the Chicago Circle campus of the University of Illinois have contributed in various ways through their personal encouragement and support. I also owe a debt to Dr. Stanley E. Boyle of Virginia Polytechnic Institute, who some years ago, in one of his lectures, aroused my interest in this subject.

I should also like to express my appreciation to the staffs of the libraries and computing facilities at Carnegie-Mellon University and the University of Notre Dame, where much of the research and writing was conducted, and to Mrs. Rosemary Onderdonk of South Bend, Indiana, for typing the manuscript. A final word of gratitude must also be said for my wife and family, who bore so patiently the burden of my unusual writing habits, my frustrations, and the other problems I encountered in the course of working on this book.

Samuel Richardson Reid

Contents

Tables

TABLE

Charts

CHART

1

Introduction: The Merger Problem

The biggest merger wave ever to hit American economic life is rolling on unabated and virtually unnoticed except for an occasional article in the business press. This is remarkable in view of the fact that almost every other facet of life in the United States is continually magnified by the various communications media, as well as by various other assorted groups and organizations. As an example, the public is warned about air and water pollution, but a serious pollution in the economic structure of the nation is ignored. The activities and values of the "hippies," a relatively small group of people with virtually no economic power, receive considerably more attention than those of another subgroup in society which is a major power bloc—the managers of large business and financial firms. This is a curious fact of life in modern America, where Flower Power generates more attention, interest, and concern than Economic Power.[1]

Perhaps the current wave of mergers has been relatively neglected because the various communications media believe it is colorless; yet a closer examination reveals an economic phenomenon of considerable interest and dimension. This phenomenon is the subject of this book, which includes an extensive study of various facets of the merger problem as they relate to the current merger wave and to each of the previous waves in American economic history. An economic and behavioral theory of merger is developed, and the interesting results of the most extensive empirical testing of hypotheses concerning merger are presented and discussed. In addition, numerous public policy proposals are suggested which, if adopted, could make important contributions to American life in the future. In harmony with the title of the book, this introductory chapter will briefly examine mergers, managers, and the role of each in the economy.

Mergers

In making a case for increased recognition of the current wave of mergers in American business, the most pertinent starting point is an examination of the magnitude of the movement. There are three measures which can be examined briefly: the number of reported mergers, the estimated dollar amount of the assets involved in the mergers, and the effects of mergers upon concentration during the wave.

A Chicago-based consulting firm reported 2,975 mergers consummated during 1967 and has forecast that the number will climb to 3,250 in 1968.[2] Manufacturing as well as nonmanufacturing firms were included. The estimated manufacturing assets involved in mergers during 1966 amounted to nearly $7 billion, or about 25 percent of the total spent for new plant and equipment by American industrial firms. During the first ten months of 1967, it is estimated that close to $12 billion was spent on merger activity, with a reported $2 billion spent in the month of September alone.[3] One consequence of all this activity is the growing control of big business over the nation's manufacturing wealth. At the moment, the largest 200 corporations control close to 60 percent of these assets, up from 54.6 percent in 1962, and 46.7 percent in 1950. Each of these measures taken independently would be cause for concern; viewed collectively, they indicate a problem of even greater importance.

Measures of magnitude are admittedly concerned with only one dimension of a multidimensional occurrence. The more pertinent and colorful aspects of the problem relate to some of the peculiar characteristics of the current wave. These characteristics are naturally not independent of various environmental conditions which have an influence upon behavior. Prior to a discussion of the various environmental conditions present during the current wave and the behavior of the various groups associated with merger, a brief discussion of the main promoters in the current wave is in order.

Mergers and Managers

A distinguishing characteristic of the current wave is the major promotional role which has been assumed by the top executives of the firms involved. Contrast this development with the major role of the "outside" professional promoters at the turn of the century, when Charles W. ("Bet-a-Million") Gates, J. P. Morgan, Daniel Reid, and others played such a prominent role. A few of the "inside" management promoters in the current wave are also flamboyant personalities, which is reflected in the diversified empires they have built. Some of the promotional activities of these firms are reminiscent of developments in the turn-of-the-century wave and the wave in the late 1920s.[4] Even the annual report becomes a promotional device for these firms; a financial weekly observed: "The emphasis in the annual reports is conceptual—Ling-Temco-Vought in 1965 took as its theme 'Building Lasting Values' from the Golden Age of Greece. The report was full of urns, chariots and pictures of Socrates."[5]

While these firms are the exceptions, they are the activists providing an example and impetus in the current wave. One has the impression that it will not be long before these "go-go type" growth firms are distributing annual reports similar to some of the currently popular magazines, complete with a foldout displaying the "acquisition of the year" and with the assets and structure made up and exposed in a most favorable light. Some of their accounting methods are also something to behold; this will be discussed in more detail in Part 2.

The method of slotting the acquisitions into various divisions in the corporate structure and strategy has given rise to a new promotional nomenclature. The acquisition of a screw and bolt company provides a "synergistic steel fabricating resource base," or the acquisition of a motel chain provides a "leisure time division," where the acquiring firm "intends to be a leader in the coming travel revolution." Numerous examples could be cited as evidence that promotional flair is still very much alive in the current merger wave and did not die during the 1920s or earlier.

The managers of many merging firms tend to view mergers romantically and consider them an economic "love affair," complete with courtship, wedding plans, and eventually marriage. It is believed that natural partnerships are formed out of mutual respect and conceived in a sort of economic heaven. By contrast, there are others who admit to the possibility of economic compatibility but who are also aware of other facts of life concerning these events, such as economic rape (forcible and statutory), prostitution, divorce, bigamy, and so on. The record provides an array of various types of happenings when mergers are undertaken as a means of growth.

One type of economic assault related to mergers which is growing in popularity is the "tender offer"—a public solicitation to buy stock of another company. A weekly news magazine reports on these propositions as follows:

> Last year, no less than 107 companies were swallowed up through the tender route as against a mere eight in 1960. . . . Tender offers—predominantly for cash in an affluent age—have grown popular because they can be sprung swiftly at comparatively small risk and cost for the attacker, are less likely than ordinary mergers to run afoul of Government antitrust obstacles. . . . to keep the advantage of surprise, bidders like to pounce on Sundays (all it takes is a press release and an order for an ad in the next day's paper), when the management of the attacked company is unready to hit back.[6]

It is interesting to note that many economists in the past have equated management's preoccupation with mergers and monopoly with a quest for a "quiet life." We all know from even casual observation that this is basically nonsense. It is my opinion (based upon the empirical results presented in Part 2) that the managers of large publicly held merging firms are more interested in affluence, prestige, community and social recognition, and continuity of their established positions of power and control.

Mergers appear to contribute more to size maximization than profitability; thus they tend to serve managers' interests and goals, independent of those of the stockholders. The interests of the stockholders are seldom aligned by management with their own self-interests in the large publicly held merging firm. Instead, there appears to be an independence of interests, and at times even a conflict of interests. This is all quite contrary to traditional economic theory concerning assumed behavior and is a cause for legitimate concern about the efficiency of these types of investment decisions made by professional managers.

Mergers and the Economy

While managerial behavior is an important aspect of the merger problem, the behavior of other groups and individuals must be recognized also.

Legislators, regulators, economists, and others contribute in varying degrees by their behavior and their influence upon the various environments in the economy. These subjects are treated in more detail later in the book; however, a brief examination of some of the environmental factors should aid in isolating the problem.

The Economic Environment

The economic environment of each of the major waves of merger activity has been characterized by relative prosperity accompanied by a buoyant stock market. Mergers are a particular problem of prosperity, and realization of this fact by the monetary and fiscal authorities would be a major step forward in the eventual recognition and control of the problem.

Virtually all the large firms in the United States have responded to the favorable economic climate by engaging in mergers as a method of growth during the past decade. *Fortune* reported that 486 of the 500 largest firms in 1965 had used the merger route during the period 1955–1965.[7] This almost universal acceptance of this method of growth during these relatively prosperous years is proof that "good times" rather than "bad times" breed merger activity. Contrast the activity in recent years with that of the depressed periods following the first wave, at the turn of the century, and the second wave, of the late 1920s. The data are presented in Table 2.1 and Chart 2.1.

The Political Environment

The current merger wave has persisted through both Democratic and Republican administrations and can be considered a bipartisan development. A general lack of recognition of the problem, coupled with the absence of an acceptable theory of merger (economic or otherwise), has contributed to a lackadaisical attitude in both the executive and legislative branches of the government. In addition, the failure to recognize the close relationship between merger activity and relative prosperity has also contributed to the problem. Even if the merger-prosperity hypothesis were accepted, the problem of generating congressional action in the absence of a crisis, particularly during prosperous times, would be formidable indeed without the powerful lobbyists which the public lacks.

Perhaps one of the most distressing political factors at the moment in the United States is the growth of government by consensus, accompanied by a coalition between big business and big government. From the point of view of the general public, it is a distressing situation of major proportions. The countervailing power hypothesis, according to which big government serves as a check on big business and big labor, is dead. We can no longer be lulled into the belief that the exercise of private economic power will be held within reasonable bounds by the Federal government. At the moment, we can only hope that those capable of wielding economic power will be prudent and charitable.

It is also a great mistake to be so naïve that we underestimate the vast potential for power existing in many big business firms. A Sunday supplement recently pictured a group of six people, of whom three were well-known governors of states who have become public figures and three were top executives of large firms who are relatively unknown outside their usual circles. Each of the latter group has control over a considerably larger amount of expenditures than the familiar state governors, and each is directly and realistically accountable to far fewer people than the public officials. This is a sign of the times, for in 1965, one United States business firm had a net profit (after taxes) which was greater than the general revenue of forty-eight states, and its sales exceeded the gross national product of all except nine foreign countries. The use of merger has helped a growing number of other firms to reach giant proportions in recent years. There were fifty-eight industrial firms with over $1 billion of assets at the end of 1966, while eighty of the giants had sales of over $1 billion. Continued prosperity will add to the growing list of "economic Pinocchios," as they continue to gain control over larger percentages of the nation's productive capacity.

What are the political realities and ramifications of these developments? As a starter, big business has learned that conflict with government (regardless of the political party in control) is outdated and that "cooperation" is the name of the game and can result in contracts to provide a growing list of goods and services in numerous programs ranging from defense to poverty. There are also indications of an unusual crossover taking place between big business and the Democratic party which permits big business and big government to become bigger, each contributing to the growth of the other in various ways.

The political environment containing various elements of cooperation between big business and big government has caused the death of the countervailing power model in America under the existing administration. Those individuals and groups which are concerned about growing business power centers (and the role played by merger in the process) and growing government power centers face a bleak future indeed.

The Legal Environment

The basic problem is that the laws have not been designed to cope with the variety of diversification-type mergers which are such a major force in the current wave. The plain truth is that the antitrust laws are outdated as they exist, and have failed to effectively halt any of our previous waves of merger activity. Changes in the economic environment have contributed more to the demise of the previous waves than either the laws or the courts.

One of the most pertinent comments concerning the antitrust laws and the current situation in the United States was made by a staff member of a congressional subcommittee, Richard J. Barber; he said:

> The government's failure to take steps through antitrust action to block the growth of conglomerate firms and to deconcentrate those industries in which a few companies occupy commanding positions is attributable to a number of factors. First, the myth persists that enterprises become more efficient as they get bigger. To break up General Motors, General Electric, or U.S. Steel thus would run counter to the public interest by destroying their supposed efficiencies of scale. Similarly, while it may not be desirable to let two direct competitors merge, it is thought that there is nothing wrong—quite the contrary—with the formation via merger of a sprawling conglomerate. The entry of Litton or I.T.T. into a new market, so the argument goes, is likely to increase efficiency by bringing in aggressive management, adding capital, and letting in the fresh breezes of modern research. While these arguments are familiar to just about everyone who reads the *Wall Street Journal* or *Fortune,* let alone the *Harvard Business Review,* they are not generally backed up by empirical evidence.[8]

In Part 2 of this book, I present results obtained from the most extensive and varied empirical tests which have been conducted to date related to the performance characteristics of merging firms, both industrial and banking. The evidence strongly suggests that traditional economic theory is not sufficient adequately to explain or predict behavior related to merger activity. Inadequate theories and inadequate laws are interrelated, and both persist in the United States at the present time.

In addition, the nation's regulatory agencies have a generally lethargic and pathetic record; they have *not* adequately defined or protected the public's interest in discharging their responsibilities. This is a serious charge, but one that can be defended rather easily since the record is readily available. Banks have been permitted to consummate a considerable amount of horizontal mergers in recent years with the approval and aid of the various banking regulatory agencies. After the Justice Department stepped in and took belated action, there was a

Supreme Court decision striking down the mergers. The result was that a powerful banking lobby persuaded Congress to change the law in favor of the bankers. This was truly a remarkable feat and will be discussed in more detail in Chapter 11.

The record of all the regulatory agencies in regard to this problem has been dismal. The Interstate Commerce Commission has actually been encouraging mergers among the giant railroads. The history of the biggest merger of all, the New York Central–Pennsylvania Railroad combine, is a case in point. The merger was originally proposed to save two roads suffering from profit problems. Prior to the consummation of the merger, each of the roads achieved record profits independently, which actually eliminated the original need for the merger. Not all the railroads' problems can be solved through merger. Favorable outside environmental factors, such as prosperity, can result in major benefits, and imaginative internal management developments would be even more helpful. Following these approved mergers, it becomes more difficult to get a train as a passenger or a freight car as a shipper. Funds are being channeled into a variety of other enterprises, while these regulated businesses experiment in nonrailroad activity.

The Federal Communications Commission has twice approved the merger of the American Broadcasting Company, a communications network and the International Telephone and Telegraph Corporation, a growing industrial giant; this would create a giant with over $2.5 billion of assets. Only the most naïve, without financial acumen or common sense, could accept the arguments for this merger. Perhaps one of the reasons why the public is not well informed about the current merger wave is that the large and powerful communications networks are involved in varying degrees. The problem is serious as well as complicated, and not for the naïve and uninformed.

Legal and regulatory reform and renewal are long overdue concerning the merger problem; yet advocates of change must be realistically pessimistic after assessing the existing economic, political, and legal environments which play a major role in our economy. It is easy for one to become discouraged and believe that he is "blowin' in the wind," as Bob Dylan laments in the lyrics of one of his songs.

The Future and Change

My rather obvious pessimism concerning the merger problem and the future is well founded and sincere. Yet there is a faint ray of hope, though admittedly not a very formidable one, considering the task. This dim light of optimism is related to what Clark Kerr calls the "exaggerated generation." My observation of many young people, both on and off college campuses, leads me to believe that they are not going to be satisfied with the existing structure of the economic world which the older generations will turn over to them. To a vast number of these young people, "bigness" per se is not relevant. The giant firm, with all its power and its stumbling attempts to develop a "consciousness," is viewed realistically as the result of an economic, as well as a political and legal, "hang-up."

These young people have challenged and tested every tradition, convention, institution, and power group they have encountered. The home, church, school, city, and military establishment are only samples of institutions which have been subjected to their questions and challenges. In the next few years, as this generation reaches adulthood, its members will be making their first personal contacts with big government and big business power centers. The process and the outcome of these encounters should be interesting and worthy of close observation.

In order to survive, legislators in the future are going to have to deal with the problems and views of these young people, as well as with those of their older constituents. Change, perhaps drastic change, will prevail in the years ahead, and this fact alone is consoling to those in favor of economic institutional renewal.

The managers of big business power centers are going to discover eventually that eras of big government and big business cooperation may be short-lived and that survival may well depend upon bold and imaginative steps originating within the business community rather than outside it. While merger and conglomeration may appear innovative to some, they may well turn out to be regressive in the long run. There are other, more relevant alternatives available; some are suggested in Part 3, which deals with public policy recommendations. Other proposals, perhaps considerably better ones, have yet to be put forth by business executives. Yet, in my opinion, it would be in the self-interest of executives of large firms (as well as in the public interest) if they were to give a high priority to considerations aimed at restoring an improved market system in this country. One of the most interesting modern economic experiments which could be undertaken in the United States would be to *actually* try a competitive, free enterprise system, rather than merely paying homage to it while digesting chicken à la king at chamber of commerce luncheons.

NOTES

[1] There are numerous reasons why big business power escapes the public eye, not the least of which is the cost of advertising. A national business magazine was interested in my research and planned to do an article con-

cerning some research findings presented in this book. The young and enthusiastic writer called later to tell me rather frankly that the editor was afraid of the reactions of some large accounts. Another magazine, *Fortune,* which caters to big business, went so far as to send me a copy of an article they were planning to print which contained passages critical of big business mergers—it was not printed in the assigned issue and has yet to appear.

[2] See "Mergers Soared in '67, and Accelerated Pace Is Expected for '68," *The Wall Street Journal,* Jan. 3, 1968, p. 15.

[3] See "Merger Wave Rising Again, Month's Deals at $2 Billion," *Mergers and Acquisitions Monthly,* vol. 1, no. 10 p. 1, Oct. 31, 1967. This relatively new journal devoted to mergers presents a roster of merger deals which will eventually be a valuable research source. They omit transactions under $700,000 in their tabulations.

[4] See "The Takeover Titans," *Finance,* vol. 85, no. 8, pp. 8f., August, 1967.

[5] Barton M. Biggs, "Day of Reckoning?" *Barron's*, vol. 47, no. 14, p. 12, Apr. 3, 1967.

[6] "Mergers," *Time,* June 9, 1967, p. 101.

[7] See Carol J. Loomis, "The 500: A Decade of Growth," *Fortune,* July 15, 1966, p. 214.

[8] Richard J. Barber, "The New Partnership," *The New Republic,* vol. 155, nos. 6 and 7, p. 19, Aug. 13, 1966.

Part One ۞

Merger Waves, Merger Facets, and a Merger Mosaic

2

The Merger Pattern

Nearly seven decades of the twentieth century have passed. This has been a most interesting period in economic history, a span of years replete with significant and spectacular developments. One of the most powerful and fascinating of these developments, and yet one of the most widely misunderstood, has to do with the cyclical nature of corporate merger and acquisition activity.

Since the turn of the century, many scholars have examined and analyzed the merger phenomenon. Unfortunately, even at this late stage in American economic development, there is no generally accepted "theory of merger" which can be utilized as an effective instrument for decision-making and public policy considerations. This is not meant to imply that there is a shortage of theories (or opinions) about mergers. The supply is abundant and varied, reflecting the biases of the groups or individuals involved. A frequency distribution of views concerning the economic and social significance of mergers upon the economy would yield large numbers at the extremes.

Prior to isolating and examining the many facets related to mergers, it is important to recognize the pattern of merger activity in this country and the data problems inherent in an attempt to construct the pattern. The purpose of this chapter is to examine both of these subjects and to identify the major waves of merger activity, thus creating a frame of reference for the discussions in the chapters that follow.

Cyclical Aspects of Merger Activity: The Merger Waves

When one examines the time series of recorded mergers, either by number or by capitalizations involved (regardless of the series), one inescapable conclusion presents itself, that is, that merger activity has been highly episodic in its occurrence. The time series data on merger activity are presented in tabular form in Table 2.1 on the next page, and a visual presentation of the same data is below in Chart 2.1.

CHART 2.1 Firm disappearances by merger in the manufacturing and mining industries, 1895–1967. *Sources:* **Data for the period 1895–1920 are from Ralph L. Nelson,** *Merger Movements in American Industry: 1895–1956,* **Princeton, N.J.: Princeton University Press, 1959. Data for the period 1919–1967 are from the Federal Trade Commission (and Temporary National Economic Committee).**

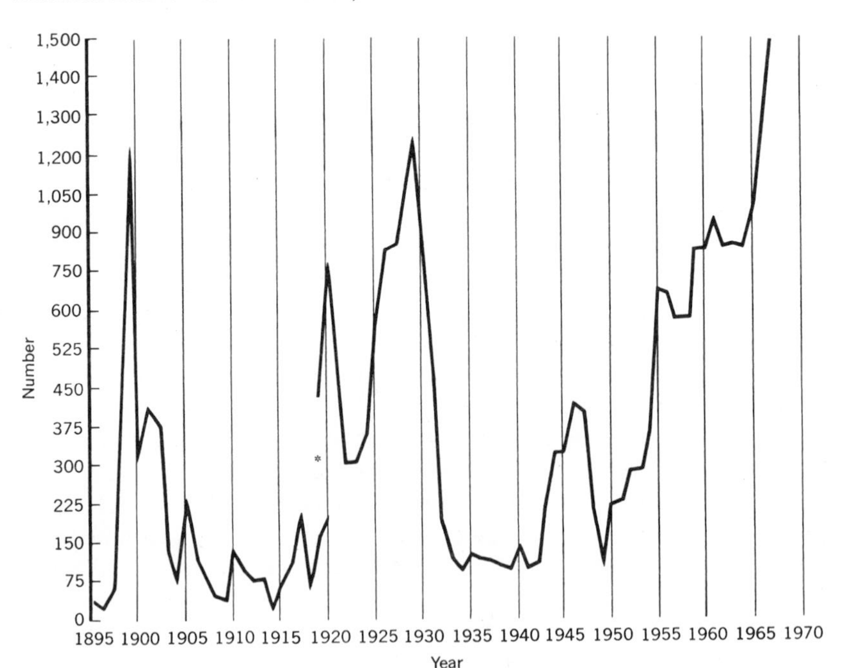

*The two series are not directly comparable.

TABLE 2.1 Number of Reported Mergers and Acquisitions in Manufacturing and Mining, 1895–1967

Year	*Annual Total*	*Year*	*Annual Total*	*Year*	*Annual Total*
1895	43	1920	206 (760)*	1945	333
1896	26	1921	487	1946	419
1897	69	1922	309	1947	404
1898	303	1923	311	1948	223
1899	1,208	1924	368	1949	126
1900	340	1925	554	1950	219
1901	423	1926	856	1951	235
1902	379	1927	870	1952	288
1903	142	1928	1,058	1953	295
1904	79	1929	1,245	1954	387
1905	226	1930	799	1955	683
1906	128	1931	464	1956	673
1907	87	1932	203	1957	585
1908	50	1933	120	1958	589
1909	49	1934	101	1959	835
1910	142	1935	130	1960	844
1911	103	1936	126	1961	954
1912	82	1937	124	1962	853
1913	85	1938	110	1963	861
1914	39	1939	87	1964	854
1915	71	1940	140	1965	1,008
1916	117	1941	111	1966	995
1917	195	1942	118	1967	1,496*
1918	71	1943	213		
1919	171 (438)*	1944	324		

* Not directly comparable.

Sources: Ralph L. Nelson, *Merger Movements in American Industry: 1895–1956,* Princeton, N.J.: Princeton University Press, 1959, p. 37; Federal Trade Commission, *Report on Corporate Mergers and Acquisitions,* 1955; and news release by the FTC dated Mar. 18, 1968.

If a merger wave is defined as a period of time characterized by relatively large numbers of mergers reported simultaneously in many industries and lines of economic activity, then three distinct and cyclical waves are discernible.[1] While there may be some minor differences among the students of mergers over the beginning and ending years of each wave, the peaks are evident whether one considers the absolute number of mergers or merger capitalizations.[2]

The three distinct waves of merger activity are (1) the turn-of-the-century merger wave, (2) the late-1920s merger wave, and (3) the current merger wave, which began in the 1950s and has continued into the present. The first two waves have been universally recognized in the literature, while the current wave has received scant attention. Perhaps this is to be expected, since interest in the two previous waves was not generated until years after the peaks of activity had been recorded. Some economists, for example, were still analyzing the turn-of-the-century wave while the second wave was being recorded during the 1920s.

The magnitude of merger waves can be determined in other ways than by an accounting of the number of reported mergers. Nelson computed the merger capitalizations for the period 1895–1920; these data are presented in Table 2.2.[3] Unfortunately, no comparable data exist for the time period since 1920. It is evident that the first wave peaked in 1899, whether one uses the absolute number of mergers, as presented in Table 2.1, or the merger capitalizations, as reported in Table 2.2.

TABLE 2.2 Merger Capitalizations, 1895–1920 (in Millions of Dollars)

Year	*Merger Capitalizations*	*Year*	*Merger Capitalizations*
1895	40.8	1908	187.6
1896	24.7	1909	89.1
1897	119.7	1910	257.0
1898	650.6	1911	210.5
1899	2,262.7	1912	322.4
1900	442.4	1913	175.6
1901	2,052.9	1914	159.6
1902	910.8	1915	158.4
1903	297.6	1916	470.0
1904	110.5	1917	678.7
1905	243.0	1918	254.2
1906	377.8	1919	981.7
1907	184.8	1920	1,088.6

Source: Ralph L. Nelson, *Merger Movements in American Industry: 1895–1956,* Princeton, N.J.: Princeton University Press, 1959, p . 37.

As a means of determining the relative magnitude of the current wave of merger activity, an estimate of the total considerations paid in mergers and acquisitions for the period 1948–1967 is presented in Table 2.3.[4] These data should dispel any doubt about the propriety of referring to the current merger movement as a major wave of merger activity. Whether judging by known considerations paid or estimated considerations paid, it is evident that many billions of dollars are involved. Close to a thousand mining and industrial firms disappeared through merger during 1965 and 1966, and it is estimated that this amount will be exceeded during 1967. Not only is there a large number of mergers, but the mergers include a number of large firms on both the buying and selling sides in the transactions. For example, during 1965, Pure Oil (assets: $750 million), Richfield Oil (assets: $500 million), Consolidation Coal (assets: $465 million), and ABC-Paramount (assets: $263 million) were acquired by Union Oil, Atlantic Refining, Continental Oil, and IT&T, respectively.

Another method of determining the relative magnitude and importance of current merger activity is to compare the estimated considerations paid for mergers with expenditures for new plant and equipment

TABLE 2.3 Acquisition of Manufacturing and Mining Firms with Assets of $10 Million and Over and Estimated Considerations Paid, 1948–1967

Year	*No. of Firms Acquired (Over 10 Million)*	*Considerations Paid**	*No. of Firms Acquired (Under 10 Million)*	*Estimated Consideration Paid**	*Estimated Total Considerations Paid**
1948	4	64.6	219	657.0	721.6
1949	5	66.8	121	363.0	429.8
1950	4	154.8	215	645.0	799.8
1951	9	201.4	226	678.0	879.4
1952	13	326.5	275	825.0	1,151.5
1953	23	678.6	272	816.0	1,494.6
1954	36	1,450.2	351	1,053.0	2,503.2
1955	68	2,156.0	615	1,845.0	4,001.0
1956	59	2,069.6	614	1,842.0	3,911.6
1957	49	1,458.9	536	1,608.0	3,066.9
1958	39	1,118.5	550	1,650.0	2,768.5
1959	63	1,944.1	772	2,316.0	4,260.1
1960	62	1,708.3	782	2,346.0	4,054.3
1961	60	2,144.6	894	2,682.0	4,826.6
1962	71	2,179.7	782	2,346.0	4,525.7
1963	65	2,791.0	796	2,388.0	5,179.0
1964	90	2,784.3	764	2,292.0	5,176.3
1965	91	3,841.1	917	2,751.0	6,592.1
1966	98	4,006.2	897	2,691.0	6,697.2
1967	155	79,69.3	1,341	4,023.0	11,992.3
Total	1064	$39,114.5	11,939	$35,817.0	$74,931.5

* In millions of dollars.

Source: Data on the number of firms with assets of $10 million and over and considerations paid for these firms were obtained from a news release by the FTC dated Feb. 11, 1966. I then arrived at the number of acquired firms with assets of less than $10 million by subtracting the number of firms with $10 million and over of assets from the total number of acquisitions as presented in Table 2.1. This number was then multiplied by an arbitrary number of $3 million. This is a rough estimate of the average consideration paid, which is probably not too different from the actual figures. Admittedly, using a constant number as the average figure for the entire time period probably results in understating some years and overstating others. Most likely, the latter part of the series, when the largest number of acquisitions were recorded, is understated. I present these data with certain reservations; however, they should give a better perspective of the magnitude of the merger movement. Data for 1966 and 1967 were obtained from news releases from the FTC dated Feb. 24, 1967, and Mar. 18, 1968. These recent releases reveal some minor changes in the data as originally reported; however, the differences are slight and have little effect upon the totals reported.

TABLE 2.4 Expenditures for New Plant and Equipment by Manufacturing and Mining Firms and Estimated Merger Expenditures, 1950–1967

	*Expenditures for New Plant and Equipment**				
Year	*Manufac-turing Firms*	*Mining Firms*	*Total*	*Estimated Total Merger Expenditures**	*%*
1950	7.49	0.71	8.20	0.80	0.10
1951	10.85	0.93	11.78	0.88	0.07
1952	11.63	0.98	12.61	1.15	0.09
1953	11.91	0.99	12.90	1.49	0.12
1954	11.04	0.98	12.02	2.50	0.20
1955	11.44	0.96	12.40	4.00	0.32
1956	14.95	1.24	16.19	3.91	0.24
1957	15.96	1.24	17.20	3.07	0.18
1958	11.43	0.94	12.37	2.77	0.22
1959	12.07	0.99	13.06	4.26	0.33
1960	14.48	0.99	15.47	4.05	0.26
1961	13.68	0.98	14.66	4.83	0.33
1962	14.68	1.08	15.76	4.53	0.29
1963	15.69	1.04	16.73	5.18	0.31
1964	18.58	1.19	19.77	5.18	0.26
1965	22.45	1.30	23.75	6.59	0.29
1966	26.99	1.47	28.46	6.70	0.24
1967	26.55†	1.50†	28.05†	12.00	0.43

* In billions of dollars. Annual total is the sum of unadjusted expenditures.
† Estimate based on anticipated capital expenditures as reported by business in late October and November, 1967.

Sources: Council of Economic Advisers, *Economic Indicators,* June, 1966, p. 9, for the years 1953 to 1965; and Council of Economic Advisers, *Economic Indicators,* January, 1958, p. 10, for the years 1950 to 1952. Estimated merger expenditures are from Table 2.3. Data for 1966 and 1967 are from Council of Economic Advisers, *Economic Indicators,* February, 1968, p. 9.

by industrial and mining firms. These data are presented and compared in Table 2.4, and while the comparison is not exact, it is possible to obtain a rough idea of the rather large role of merger in the investment decisions of these firms. An estimated $74 billion has changed hands as a result of mergers since 1950, and the majority of this amount was recorded in the period from 1955 to the present. The data suggest that merger expenditures are a significant aspect of business "investment" spending, running as high as one-third of the expenditures for new plant and equipment. Admittedly, the data are not exact, and yet they are suggestive of the relative importance of merger activity.

A Recent Merger Ripple

An upturn in merger activity during and immediately following World War II caused some authors erroneously to consider this period a major merger wave,[5] and some interesting studies were generated by the upswing in mergers during the period 1940–1947. Perhaps the most widely quoted study was that done by the Tax Research Program group at Harvard.[6] Another extensive study of this period was undertaken by the Federal Trade Commission.[7] In many respects, this ripple of merger activity during the period 1940–1947 has received more attention than the current wave of mergers.

Both of these studies—the Butters, Lintner, and Cary study and the FTC study—are interesting, particularly the one by the Harvard group. However, since the period they studied represented the war years and immediate postwar period as well as a period of a relatively small amount of merger activity, their findings must be appropriately discounted.[8] Markham discussed the period 1940–1947 in a paper published over a decade ago, and he concluded:

> When viewed against these overriding forces, some doubt is cast upon the propriety of characterizing the 1940–1947 mergers as a "merger movement." Unfortunately, the English language provides us with no descriptive term for movements of a diminutive sort. But if previous (and future) merger movements are still to be associated with waves of mergers, the 1940–1947 movement might be viewed as a *ripple* [italics supplied].[9]

Another period, extending from the post-World War II years to 1955, has received special treatment as a merger wave.[10] While these were years of increasing activity, future students of the current wave will most likely consider the starting point to be the beginning of the 1950s or perhaps the middle of that decade, depending upon the magnitude of the current wave, which shows no signs of abating at the present time.

Many of the more recent writers have emphasized the distinctive aspects of each major merger wave, suggesting that each wave has had unusual characteristics peculiar to it.[11] While this is true, it is also important and imperative to determine the reasons for the differences as well as the possible existence of similarities. Since the major waves of mergers can be distinguished (despite the shortcomings of the data), the remainder of Part 1 will be devoted to an analysis of the relevant facets and their relationships to each wave.

Merger Data

Frequently the reason cited for the lack of empirical testing on the merger problem is the lack of complete data about mergers and their occurrence. A common problem encountered by all scientists, particularly social scientists, is that the data are incomplete; yet the failure to state hypotheses and test them by empirical research cannot be blamed entirely on lack of complete data. Markham recognized this when he observed: "In the face of incomplete data, economists might be expected to behave a little like the six blind men of Indostan and develop entirely different apperceptions about something big—whether it be elephants or mergers. The data, however, are not so faulty as this. The principal causes of divergent conclusions on mergers lie elsewhere."[12]

The problem of determining the timing and magnitude of merger activity centers around the validity and accuracy of the number of reported mergers. As one might expect, during the years when mergers were first being recorded, the problem was related to the definition of a "merger." This difficulty led to an inevitable result—researchers examining the same time period calculated different totals. Unfortunately, a single agency, using set definitions and techniques to collect comparable data for the complete time series has never existed.

Data for the first merger wave at the turn of the century are a product of truncated sampling and are not comparable with those of later years. Annual merger series for this period have been compiled by Moody, Conant, Watkins, the Bureau of the Census, and Nelson.[13] Prior to the Nelson study there was a void in the data from 1904 to 1919; however, this was corrected when he compiled a new series extending from 1895 to 1920. Thorp compiled a list of mergers for the period 1919–1939 from the daily reports of the Standard Statistics Company.[14] The FTC has since extended the Thorp series of manufacturing and mining mergers utilizing reports made by Moody's Investors Service and the Standard and Poors Company for the period from 1940 to the present.[15] Thus, there are two series—the Nelson 1895–1920 series and the Thorp-FTC series, extending from 1919 to the present—which, while not comparable, can at least give indications of trends in merger activity.

Much of the criticism of present recording methods used by the FTC is centered around the fact that mergers involving small firms are not likely to be reported. Additional doubt has been expressed about the reliability of the statistics involving some large firms and also certain industries.[16] Admittedly, this is a shortcoming of the series since one may be dealing with only the upper portion of the frequency distribution of mergers. However, it is this portion that generally contains a disproportionately large share of mergers that have resulted in increases in market control, in the creation of conglomerate firms, or in "oligopoly-hedging" (the attempt by a firm to eliminate smaller competitors, either actual or potential, in order to maintain or strengthen its oligopolistic position). Actually, the omission of mergers involving small firms is a concern only because the result would be an understatement of the magnitude of the movement. A merger involving small firms would make but a small dent in our economic structure and the pattern of competition. Thus, it is the aggregate of firms that are large enough to be listed in the financial manuals and whose mergers are reported in the financial journals that receive primary attention.[17] Despite these shortcomings, it is possible to discern major trends in merger activity.[18]

Perhaps a more serious problem in attempting to construct a theory of merger is that related to the research methodology employed and the inferences drawn from the *limited* uses of data, or from no data at all. The literature on mergers is replete with case studies and armchair theorizing, with an extremely limited amount of empirical research. It is not surprising that there is a considerable amount of confusion in the field, which frequently is compounded by the reporting of limited and useless findings. Obviously, Markham encountered this problem also; he commented: "It was stated earlier that researchers on mergers have tended to act like the six blind men of Indostan—on examining different parts they reach different conclusions about the whole."[19]

In addition to problems related to the recording of mergers (the "numbers game"), there are other serious data problems. We do not know the pertinent financial data about most of the acquired firms, such as assets, market price of stock (if traded), profits, and sales volume. Further serious research problems result from the practice of reporting financial results in consolidated form, which makes it virtually impossible to isolate the results and evaluate the performances of many consummated mergers. Data problems thus plague the researcher, the investor, the financial analyst, the government official, and other interested individuals and groups concerned with the merger problem.

Some Facets of Merger Activity

Since mergers are multidimensional economic events, they naturally possess a number of facets which are of interest to the observers of these combinations. Part 1 of this book is devoted to an examination of the various facets of merger in the setting of each wave of activity, as identified previously in this chapter. A brief examination of each facet of merger should help in the development of a frame of reference which will be useful in reading the next three chapters as well as in developing an understanding of the various dimensions of the topic. The various facets related to merger activity will be identified in this section.

The Magnitude of the Movement

The various shortcomings of the data concerning mergers and merger activity have already been discussed in this chapter. Despite these problems, it is possible to examine the time period during which each of the major waves occurred and to determine the relative magnitude of the movement in terms of reported *numbers* of mergers, as well as to make an approximate calculation of the assets involved in the activity. Even if the comparable data are not precise, our understanding of the relative importance of the merger waves is improved somewhat in the process.

Merger Forms and Types

The term "merger" is used to describe a number of different types and forms of combination activity, ranging from the consolidation of 100 or more firms, at one extreme, to the acquisition of one firm by another in the same basic industry or in completely unrelated lines of business activity, at the other.

There are two general types of classification for mergers; one relates to the *form* of the particular merger (i.e., whether it is a consolidation of firms or an acquisition of one firm by another), and the other relates to the *type* of merger, which depends upon the industrial or commercial relationship of the firms involved.

While mergers may take a number of various legal forms, they are usually referred to as either "consolidations" or "acquisitions." A merger-consolidation is an amalgamation or fusion of two or more firms into a new firm with a different capital structure. It is generally considered the "many-at-once" form of merger. The merger-acquisition may be viewed as the "one-at-a-time" form of merger; generally a larger firm absorbs a smaller firm. The larger, acquiring firm retains its identity and accomplishes the merger-acquisition merely by expanding its own capitalization or by using cash reserves, if available for the purpose.[20]

Classifying mergers by the industrial or commercial relationships of the firms involved is largely a matter of definitions. A *horizontal merger* is considered one involving firms which are engaged principally in the same industry.[21] An example would be the combination of two firms in the cement industry. There may be geographical diversification aspects to horizontal mergers when firms making the same products are located in and serve different markets. A *vertical merger* is consummated either to provide facilities to supply goods or services that were formerly purchased (such as an automobile manufacturer buying a tire producer) or to provide facilities to process or distribute goods at different levels in the distribution process (such as a shoe manufacturer buying a chain of retail shoe stores). A *circular merger* involves product extension; that is, it provides a firm with nonsimilar products or services that utilize the same distribution channels.[22] An example would be a razor manufacturer buying a ball-point pen maker, with both products being distributed in the same type of retail outlets. A *conglomerate merger* is the fusion of firms with no apparent similarities in producing or marketing activities (such as a mining company buying an ice-cream producer).[23]

Mergers and Concentration

The word "concentration" as used in economics refers to the share of an economic activity accounted for by a small group of firms performing a large share of that activity. Measures of concentration have been based on such indicators of economic activity as sales, total assets, profits, income generated, employment, and value added by manufacture.[24] Concentration may be examined for the economy as a whole; for particular industries, geographical areas, or markets; and for individual products or services.

Mergers have been linked with studies of concentration since they are generally considered to be a facilitating cause of increased levels of concentration. The most appropriate method of determining the effects of merger waves upon the levels of concentration would be to measure the level of concentration at the beginning and end of each wave and determine the resulting change in concentration. Ideally, this should be done for the economy as a whole and for each subgroup in the economy (various industries, utilities, banks, etc.). Unfortunately, evidence of this type has not been accumulated in a systematic way for each wave. However, a considerable amount of time and energy has been expended on various concentration studies over the years, which contribute some evidence about the relative impact of the various waves upon industrial structure. Each merger wave will be examined separately with the objective of determining whether the mergers consummated during these periods of increased activity have contributed to increased concentration in American industry.

The Promoters of Mergers

A merger is an economic happening which can assume an array of alternative forms, types, sizes, and shapes. Since it is so nonstandardized, there can be a wide variance in the difficulty of the task of consummating the transaction. Certainly, complications could be compounded when consummating a consolidation composed of a large number of independent firms, a situation conspicuous at the turn of the century. Contrast this with the relative simplicity of writing a corporate check to consume a small but comely competitor or an attractive firm in another industry. Regardless of the relative complexity inherent to the transaction, there is always an initiator—the merger *promoter.* In this book, the various promoters will be identified and their role during each of the merger waves discussed.

An amusing approach to a description of the merger process appeared in the opening paragraphs of a publication of the Federal Reserve Bank of Philadelphia:

> Corporations marry for money. Simon Pure, unabashed gold-digging is the sole motive behind every business merger. How they meet is a matter of chance or choice. Sometimes the marriage is the culmination of a long and mutually profitable business relationship; in other instances, they may meet on a stratoliner, or a golf course, or at a convention. Then, too, some mergers are arranged by the John Aldens of business; some would-be brides even put an ad in the newspapers where they put their best foot forward, so to speak with the objective—matrimony. Corporate mores sanction initial advances by the bride.
>
> The groom is usually bigger and often, although not always, older, worldlier, and wealthier. Reliable records and ratings on substance and prenuptial debts outstanding are readily available to both parties upon consulting the well-known financial services. Debutantes are not necessarily the most attractive. While they may have good corporate configuration and a glint of profit in their eyes, they must compete with their older sisters of demonstrated profitability and good connections in the business world.[25]

This rather casual approach to a serious and complicated problem is somewhat indicative of the attitude of the Federal Reserve System and the regulatory agencies (in general) concerning the merger problem. The behavior and record of the bank regulatory agencies will be analyzed in more detail in later chapters. However, the implication that corporations "marry for money" raises a number of related questions concerning money and its distribution among various interested groups, including the promoters of these economic marriages as well as the stockholders and others. The major promoters active in each wave of merger activity (those who are instrumental in arranging the event) will be identified to determine the changes which have occurred over the years as well as the reasons for the changes.

Mergers and Growth of Firms

Discussing the role of mergers in the absolute growth of firms is related to, yet quite different from, discussing mergers and monopoly or oligopoly or concentration caused by mergers. In handling the latter problem, we must deal with the proportions of "overall" industry or of particular industries and markets supplied by individual firms or groups of firms. The purpose of including this facet is to examine the role and the impact of mergers upon the absolute growth rate of firms. Stigler has emphasized the importance of this development: "The growth of individual firms to great size through merger with rivals is an outstanding development of modern economic history."[26]

It appears rather obvious that when one firm acquires another firm, it will grow instantaneously in absolute size. One possible exception could arise when measuring total assets, if the acquiring firm purchases the acquired firm for cash and then the surviving firm simply reduces liquid assets and increases fixed assets by a corresponding amount. However, the other size variables will increase, such as sales volume, number of employees, etc., when "going concerns" are combined by either consolidation or acquisition.

The determination of the relative growth of a firm that is induced by the use of merger and by internal growth is a difficult task.[27] In one widely quoted study designed to measure the role of merger in the growth of a sample of large firms, made by Weston,[28] the conclusion regarding the role of mergers upon the absolute size of firms is that "for only a small proportion of the firms does external growth represent a high percentage of total growth. The direct effect of merger on the absolute size of large firms appears to have been small."[29] The impression created by the Weston study is that mergers do not play an important role in the growth of firms. Some of the shortcomings of the Weston study have been discussed by Nutter and Stigler.[30] Perhaps the most noticeable shortcoming of the Weston study (in addition to those discussed by Nutter and Stigler) has to do with the time period covered, which is "from roughly the turn of the century through 1948."[31] The study covers the period from the end of the first merger wave, when many firms had completed their merger activity, to 1948, a span of time that included two world wars and the Great Depression, when there were relatively few mergers. Hence, it would not be safe to conclude on the basis of Weston's evidence that mergers do not now play a major role in the growth of many firms. The problem here is similar to that encountered with the concentration studies that used interwave time periods; that is, the effects of mergers during merger waves are not isolated. Since we are basically examining merger waves and the resultant growth of firms in these restricted periods of time, we shall examine the studies concerned with the absolute growth of firms in these time periods.

The Relative Success of Mergers

The question of determining the degree of "success" of mergers is important to a variety of interested individuals and groups, including businessmen, stockholders, government officials, and others such as employees, union leaders, suppliers, and customers. A fact which is almost universally overlooked is that much of the evidence resulting from studies designed to determine the success of mergers casts doubt on whether success has in fact been realized by a majority of merging firms. This rather basic fact concerning mergers has not been sufficiently recognized and appreciated in business, academic, and government circles. This is particularly distressing since a new generation of young people (who either have entered the managerial ranks or are studying in academic institutions with the purpose of becoming managers) have, for the most part, been exposed to a distorted picture concerning the relative success of mergers. The examples of mergers presented in the textbooks as case studies generally concern the few well-known successful firms. Perhaps this is natural, since the concept of "failure" has very limited acceptance among students and young people, to say the least. The situation has not changed much since Markham recognized this development more than a decade ago; he said:

> Recent textbooks on business finance indicate a widely-held view that mergers have come about largely to reduce the cost of production, distribution, administration, etc.; and where the authors of such texts pass judgment on the social significance of mergers, the reader is frequently more impressed with their desirable than their undesirable consequences.[32]

This is a most unfortunate and regrettable development since if change is to occur, it most likely will have to originate with those people who are willing to take the initiative to cause change, and these are precisely the people who have not been properly exposed to the problem. Today's college students want answers, and they are not content with many ideas and institutions unless they are proved superior to the alternatives. With this consideration in mind, we shall examine the evidence available from the various studies made either after merger waves or during them which were designed to determine the relative success of mergers.

Problems of Defining Success Every author who has attempted to measure the relative success and failure of mergers has been faced with the problem of defining a successful merger. Dewing, a widely quoted student of the consolidations in the first merger wave, discussed the problem as follows:

> The term "success," when applied to a business, may mean a variety of things. A successful business may be one which is conducted so economically that the commodities it deals in reach the ultimate consumer at a low price relative to the competitive cost of production. It may be one that endures through a longer period of time. It may be one that grows in mere size without reference to the relative yield to invested capital or to business ability. And finally it means—in fact usually does—a business that yields a relatively large profit to the managers. In the end all these usages are reducible to the last.[33]

Dewing's emphasis on profitability led him to establish the following criteria for determining whether or not a consolidation is successful:

> I shall assume that an industrial combination in order to be called successful, should yield a larger net profit than the sum of the net profits of the component elements that entered the combination. This is our first criterion. A second assumption will be that the combination should yield a net profit at least approximately equal to what its proponents, including its bankers, owners, and promoters, estimated it would yield. And lastly it must be assumed that the average net earnings over a considerable period of time—say ten years—should show a conspicuous increase over the net earnings prior to the combination and during its first year. In other words, there must be a sustained increase.[34]

All three of Dewing's criteria for determining whether a merger is successful are related to the realization and sustainability of net profits. The Dewing criteria were not without critics, however, and one of them, Shaw Livermore, made the following observation concerning these criteria:

> It would be nearly as logical to test the careers of political leaders solely by their campaign promises! His second yardstick *(ibid.)*, the earnings of constituent units *versus* their earnings as a consolidated entity, might be used quite as well to prove that certain earlier years were more prosperous in various lines of industry than the later years when consolidations were in operation.[35]

Both Livermore and Mead avoided the problem of defining "success" in their studies. The problem was discussed by Livermore, but he did not formulate a clear test. He disclosed that he studied "earnings on capitalization" and "dividend records and company histories," but he gave no indication of how these were used to determine whether a merger was a success or a failure.[36]

Some other studies have appeared in the post–World War II period. Edith Penrose did not test any hypotheses regarding mergers and success, but in theorizing about mergers and the growth of firms, she defined a "successful merger" as follows: "From our point of view a merger is 'successful' if it creates a larger industrial organization than before and one that survives and provides a basis for future growth. But even on this criterion there have been many failures."[37]

My doctoral dissertation compared the performance of a sample of firms that merged during the period 1950–1959 with the "average" firm in their industry. The relative performance of five variables was examined: growth of sales, assets, net profits, earnings on common stock, and market price of common stock.[38] Bossons, Cohen, and I used a sample of 478 large firms and compared the results of merging and nonmerging firms by merger intensity groups and the results of these groups of firms within their basic industries for the period 1951–1961. The results of this empirical study of industrial and mining firms, as well as those of other studies by Cohen and me of commercial banks, will be presented later. These studies cast serious doubt on the question of whether the stockholders of merging firms have (on the average) benefited from this activity.

Another study by Kelly compared the performance of twenty merging firms for five years prior to a major merger with their performance for five years after the merger.[39] The merging firms were compared with a "similar" firm with little or no merger activity to determine relative performance. Success was determined by comparing the performance of matched pairs of firms in similar industries.

Another interesting study was undertaken by Johan Bjorksten, a management consultant, who kept a record of known merger failures which were reported in the press.[40] Naturally, many failures are not reported; however, the chronicles of *known* failures are suggestive. Bjorksten made no attempt to measure success in this study.

Thus, the concepts of what constitutes a successful merger are many and varied. Growth in net profits is a criterion, or success can be judged on the basis of a subjective study of earnings, dividend records, and company history. Other criteria include increase in size, providing a base for future growth, and the amount of relative benefits accruing to interested groups.

Mergers and Antitrust

Large segments of the American public believe that the antitrust laws are the bulwark of an economy in which competition is considered necessary (as well as important) and in which concentration is not necessarily viewed with favor. The combination of firms through merger is one method of eliminating either a direct competitor or a potential competitor if a firm is expanding to diversify into a different area. Thus, merger must be considered to be anticompetitive unless it can be proved that in some way competition has been improved by the combination of firms. Proponents of mergers often state that mergers permit firms to become more effective competitors; however, we have no empirical evidence that this result has actually occurred except in isolated case studies which are not in themselves conclusive. The competition to which I am referring is naturally price competition, and not the nonprice competition waged on advertising gimmicks, games, packaging, and the like.

Each of the various antitrust laws specifically mentions mergers and their potential consequences; yet it is a curious fact of economic life that each of the major waves of mergers has developed following the passage of an antitrust law. There is no doubt that these laws have influenced the shape and scope of the movements, and yet they have not resulted in the abandonment of this external method of growth. The record clearly shows that the turn-of-the-century wave developed in the decade following the passage of the Sherman Act in 1890; the late-1920s wave was recorded following the passage of the Clayton Act and the Federal Trade Commission Act in 1914; and the current wave developed following the passage of the so-called antimerger amendment to the Clayton Act in 1950. Some of the reasons for this development will be discussed in more detail in the chapters that follow.

The Environment for Mergers

The time series data on merger activity reveal that mergers are not necessarily randomized events and that they have definite cyclical characteristics. Consequently, it becomes important to determine the environmental factors which contribute to this cyclical pattern.

Unfortunately, the development of a theory of merger has been hampered by a considerable amount of confusion which has been generated (and compounded) over the years concerning the relative roles of various factors that have a causal effect in the development of major waves of activity. The basis for much of the confusion is that the environmental conditions and the motivations for merger are seldom analyzed separately.

The rather obvious cyclical pattern of merger activity should be noticeable even to the casual observer. Yet Weston, one of the leaders in merger research, has reported that mergers do not appear to exhibit cyclical characteristics; he said:

> The timing of mergers does not appear to exhibit cyclical characteristics. Certainly the periodicity of the movements does not bear similarity to the widely familiar reference cycles. The changed relationship between mergers and stock prices and the (statistically) tenuous relationship between mergers and the other variables indicate the absence of a mechanism producing cyclical patterns in merger activity. The possibility of long waves in mergers also seems controverted by the absence of systematic forces operating to produce the variations in merger activity which did take place. The three major merger movements which have been described seem to be accounted for in each case by a special combination of factors. *Any factors common to the different periods have operated with considerably different force and effect at the different times* [italics supplied].[41]

The shortcoming of this finding by Weston is that he observed the time period 1919–1941, which included only the second merger wave, as well as a span of years preceding and following the wars. Markham, in his widely quoted article, compounded the confusion resulting from the Weston study when he relied upon Weston's findings for this period, which led him to conclude that ". . . the widely expressed view that mergers are causally connected with general economic fluctuations is only weakly supported by the available statistical data."[42]

Adams, another respected industrial organization economist, discounts the cyclical aspects of merger activity and focuses upon the role of government; he said:

> It seems to me that further investigation may well reveal that mergers are not inevitable, either technologically or economically; that they are not merely the product of promoters' dreams and rising stock prices; but rather that their occurrence is intimately connected and inextricably intertwined with the permissive, protective, or promotive policies of government toward the monopolization of the economy.[43]

Adams's recognition of the role of government is interesting. It is possible for government to play a direct and an indirect role in creating an environment conducive to merger activity. If mergers are a product of prosperous times and if the prosperity is promoted by the government, the role of the government could be more indirect than an outright promotion of monopolization of the economy through lax enforcement of the antitrust laws and selective government procurement policies.

In developing a theory of merger activity, it will be helpful to concentrate upon the environmental factors present during the major waves of mergers. The determination of the role of prosperity as related to mergers has important public policy considerations which cannot be overlooked. Markham recognized this fact when he said: ". . . if it can be clearly demonstrated that mergers are a product of booms (or a product of a depression-prosperity sequence) effective control over merger activity may be sought through fiscal measures as well as through the antitrust laws."[44]

The economic environmental factors associated with each major wave are an important facet of merger activity and will be examined in detail in the three chapters that follow, each of which is devoted to an examination of one of the merger waves.

Mergers and the Economy

In addition to the question of environmental factors conducive to the stimulation of a merger movement, the related question of the impact of mergers upon business conditions or the cyclical character of the economy looms large on the economic scene. This question has not been treated in the economic literature.

The fact that a recession or a depression has followed each of the previous merger waves—the turn-of-the-century wave and the late-1920s wave—suggests that these merger waves may have been a contributing factor to the subsequent happenings.[45] Obviously, dollars spent on mergers are dollars that have been (at least partially) diverted from the spending stream for new plant and equipment. There is little reason to believe that the antitrust laws stopped the previous waves, and there is reason to believe that perhaps the previous waves were self-destructive instead. This facet of merger is important and worth examining even if the results are only suggestive and not conclusive.

Mergers and the Economist

The most famous worldly philosopher of all, Adam Smith, in his *Wealth of Nations* put forth the theory that the self-interest of men levering against one another and controlling one another through competition results in a splendid ethical balance wheel, the free market. Since the days of Smith, economists have worked with various models designed to describe markets and the behavior resulting from different market structures. Because of this natural concern with competitive models, one would expect that the economics profession would, as a group, be most vitally interested in the preservation and promotion of competition. In reality, it appears that the legal profession and the lawmakers have shouldered most of the burden in the practical area of issues related to competition. The record of all three groups, not to mention that of the regulatory agencies, leaves much to be desired. Certainly the lack of economic analysis and policy recommendations has been a contributing cause to the inconsistency and confusion which abound in the decisions of each of these groups.

Since the legislators and the courts are dependent upon the theories and analyses of economists in the industrial organization area, the contributions and the concern of this professional group will be examined as a facet of merger activity. The professional economists are capable of influencing the direction of public policy regarding economic matters related to the structure and performance of the economy, and the record should be examined.

Summary

An examination of the time series of recorded mergers reveals three distinct major waves of activity. The current wave of mergers is of considerable magnitude whether measured by numbers or "estimated" considerations paid. In addition, it has persisted longer than each of the previous major waves.

A major reason for the lack of empirical research on this important problem (in addition to lack of interest) is the scarcity of consistent and useful data. While this is not necessarily a legitimate or valid excuse for ignoring this economic phenomenon, it has served as a deterrent to progress in the development of a theory of merger activity.

Since mergers are economic events with numerous dimensions, the various facets associated with them should be examined in the context of each of the major waves of activity. The following three chapters will be devoted to this analysis as an aid in developing a merger mosaic, which is presented as the concluding chapter in Part 1.

NOTES

[1] A flurry of merger activity was reported in the period following the Civil War in the United States; however, the lack of data precludes any orderly analysis.

[2] A "merger capitalization" is defined by Ralph L. Nelson in his book *Merger Movements in American Industry: 1895–1956,* Princeton, N.J.: Princeton University Press, 1959, p. 18, as follows: "Conceptually this designation comes closest to being the sum of the sizes of the merging firms." If this concept was used with merging firms during the current wave, the figures would dwarf these early capitalization estimates, even allowing for price level adjustments.

[3] For a detailed description of the process of determining the merger capitalizations, see *ibid.,* chap. 2.

[4] Admittedly this is a rough estimate; however, no other data exist which can give the student of mergers an idea of the relative importance of this economic phenomenon.

[5] This period was reported as the "third wave" by J. Fred Weston in his book *The Role of Mergers in the Growth of Large Firms,* Berkeley, Calif.: University of California Press, 1953, pp. 50–61, and in his article "The Recent Merger Movement," *Journal of Business,* vol. 25, no. 1, pp. 30–38, January, 1952, and also by John Lintner and J. Keith Butters, "Effects of Mergers on Industrial Concentration: 1940–1947," *Review of Economics and Statistics,* vol. 32, no. 1, pp. 30–48, February, 1950.

[6] J. Keith Butters, John Lintner, and William L. Cary, *Effects of Taxation: Corporate Mergers,* Cambridge, Mass.: Harvard University Press, 1951.

[7] Federal Trade Commission, *The Merger Movement: A Summary Report,* 1948.

[8] M. A. Adelman has stated that "a generous estimate is that not over $5 billion was involved in all manufacturing and mining mergers during 1940–47." See his article entitled "The Measurement of Industrial Concentration," *Review of Economics and Statistics,* vol. 33, no. 4, p. 294, November, 1951.

[9] Jesse W. Markham, "Survey of the Evidence and Findings on Mergers," in National Bureau of Economic Research, Inc., *Business Concentration and Price Policy,* Princeton, N.J.: Princeton University Press, 1955, p. 179.

[10] See A. D. H. Kaplan, "The Current Merger Movement Analyzed," *Harvard Business Review,* vol. 33, no. 3, pp. 91–98, May–June, 1955; Joseph P. McKenna, "The Current Merger Movement," *Review of Social Economy,* vol. 16, no. 1, pp. 11–18, March, 1958; and Federal Trade Commission, *Report on Corporate Mergers and Acquisitions,* 1955.

[11] See, for example, Federal Trade Commission, *Report on Corporate Mergers and Acquisitions,* p. 1; Kaplan, *op. cit.,* pp. 94–95; and Markham, *op. cit.,* p. 154.

[12] Markham, *op. cit.,* pp. 142–143.

[13] John Moody, *The Truth about the Trusts: A Description and Analysis of the American Trust Movement,* New York: Moody Publishing Company, 1904, pp. 453–469; Luther Conant, Jr., "Industrial Consolidations in the United States," *American Statistical Association Publications,* vol. 7, no. 53, pp. 1–20, March, 1901; Myron W. Watkins, *Industrial Combinations and Public Policy,* Boston: Houghton Mifflin Company, 1927, pp. 317–324; U.S. Bureau of the Census, *Twelfth Census of the United States,* 1900, vol. VII, part L, pp. XXVff; and Nelson, *op. cit.,* p. 37.

[14] Willard L. Thorp, *Recent Economic Changes in the United States,* New York: National Bureau of Economic Research, Inc., 1929, vol. 1, pp. 181–187; and "The Merger Movement," *The Structure of Industry,* Temporary National

Economic Committee Monograph No. 27, 1941, part 3, pp. 231–234. There are two years of overlap between the Nelson and Thorp series, 1919 and 1920; the Thorp series includes considerably more mergers than the Nelson series for these years. Each used a different source; Nelson utilized the *Weekly Commercial and Financial Chronicle,* while the Thorp series was based on mergers reported in the *Standard Daily Trade Service.*

[15] See Federal Trade Commission, *Report on Corporate Mergers and Acquisitions,* p. 33, and annual press releases by the FTC.

[16] For example, see Willard F. Mueller, "A Comment on the F.T.C.'s Report on Mergers with Special Reference to Dairy Mergers," *Journal of Farm Economics,* vol. 39, no. 1, pp. 140–152, February, 1957. Mueller examined the dairy industry and found that the FTC tended to underestimate the number of acquisitions by the large firms as well as the smaller firms in the industry. In recent years, Mueller has been Chief Economist for the FTC and has some responsibility for the data collection activities.

[17] In two separate studies, the accuracy of the FTC's reporting of mergers involving large firms was checked and was found to be highly accurate. In the process of verifying the merger activity of over sixty firms for the period 1950–1959, I found the FTC data to be about 98 percent correct. Several mergers were reported that were never consummated, while other small acquisitions by firms that were active in the merger movement were not recorded. Kalman J. Cohen and I obtained similar results when we checked the acquisitions of the 500 largest industrials during the period 1951–1961. We also examined the merger activity of 165 large commercial banks during the decade 1952–1962. Since commercial banks are regulated and mergers must be approved by the relevant regulatory agency, information concerning mergers *must* be reported. Our experience with the financial manuals in this study was similar to that of the above studies involving unregulated firms. The results of these studies will be presented in Chapters 10 and 11.

[18] The merger data referred to are for manufacturing and mining firms, since there is no continuous comprehensive series which included all business, banking, transportation, and utility firms.

[19] Markham, *op. cit.,* p. 174.

[20] For a more complete discussion of the corporate organization forms used in mergers, see Federal Trade Commission, *Report on Corporate Mergers and Acquisitions,* pp. 91–93.

[21] It is very difficult to classify mergers in some cases since many firms are classified in more than one industry. Much depends upon the Standard Industrial Classifications used, which may range from the broadly defined two-digit classifications to the more narrowly defined three- and four-digit categories. An example is industry number 20, food and kindred products, which would include bakers, brewers, canners, packers, etc. If another digit is added (208), only beverage firms would be included. If a fourth digit is added (2082), then only brewers would be included.

[22] For some unexplained reason, the *circular* type of merger is not mentioned by the FTC or by most of the current writers on the subject. This is unfortunate since it has become the most widely used type of merger in the current wave. The Procter & Gamble acquisition of Clorox was a circular merger and *not* a conglomerate acquisition, as reported in the press. Industrial organi-

zation economists are familiar with the definition of this type of merger as used in the literature. See Harvey A. Toulin, *Millions in Mergers,* New York: B. C. Forbes, 1929, chap. 5; William R. Basset and J. Heywood, *Operating Aspects of Industrial Mergers,* New York: Harper & Brothers, 1930, chap. 2; Harry W. Laidler, *Concentration of Control in American Industry,* New York: Thomas Y. Crowell Company, 1931, p. 444; and Charles S. Tippetts and Shaw Livermore, *Business Organization and Control,* 2d ed., Princeton, N.J.: D. Van Nostrand Company, Inc., 1941, p. 481.

[23] H. Igor Ansoff and J. Fred Weston use four classifications for mergers: horizontal, vertical, concentric, and conglomerate. Their definitions of horizontal, vertical, and conglomerate mergers are similar to those presented above; however, they define concentric mergers quite differently. According to them, concentric mergers may be either vertical or horizontal, although the majority would most likely be in the circular category. Their definition of a concentric merger, which appears in their article "Merger Objectives and Organizational Structure," *Quarterly Review of Economics and Business,* vol. 2, no. 3, pp. 51–52, August, 1962, follows: "Concentric mergers involve a common thread in the relationships between the firms. The existence of a common thread in their relationships will produce two-plus-two-equals-five effects. To achieve these multiplicative rather than merely additive effects requires a complementary relationship which, in turn, reflects the degree of fit between the operations joined. . . . The criteria for the measure of fit are basically three in number. One is the increase in each Company's product-market strength as a consequence of the merger. . . . A second criterion for measure of fit is the potential for joint product development. . . . The third criterion is operational compatibility." To classify mergers using their criteria would indeed be difficult without a knowledge in depth of all firms engaging in merger activity. In reporting on their tests to determine stability under concentric and conglomerate strategies, they identified only five firms as using a concentric strategy.

[24] For a discussion of four of the principal dimensions of size used to measure concentration, see Adelman, *op. cit.,* pp. 272–273.

[25] Evan B. Alderfer, "Corporate Courting, and After," *Business Review,* p. 3, Federal Reserve Bank of Philadelphia, May, 1962.

[26] George J. Stigler, "Monopoly and Oligopoly by Merger," *American Economic Review,* vol. 40, no. 2, p. 23, May, 1950.

[27] Perhaps this partially explains why the role of mergers in the growth of firms has been given scant attention; as R. B. Heflebower observed: "The literature on mergers is abundant but the theoretical analysis of growth by mergers almost nonexistent. Recent statistical studies of factors related to growth of firms do not introduce method of growth as a variable." R. B. Heflebower, "Corporate Mergers: Policy and Economic Analysis," *Quarterly Journal of Economics,* vol. 77, no. 4, p. 553, November, 1963.

[28] Weston, *op. cit.*

[29] *Ibid.,* p. 30.

[30] See G. W. Nutter, "Growth by Merger," *Journal of the American Statistical Association,* vol. 49, no. 267, pp. 448–466, September, 1954; and G. J. Stigler, "The Statistics of Monopoly and Merger," *Journal of Political Economy,* vol. 64, no. 1, pp. 33–40, February, 1956. Nutter (pp. 450–455) discusses a major shortcoming in the Weston study, that is, the fact that the value of the assets

was not deflated to allow for changing price levels. This was particularly serious since most of the mergers occurred in the early years under study. Stigler discusses the same problem and gives examples (pp. 38–40) in his article.

[31] Weston, *op. cit.,* p. 101. Weston admits to the possibility of bias since some of the firms had been formed and had attained considerable size through the use of merger prior to the initial years used in his study.

[32] Markham, *op. cit.,* p. 142.

[33] Arthur S. Dewing, "A Statistical Test of the Success of Consolidations," *Quarterly Journal of Economics,* vol. 36, no. 4, p. 85, November, 1921.

[34] *Ibid.,* pp. 85–86.

[35] Shaw Livermore, "The Success of Industrial Mergers," *Quarterly Journal of Economics,* vol. 50, no. 4, p. 69, footnote, November, 1935.

[36] *Ibid.,* p. 74.

[37] Edith Penrose, *The Theory of the Growth of the Firm,* Oxford: Basil Blackwell & Mott, Ltd., 1959, p. 192.

[38] Samuel R. Reid, *Corporate Mergers and Acquisitions Involving Firms in Missouri: Some Economic Results and Administrative Policies and Procedures,* Ann Arbor, Mich.: University Microfilms, 1962, pp. 219–248.

[39] Eamon M. Kelly, *Profitability of Growth through Mergers,* University Park, Pa.: The Pennsylvania State University, 1967.

[40] Johan Bjorksten, "Merger Lemons," *Mergers and Acquisitions: The Journal of Corporate Venture,* vol. 1, no. 1, pp. 36–41, Fall, 1965.

[41] Weston, *op. cit.,* pp. 81–82.

[42] Markham, *op. cit.,* p. 154.

[43] Walter Adams, "Comment," in *Business Concentration and Public Policy,* National Bureau of Economic Research, Inc., Princeton, N.J.: Princeton University Press, 1955, p. 190.

[44] Markham, *op. cit.,* p. 146. I also advocated the use of fiscal measures along with antitrust law enforcement as a merger deterrent in a paper presented to the Midwest Economics Association in April, 1964, and before the Senate Subcommittee on Antitrust and Monopoly in September, 1966. This paper is published as part of the proceedings of the Committee on the Judiciary, Senate Subcommittee on Antitrust and Monopoly, *Economic Concentration,* 89th Cong., 1st Sess., 1967, part 5.

[45] There are obviously other variables to be examined, such as money supply changes, etc.; however, one need not be as conservative as Josef Schumpeter, who said that "like every other individual phenomenon, a given depression can only be explained by many factors, the number of which depends on the accuracy desired and, therefore, is indefinitely large." See his article entitled "The Present World Depression: A Tentative Diagnosis," *American Economic Review,* supplement, vol. 21, no. 1, p. 179, March, 1931.

3

The Turn-of-the-century Merger Wave

Many important historical events in American history occurred during the nineteenth century. Perhaps the most important economic event was the huge merger wave which developed at the close of the gay nineties. The prose used to describe this first merger wave in the United States is rich with such descriptions as "one of the most significant chapters in the history of the country," "a classical era in economic development," and "a movement of gigantic proportions," to mention but a few. The activity which took place in this period has had a profound and lasting effect upon the industrial structure of this nation. In order to develop a deeper understanding of this important movement and of the impact of mergers upon the economy, each facet of merger will be discussed in the context of this first wave.

The Magnitude of the Movement

An examination of the record leads one to the inevitable conclusion that the merger wave at the turn of the century was significant. The action in this movement was extensive and rapid since this was the shortest major merger wave on record. Although historians have disagreed slightly concerning the duration of the activity, an examination of the data suggests that the main thrust was in the period 1898–1902. As shown in Table 3.1, during this five-year span there were 2,653 reported mergers, with 1,208 mergers reported in 1899 alone, and capitalizations of $6.3 billion, with twin peaks evident in 1899 and 1901. Over $2 billion of activity, accounting for the majority of the reported activity, occurred in each of these years.

TABLE 3.1 Distribution of Merger Activity by Form of Merger, 1895–1902

		Merger Capitalizations			*Firm Disappearances*	
Year	*Total*	*% by Consolidation*	*% by Acquisition*	*Total (Firms)*	*% by Consolidation*	*% by Acquisition*
1895	40.8	84.6	15.4	43	86.1	13.9
1896	24.7	89.1	10.9	26	84.6	15.4
1897	119.7	92.4	7.6	69	89.9	10.1
1898	650.6	94.6	5.4	303	93.1	6.9
1899	2,262.7	92.1	7.9	1,208	91.7	8.3
1900	442.4	88.1	11.9	340	85.9	14.1
1901	2,052.9	92.4	7.6	423	83.2	16.8
1902	910.8	76.2	23.8	379	70.7	29.3

* In millions of dollars.

Source: Adapted from Ralph L. Nelson, *Merger Movements in American Industry: 1895–1956,* Princeton, N.J.: Princeton University Press, 1959, p. 60.

In relation to the total economy of that period, this was a considerable amount of activity in a brief period of time. According to Moody, there were 318 important industrial consolidations in existence in 1903 with total capital of $7.2 billion and over fifty-two hundred plants.[1] Of the total, 236 had been formed since the beginning of 1898, accounting for about $6.1 billion of the total capital.[2] Seager and Gulick indicated the relative importance of these figures to the economy when they observed that ". . . it appears that by 1904 the trusts controlled fully two-fifths of the manufacturing capital of the country."[3] Another source has observed that ". . . it can be roughly estimated that the 1887–1904 combination movement accounted for approximately 15 per cent of the total number of plants and employees comprising manufactures in 1900."[4] Needless to say, the gay nineties culminated with an explosion of combination activity which carried over into the initial years of the twentieth century and which was the first of the three major merger waves that have had an impact upon the structure and performance of the economy during the fascinating and turbulent years of this century.

Merger Forms and Types

One of the few aspects of this period of merger activity about which almost all writers agree is that this was the classical era of consolidations. The merger-consolidations in this period were comprehensive and included a large number of firms in an industry, with the purpose of establishing a dominant firm. It was these early consolidations that led to the linking of mergers in the economic literature to monopoly and oligopoly.[5] Some of these consolidations assumed gigantic proportions, such as the combination resulting in the United States Steel Corporation in 1901, which reportedly "included 11 trusts with aggregate capital of $900 million and a total of 800 properties employing 168,000 persons."[6] Of the 318 important industrial combines in existence in 1903 (representing a total capital of $7.2 billion), at least 236 (accounting for $6 billion of this total) had been incorporated since January 1, 1898. Nelson reports that during this period (1895 to 1904), ". . . consolidations dominated the merger activity of all but one of the two-digit industries. . . ."[7] The data presented in Table 3.1 show the relative importance of the merger-consolidation (many-at-once form) and the merger-acquisition (one-at-a-time form) during the first merger wave.

Since many of these consolidations were comprehensive in nature, encompassing large numbers of firms in the same industry, it is reasonable to conclude that the majority of mergers were horizontal. Certainly some of the consolidations had vertical and circular aspects, but it seems reasonable to assume that they played a subservient role to the horizontal type during the turn-of-the-century merger wave.

Mergers and Concentration

There is a general consensus among the various students of the first great wave of mergers that concentration was increased considerably during this period. Weston stated that ". . . the merger movement of 1898–1903 resulted in a high degree of concentration in many industries."[8] Markham said that ". . . of all those forces unleashed in the latter part of the nineteenth century that tended to make for larger size and greater concentration, the industrial combination was clearly the most important."[9]

Studies concerning monopolies may or may not be concerned with concentration effects; however, by definition a monopolist has attained a high degree of concentration. Regarding the monopolies formed in this period, Stigler said: "In this country mergers for monopoly began on a large scale only in the eighties, they reached a minor peak at the beginning of the nineties, and they attained their pinnacle at the end of the century."[10] Of the ninety-two large industrial mergers studied by Moody, seventy-eight controlled 50 percent or more of the output in their industry, and twenty-six controlled 80 percent or more.[11]

Considering the magnitude of the consolidations during this period, it is not surprising to discover that concentration increased in American industry. This was the era when most of the dominant firms in steel, petroleum, smelting, and tobacco and most of the shipping industries were formed. The highly concentrated nature of American business which persists to the present time was the aftermath of this relatively brief but explosive period in our economic history.

The Promoters of Mergers

The literature devoted to this era reveals a common thread of agreement—that the outside professional promoter (stimulated principally by the desire for personal gain) played an important role in the consummation of the mergers. This finding has been documented by numerous students of this merger movement. Stigler, for example, observed this development when he said: "I am inclined to place considerable weight upon one other advantage of merger: it permitted a capitalization of prospective monopoly profits and a portion of these capitalized profits to the professional promoter."[12]

The *modus operandi* of these flamboyant outside professional promoters in exploiting the market was conceptually simple. The discounted values of the expected future earnings were presented so that they greatly exceeded the existing book value of the assets of the constituent firms. This "puffery" was accomplished by promoter advertising and, in some cases, by the added inducement of potential monopoly power. The formation of a merger-consolidation or a holding company permitted the promoters and cooperating participants to float additional securities against the same assets. Thus the supply of securities was increased by the difference between the amounts of the old and new issues, with the difference usually expressed as "goodwill" (which was the promoter's gross profit). While the personal gain to the promoter was substantial, these practices resulted in a definite obstacle for the operating management of these firms which, in many cases, was never overcome. The dilution of the stock coupled with a decline in business conditions following this wave were severe handicaps to management.

In the large consolidations formed during this period, it was frequently necessary to have an outsider who could reconcile the differences between the various constituents being formed into a consolidated firm. This outsider acted as an intermediary between parties, as well as the prime mover in consummating the mergers. Nadler provides us with the following example:

> In the consolidations formed around 1900, the professional promoter took an important part in numerous instances. Charles R. Flint, frequently mentioned as the prototype of the professional promoter of industrial consolidations, was one of the most active promoters of consolidations at that time, standing sponsor to scores of individual combines and thus gaining the cognomen of "father of trusts." Among the large transactions he consummated was the formation of the United States Rubber Company, and it is significant that he accomplished this consolidation only after the individual rubber manufacturers had negotiated in vain for months in an effort to reach an agreement.[13]

In contrast to the current situation, in which stock ownership is diverse, during this period individuals possessed large blocks of stock as well as a high percentage of ownership of a firm. In some cases these stockholder-speculators promoted mergers since they were in a strategic position to exercise their power. Nadler again illustrates this situation:

> During the great consolidation movement in the early part of the century, such speculators took a leading role in several large combinations. Large profits accumulated in market operations, and a desire to have new stock issues to sponsor made them turn promoters of combinations. The American Can Company and many other great combinations of the time were involved under the auspices of such large-scale market operators as Daniel Reid and Charles W. Gates.[14]

A considerable amount of attention has been devoted to the role of the outside promoter during this first wave; however, the fact that students of this wave have described the picturesque position of these flamboyant personalities does not mean that others, such as investment bankers and the managements of the firms involved, were inactive. However, the methods of operation of the inside and outside promoters could vary considerably. In most cases, the outside promoter was interested in getting the consolidation consummated and under way (taking out the promoter's profit) and not in managing it after formation. In other cases, individuals who helped to organize a consolidated firm from the outside stayed on as executives.

Markham has formulated an interesting hypothesis concerning the role of the professional promoters in the first merger wave. He attributes the high incidence of mergers to their general speculative character. He formulates his hypothesis as follows:

> Presumably a large proportion of the profitable mergers were provided with a real basis for merger (market control or production and distribution economies) while a corresponding proportion of the unprofitable ones were not. The professional promoter was likely to have played a less important role in the formation of mergers falling in the former than in the latter group.[15]

Markham identifies a small sample of firms which he uses to test this hypothesis. Unfortunately, he does not define "success" or "failure," nor does he provide any statistics or significance tests to determine the relevancy of his findings. However, an interesting footnote in his paper provides us with some illumination; Markham states:

> This hypothesis finds its origin in a very simple line of logic. The mergers that actually turned out to be profitable operating firms were *expected* to be more profitable than those that did not. Where expectations of operating profitably were high, however, less professional promotional services were needed. While readily available data on this point include a very small proportion of the total number of mergers, they seem generally to support the hypothesis. Ten mergers that were either promoted by banks, syndicates, or other persons outside the industry, or gave rise to large promotional profits, were early failures . . . [and] of 11 mergers in which outside promoters played a negligible role, 7 were successes . . . 1 was a limping success . . . 1 was a rejuvenated success . . . and 2 were early failures. . . . Data for 4 other mergers can be used, depending on the aspects of the mergers given emphasis, either to support or refute the hypothesis.[16]

In summary, it is apparent that outside professional promoters played a leading role in the formation of the large consolidations during the first merger wave. The role of the operating management of the firms engaging in mergers during this period is not as well documented; however, it is likely that they played an important role, particularly in the smaller mergers and (as noted by Markham) in some of the larger consolidations. Yet the impression gained from a survey of the literature is that the management groups played a subservient role to that of the colorful professional promoters during this period. Since most of the mergers during the first merger wave were consolidations of the horizontal type, the promoters were emphasizing the expected advantages to be gained from economies of scale and/or market control. According to the available evidence concerning postmerger performance, it is doubtful that these advantages were generally realized.

Mergers and the Growth of Firms

Obviously, the use of merger is a powerful method of rapidly increasing the size of individual firms or creating new, larger business units. The numerous large consolidations at the turn of the century gave birth to new industrial giants; for example, we have already noted that of the 318 important industrial combines in existence in 1903, at least 236 had been incorporated since January 1, 1898.[17]

Weston, who has made the most extensive study of the role of mergers in the growth of large firms, found that mergers played an important part in the growth of firms during this first merger movement.[18] Markham also recognized the role of mergers in the growth of firms during this period when he said that ". . . it seems safe to conclude that a significant number of the large horizontal mergers greatly increased the size of particular firms and their proportionate control over both total production capacity and the market, however defined."[19]

Nelson provides us with a study designed to evaluate the importance of mergers in the growth of large firms by pinpointing their occurrence in the history of the largest manufacturing firms as of 1955.[20] The results of Nelson's study are presented in Table 3.2. Nelson considered

TABLE 3.2 Distribution of the 100 Largest Manufacturing Corporations of 1955 by Date of Most Important Merger*

Corporations having important mergers:		
Before 1895	11	
1895–1904	20	
1904–1915	7	
1915–1924	5	
1925–1934	11	
1935–1944	0	
1945–1955	9	63
Corporations having no important mergers		37
		100

* Size of corporations measured by assets.

Source: Ralph L. Nelson, *Merger Movements in American Industry: 1895–1956,* Princeton, N.J.: Princeton University Press, 1959, p. 4.

only *important* mergers in the history of these firms, and he defined them as follows:

> A merger was considered important if (1) it represented the consolidation of a number of small or medium-sized companies into one firm occupying a leading position in its industry, or (2) a leading large firm acquired another large firm, thus markedly increasing both its absolute size and its leadership in the industry, or (3) a firm acquired a number of firms—large or small—in succession, thus rapidly increasing its size and its position in the industry.[21]

Nelson admits that his classifications were arbitrary in some cases but that he was erring on the side of rejecting mergers of uncertain performance.[22] Despite following the approach of the cautious scholar, Nelson noted that more than three-fifths of these firms had at least one important merger in their history, with most of the important ones coming during the major waves; he says:

> The decade spanning the wave at the turn of the century shows the largest number (twenty), and the decade spanning the wave of the late twenties shows the second largest (eleven). The third largest number of foundation-laying mergers (nine) came in the decade following World War II; in eight of these nine corporations the mergers occurred either in 1953, 1954, or 1955.[23]

Mergers at the turn of the century not only created large new firms instantaneously but also provided large increments of growth to other firms. Subsequent growth following mergers depends upon a number of factors, including general business conditions, the industry life cycle, the subsequent merger activity of the firm, and the preferences and objectives of the firms' management, among others. As noted previously, many of these large firms created by merger during the first wave either failed or declined in relative importance in the period *between* merger waves, when recessions and other adverse economic conditions were present.

The Relative Success of Mergers

Following the first merger wave, some interesting empirical studies were made that attempted to measure the success of these mergers in terms of their relative profitability. The best-known and most widely quoted study of the performance of mergers by consolidation during this period was by Dewing.[24] He selected thirty-five consolidations organized between 1893 and 1902, and his findings were as follows: (1) The earnings of the constituent companies before consolidation were nearly one-fifth greater than the earnings of the consolidated company for the first year after consolidation and between one-fifth and one-sixth greater than the average earnings of the ten years following the consolidation. (2) Promoters' estimates of probable earnings were 150 percent of the actual earnings of the first year and 200 percent of the actual average earnings during the decade following the consolidation. (3) After sufficient time had elapsed to permit the consolidation to perfect its organization and other anticipated economies, earnings actually diminished; the earnings of the first year were 7 percent greater than the earnings of the tenth year after the consolidation.[25]

Mead studied the subsequent histories of the combinations whose operations for the first ten years had been summarized by Dewing.[26] Mead observed that most of the companies had been formed in anticipation of securing a high degree of monopoly, and while this was not accomplished, a majority of the consolidations achieved "conspicuous success," reflecting the advantages of large-scale operations. Mead did not define "success," and Weston does not believe that the evidence presented by Mead supports his conclusions.[27] Both the Dewing and the Mead studies were limited to merger-consolidations.

Another extensive study of the relative success of consolidations was made by Livermore.[28] His sample included 328 firms which had merged during the period 1890–1904. Of the 156 firms classified in the primary group (those which obtained a high degree of market control), Livermore judged 40.4 percent failures, 10.9 percent marginal, and 48.7 percent successes. Included in his secondary group were 172 firms (that did not obtain a high degree of market control); 45.3 percent of these firms were classed as failures, 6.4 percent as marginal, and 48.3 percent as successes. Livermore concluded that the general impression created by Dewing's study—that mergers were typically unsuccessful—needed reappraisal. He suggested that the number of successful mergers was higher than generally supposed.[29]

It is interesting to note that in both groups, the successful mergers were less than 50 percent of the total. It is doubtful that the managers and stockholders of these firms would have considered the probabilities of success of their mergers at less than 0.5 (on the average) at the time of consummation.

None of these studies examined an important aspect of the financial experience of the early consolidations, that is, their dividend record and the effects of the mergers upon the market price of the common stock of these firms. Nelson made a limited study of these two factors for a small sample of thirteen firms organized between 1899 and 1901. He chose an interval ending in December of either 1908 or 1910 and found that if "an individual had invested the same amount of money in each of the 13 stocks, his return on his investment over this hybrid nine-year period would have been 5.9 percent."[30] Of the thirteen stocks chosen by Nelson, seven paid dividends and seven offered a positive return on the investment.[31] Again, there was an almost equal number of gainers and losers, and we do not know the relative performance of these merging firms compared with that of the nonmerging firms in that time period.

The National Industrial Conference Board conducted a study of the earnings of forty-eight consolidations which had a continuous existence during the greater part of the period from their inception to 1914.[32] The general conclusions drawn from the NICB survey of the record of earnings of these surviving consolidations were as follows: (1) When whole industries have been subject to stagnation, the mergers have been unable to escape the prevalent drift toward ruin; (2) in new industries experiencing rapid growth, the mergers have participated in the general prosperity; (3) industrial consolidations have not been able to avoid sharp decreases of profits in years of general business depression; (4) when consolidations have been handicapped by an unmanageable financial structure, involving excessive fixed charges above their minimum earning capacity, they have been unable to adapt themselves to new situations and have thus forfeited their industrial leadership; and (5) business mergers offer no substitute for competent management.[33]

If there is any one dominant factor which emerges from a review of these studies concerned with the mergers of the first great wave, it is the general lack of success of these mergers, which (in many cases) were designed to secure a high degree of market control and/or scale economies.

Mergers and Antitrust

The first of the antitrust laws applicable to mergers was the Sherman Act of 1890, which was directed at monopoly and monopoly practices. Ironically, this law not only failed to halt monopolies and an increased degree of concentration, but has been considered by some to be a partial cause of the development. Markham concluded: "The Sherman Act of 1890 made collusion illegal and put an end to the trustee device, thereby forcing industrialists seeking market control to resort to complete fusion of their separate companies."[34] This was an ironic turn of events which was aided by the interpretation of the courts, among other factors. In discussing the crucial E. C. Knight decision by the courts, Adams states:

> Yet it was this decision which provided the first significant test of the Sherman Act's effectiveness in combatting mergers. It was this decision ("manufacturing is not commerce"), which reassured lawyers and businessmen that mergers in manufacturing and mining were quite safe under the new law. It was this decision—combined with President Cleveland's subsequent statements that it made trusts a state rather than a federal problem—which served as a powerful impetus to the merger movement of the late 1890's. On the basis of the available evidence it appears that public policy—both the favorable ruling in the Knight case and the "adverse" dictum in the *Northern Securities* case—had a profound influence on the scope and limits of this admittedly gigantic merger movement.[35]

Another factor which contributed to the ineffectiveness of the first antitrust law was the fundamental change in the corporation laws which took place at about the time the legislation was passed. It became legal for one corporation to acquire and hold the stock of another corporation, a development which effectively defeated the purpose of the legislation. A distinguished economist, Arthur R. Burns, summed up the situation when he said that "although federal antitrust legislation has been on the books since 1890, there is little doubt that we have failed to achieve a competitive system at all closely resembling that which was in the minds of the economists of the last century and which provided the background for the legislation."[36]

An examination of the record for the first merger wave leads to the obvious conclusion that the first of the antitrust laws, the Sherman Act, did not deter the first wave of merger activity in the United States at the turn of the century. One of the most interesting facts about the first merger wave is that it occurred *following* the passage of legislation designed to prevent concentration of control in industry. The interpretations of the courts during this period must be considered a contributing factor to the ineffectiveness of the Sherman Act in curbing this development in the American economy.

The Environment for Mergers

The buoyant securities market during the period of the first merger wave has been recognized as an important factor in the economic environment at that time. Markham recognized this when he said:

> The literature provides convincing evidence that the abnormally large volume of mergers formed in 1897–1900 stemmed from a wave of frenzied speculation in asset values. Several students of the early merger movement agree that excessive demand for securities

> was an impelling force in the mass promotion of mergers after 1896. Average stock prices increased from $40 in the second quarter of 1897 to nearly $80 by the fourth quarter of 1899. Most of this rise in stock prices occurred between mid-1897 and the closing months of 1899.[37]

Nelson, another student of the first merger wave, also recognized the role of a buoyant stock when he said: "The high correlation between merger activity and stock prices suggests that much of the merger activity of the period had its origin in, or was influenced by, the stock market."[38]

Both Markham and Nelson recognized that prosperous business conditions were also a factor during the first merger wave. Markham found that ". . . the high value of the Fechner-Weber index for the period 1887–1904 is almost wholly accounted for by the identical directional movements of the merger series and the business cycle for all the years between 1897 and 1904."[39]

It was apparent, however, that the business cycle was important in the timing of the first merger movement. Revival of merger activity did not occur until the depressed conditions of the mid-1890s had passed and the prosperous turn-of-the-century years were reached. Also, the merger expansion occurred during a period of a cyclically rising stock market.[40]

Some of the merger literature leaves one with the impression that prosperity and rising stock prices are independent. This is certainly not a valid assumption, since both factors generally move in the same direction, with stock prices considered a leading indicator of business conditions. The fact that the environment at the turn of the century included both of these factors was recognized by both Markham and Nelson. Markham observed that "in view of the moderately high positive correlation that exists between merger activity and stock prices, it is worth pointing out that the movement conformed closely to a general statistical pattern."[41]

Nelson's research dispels the view that mergers during this period were prompted by industrial stagnation or retardation. He tested the retardation hypothesis, and his conclusions were as follows:

> Statistical examination of the growth-retardation–merger relationship indicates that there is little empirical basis for believing that the turn of the century merger wave was caused by a general retardation in industry growth thought to be prevalent at that time. The last one and one-half decades of the nineteenth century saw the halting and reversing of the previous decline in growth rates for industry in general. In the industries of high merger activity, the reversal of retardation was even more pronounced than it was

> for industry in general. Measured on an industry-by-industry basis, retardation was generally absent from industries of highest merger activity in the decade and one-half preceding the merger wave. Indeed these findings suggest that more satisfactory explanations of merger movements may be found in periods of accelerating growth than in periods of retardation.[42]

Certainly our subsequent history has tended to confirm this fact. Witness the increase in mergers during the roaring twenties and soaring sixties and the decline in activity during the dismal thirties and war-torn early forties, when industrial retardation was present.

Butters, Lintner, and Cary recognized the dual role of the economic and legal environment of the first merger wave; they observed:

> Court decisions outlawing the trust form of organization and the business depression of 1893 produced a temporary lull in merger activity, but the revival in general business conditions in 1897 ushered in an even greater wave of combinations, based upon the direct merger or consolidation of large numbers of leading competitors in each industry rather than upon the abandoned trust device. The whole movement reached its peak in 1901 with the formation of the billion-dollar United States Steel Corporation and finally ended like the first with the sharp depression of 1903 and the Northern Securities decision in early 1904.[43]

Perhaps the most extensive tests of the various factors contributing to the first merger wave were conducted by Nelson. His conclusions concerning the results of these empirical tests confirmed the important environmental role of relative prosperity and a buoyant stock market; he said:

> Empirical investigations of such factors as the rate of industrial growth, the rise of technological innovation, and the growth of interregional transportation indicated that they were not likely to have been important immediate factors in the merger wave. The leading factors of immediate importance appeared to be the newly-achieved development of a broad and strong capital market, and the existence of institutions which enabled organizers of mergers to utilize this market. The generally favorable conditions of business and a rising buoyant securities market made practicable larger and larger units of business enterprise. This in turn permitted the centralization, in one corporate structure, of control of a large part of an industry, and made possible a more effective rationalization of industry output by business leaders.[44]

In summary, it appears that a period of relative prosperity coupled with a buoyant securities market were major economic environmental factors during this first great merger wave at the turn of the century. The wave subsided only after the collapse of the stock market and a decline in business conditions. A less important but contributing factor could also have been the exhausted merger opportunities, since a large portion of industry was involved in this wave.

Mergers and the Economy

The importance of the environmental factors of prosperity and a buoyant market for securities in providing the stimulant for merger waves was emphasized in the previous section. A related question which has never been examined is the resulting impact of mergers upon the business cycle or business conditions. In other words, the mergers in the first wave were consummated during a period of prosperous business conditions, and the wave was terminated mainly by declining business conditions, which may have been influenced by the mergers in the preceding period.

Actually, the first great merger wave had declined prior to the "sharp depression of 1903," as had stock prices. Isolating the factors which determine the prices of stocks is a difficult task; however, it is safe to assume that expectations about future streams of income are one of the factors. I have already noted that professional promoters used a considerable amount of "puffery" in their promotional efforts at the turn of the century. It may well be that investors became skeptical when the financial results of these early combinations were below their expectations. Dewing pointed out that many of the combinations fell short of promoters' projections for the first year as well as for the tenth year after consolidation. Thus the securities market reacted to these less-than-spectacular results produced by the early consolidations.

Aggregate demand during this period was also almost solely dependent upon business investment spending and consumer spending. The role of government spending was of minor importance during this period. One would not expect business investment spending to provide much impetus to the economy during the latter part of this period since many large firms (which were the result of consolidations) were still trying to determine their existing capacity rather than expand capacity through new capital expenditures. Remember that a large number of these firms were formed with the purpose of gaining control over production and not necessarily to add productive capacity to an industry. I submit that these two factors—the disappointing performance of the early consolidations (which could have been a factor in the sharp decline of stock prices) and reduced capital expenditures by the large consolidations—may have been contributing causes to the depression of 1903. Markham noted the decline in the stock market and the role of unrealized gains expected by investors in the depression following the first merger wave when he said:

> As one would expect, the merger-creating industry did not thrive for long. Bankers, industrialists, and the stock-buying public, on whose support the promoter relied, soon had their expectations shattered. In the eighteen-month period preceding October, 1903, the market value of 100 leading industrial stocks shrank by 43.4 percent. Much of this shrinkage was undoubtedly a downward adjustment of stock prices to reflect the difference between *expected* and *actual* earnings. The result was the "Rich Man's Panic" of 1903, by which time the early merger movement had run its course.[45]

Thus we had a situation in which expected profits were not realized by the merging firms, which contributed to a new appraisal by investors concerning future prospects. In addition, there was a slack in aggregate demand as a result of the decline in capital investment spending for new plant and equipment by the large consolidated firms at that time, which contributed to the depressed business conditions.

Mergers and the Economist

The burst of merger activity which occurred during this period undoubtedly caught the economists of the time without the analytical tools and the data to properly assess its magnitude. No doubt many economists and others believed that the passage of the Sherman Act some years prior to the wave would be sufficient protection against the development of a high degree of concentration. In addition, this merger wave was of relatively short duration. One can only conclude upon examining the literature concerning mergers in this period that there was a coincident silence among the economics profession. Certainly there were some early works concerned with the trust problem, but it was a decade or more before the story of this great wave was finally pieced together.[46] In defense of the profession, it must be understood that this was the first great wave of mergers in this country, and it would not be unusual to expect a lag in research and analysis.

It is interesting to note that Stigler, one of the current leaders in the economics profession, has taken the early economists to task for their passive attitude during the first wave; he observed:

> It is sobering to reflect on the attitudes of professional economists of the period toward the merger movement. Economists as wise as Taussig, as incisive as Fisher, as fond of competition as Clark and

Fetter, insisted upon discussing the movement largely or exclusively in terms of industrial evolution and the economies of scale. They found no difficulty in treating the unregulated corporation as a natural phenomenon, nor were they bothered that the economies of scale should spring forth suddenly and simultaneously in an enormous variety of industries—and yet pass over the minor firms that characteristically persisted and indeed flourished in these industries. One must regretfully record that in this period Ida Tarbell and Henry Demarest Lloyd did more than the American Economic Association to foster the policy of competition.[47]

The situation changed considerably in the decades following the first merger wave, when economists discovered the vast increases in concentration which had resulted from this brief but explosive movement.[48] It gave rise to a stream of literature which by 1920 was probably equal in volume to that on the industrial revolution, international trade, or the business cycle.[49] In the period 1904–1914, complete books were written by Moody, Ripley, Van Hise, Dewing, and others.[50] A number of other works concerned with the first wave appeared years later, even after the second wave had begun. In addition, economists knew virtually nothing about the period 1905–1920 until a relatively recent study of this period was conducted by Nelson.[51]

In summary, it appears that the first great merger wave at the turn of the century was an accomplished fact before the economists of that period realized what had happened. Most of the economists' traditional concern for a competitive market structure was expressed only within ivy-covered lecture halls and did not reach the public forum until years later, when new descriptive models were formulated.

NOTES

[1] John Moody, *The Truth about the Trusts: A Description and Analysis of the American Trust Movement,* New York: Moody Publishing Company, 1904.

[2] *Ibid.*

[3] Henry R. Seager and Charles A. Gulick, Jr., *Trust and Corporation Problems,* New York: Harper & Brothers, 1929, p. 61. See also Moody, *op. cit.,* p. 487.

[4] Jesse W. Markham, "Survey of the Evidence and Findings on Mergers," in National Bureau of Economic Research, Inc., *Business Concentration and Price Policy,* Princeton, N.J.: Princeton University Press, 1955, p. 157.

[5] The literature on this subject is extensive. See, for example, Markham, *op. cit.,* pp. 154–158; and George J. Stigler, "Monopoly and Oligopoly by Merger," *American Economic Review,* vol. 40, no. 2, pp. 23–34, May, 1950.

[6] A. D. H. Kaplan, "The Current Merger Movement Analyzed," *Harvard Business Review,* vol. 33, no. 3, p. 92, May–June, 1955.

[7] Ralph L. Nelson, *Merger Movements in American Industry: 1895–1956,* Princeton, N.J.: Princeton University Press, 1959, p. 64. For a more complete discussion of interindustry and intraindustry effects, see pp. 40–50.

[8] J. Fred Weston, *The Role of Mergers in the Growth of Large Firms*, Berkeley, Calif.: University of California Press, 1953, p. 34.

[9] Markham, *op. cit.*, p. 156.

[10] Stigler, *op. cit.*, p. 28.

[11] Moody, *op. cit.*, pp. 453–467.

[12] Stigler, *op. cit.*, p. 30.

[13] Marcus Nadler, *Corporate Consolidations and Reorganizations,* New York: Alexander Hamilton Institute, 1930, p. 121.

[14] *Ibid.,* p. 122.

[15] Markham, *op. cit.,* p. 163.

[16] *Ibid.,* pp. 163–164, footnote. While Markham is looking at groups of firms, he makes no provision for, or mention of, industry influences. Perhaps this was because the firm was the industry; however, we can only speculate since no time period is specified.

[17] Kaplan, *loc. cit.*

[18] Weston, *op. cit.,* pp. 48–49.

[19] Markham, *op. cit.,* p. 158.

[20] Nelson, *op. cit.,* p. 4.

[21] *Ibid.,* p. 4, footnote to table 1.

[22] *Ibid.,* pp. 4–5. Nelson gives some examples on this point; he says: "The early Alcoa (then Pittsburgh Reduction) mergers, which brought in all the critical aluminum-making patents, were not classified as important on the ground that the acquired companies were really only patent holders, and not important aluminum producers. On the other hand, the early Westinghouse mergers, by which producing facilities were acquired, were not classified as important on the ground that the critical factors in the company's future growth were the inventions of George Westinghouse, not the producing facilities acquired through merger."

[23] *Ibid.,* p. 5. Nelson lists the firms included in his study in his appendix table C-1. In the last decade of increased merger activity, many of the firms listed (including those classified as not having previously had important mergers) have been engaged in mergers. The cutoff year in the Nelson study was 1955, the point at which the current wave began to accelerate.

[24] Arthur S. Dewing, "A Statistical Test of the Success of Consolidations," *Quarterly Journal of Economics,* vol. 36, no. 4, pp. 84–101, November, 1921.

[25] *Ibid.*

[26] Edward S. Mead, *Corporation Finance,* New York: D. Appleton & Company, Inc., 1930, pp. 473–478.

[27] Weston, *op. cit.,* p. 69.

[28] Shaw Livermore, "The Success of Industrial Mergers," *Quarterly Journal of Economics,* vol. 50, no. 4, pp. 68–69, November, 1935.

[29] Markham made a further study of Livermore's list of "influential" mergers (those mergers which succeeded because of monopoly control or unfair and vexatious practices) and found that considerably more had attained a dominant position in their industries than Livermore recognized. See Markham, *op. cit.,* pp. 158–160.

[30] Nelson, *op. cit.,* p. 97.

[31] *Ibid.,* p. 98.

[32] *Mergers in Industry: A Study of Certain Economic Aspects of Industrial Consolidation,* New York: National Industrial Conference Board, Inc., 1929. See chap. 3.

[33] *Ibid.,* pp. 40–41.
[34] Markham, *op. cit.,* p. 167.
[35] Walter Adams, "Comment" (following Markham's paper), National Bureau of Economic Research, Inc., *Business Concentration and Price Policy,* Princeton, N.J.: Princeton University Press, 1955, pp. 189–190.
[36] This statement appeared in Dexter M. Keezer, "The Effectiveness of the Federal Antitrust Laws: A Symposium," *American Economic Review,* vol. 39, no. 4, p. 691, June, 1949. Mr. Burns was associated with Columbia University at the time of the symposium, and he later served on the Council of Economic Advisers as chairman under President Eisenhower.
[37] Markham, *op. cit.,* p. 162.
[38] Nelson, *op. cit.,* p. 6.
[39] Markham, *op. cit.,* p. 152.
[40] Nelson, *op. cit.,* p. 106.
[41] Markham, *op. cit.,* pp. 166–167.
[42] Nelson, *op. cit.,* pp. 77–78.
[43] J. Keith Butters, John Lintner, and William L. Cary, *Effects of Taxation: Corporate Mergers,* Cambridge, Mass.: Harvard University Press, 1951, p. 288.
[44] Nelson, *op. cit.,* p. 6.
[45] Markham, *op. cit.,* p. 166.
[46] Among the authors of the early works concerning the trust movement were Richard T. Ely, *Monoplies and Trusts,* New York: The Macmillan Company, 1900; Jeremiah W. Jenks, *The Trust Problem,* New York: McClure, Phillips and Co., 1903; James E. LeRossignol, *Monopolies Past and Present: An Introductory Study,* New York: Thomas Y. Crowell Company, 1901; and William W. Collier, *The Trusts: What Can We Do with Them? What Can They Do for Us?* Hillside, N.J.: The Baker & Taylor Company, 1900.
[47] Stigler, *op. cit.,* pp. 30–31.
[48] The subject of combinations and trusts was discussed at the twelfth annual meeting of the American Economic Association held at Ithaca, N.Y., Dec. 27 to Dec. 29, 1900. The following three papers were presented: James B. Dill, "Some Tendencies in Combinations Which May Become Dangerous"; Charles S. Fairchield, "The Financiering of Trusts"; and Sidney Sherwood, "Influence of the Trust in the Development of Undertaking Genius." Discussion of the papers was by E. W. Bemis, J. W. Jenks, S. M. Lindsay, J. H. Gray, P. H. Giddings, T. N. Carver, Theodore Marburg, D. R. Dewey, H. B. Gardner, and Allen Ripley Foote. See *Publications of the American Economic Association,* Third Series, vol. 1, no. 1, pp. 149–211, February, 1900.
[49] Markham, *op. cit.,* pp. 154–155.
[50] See, for example, Moody, *op. cit.;* William Z. Ripley, *Trusts, Pools, and Corporations,* Boston: Ginn and Company, 1905; Charles R. Van Hise, *Concentration and Control: A Solution of the Trust Problem in the United States,* New York: The Macmillan Company, 1912; and Arthur S. Dewing, *Corporate Promotions and Reorganizations,* Cambridge, Mass.: Harvard University Press, 1914.
[51] The title of the Nelson book, *Merger Movements in American Industry: 1895–1956,* is slightly misleading since the bulk of the study is concerned with the period between the first wave, at the turn of the century, and the second, late-1920s wave. Needless to say, it is a valuable contribution to the literature on mergers.

4

The Late-1920s Merger Wave

The second great wave of merger activity did not get underway until nearly three decades after the initial burst of activity. The nation had experienced an economic recession and World War I in the intervening years. A number of relatively important mergers were consummated during these intrawave years, particularly the numerous acquisitions which resulted in the formation of such industrial giants as the General Motors Corporation. Firms such as Chevrolet, Fisher Body Corporation, Buick Motor Company, Olds Motor Works, Oakland Motor Car Company, Cadillac Automobile Company, and numerous other car and truck manufacturers and parts suppliers were acquired by General Motors in this period. These mergers played an important role in the development of this holding company into its dominant position in the transportation equipment industry.

While there was an increase in merger activity in the early 1920s, the real thrust did not take place until the middle and later years of this spectacular period, which has been termed the "roaring twenties." Some facets of merger during this period resembled developments in the first great wave; yet an examination of this period reveals some particularly unique characteristics peculiar to this second great merger wave in the late 1920s.

The Magnitude of the Movement

While there is an insufficient amount of data on each of the major merger waves, the particular lack of data on the second wave makes it an especially difficult one to measure. An examination of the number of reported mergers reveals that from 1925 to 1931 there were 5,846 mergers, with a peak reached in 1929, when 1,245 mergers were recorded. Measured by numbers alone, more than twice as many reported mergers occurred during this seven-year period than during the turn-of-the-century wave. Since most of the mergers in this period were acquisitions rather than consolidations, the average size of the mergers was most likely smaller than during the first wave.

Since there has been no systematic record kept of the assets involved in the mergers during this period, it is difficult to compare the relative importance of this wave. The existing data are fragmented, and yet it is possible to piece together enough scraps to see that the wave was important in many ways. Means kept a record of those companies on the list of the 200 largest which were acquired by another firm on the list during the period 1922–1929.[1] If we consider the five-year period from 1925 to 1929, a total of thirty-seven giant firms were merged, involving assets totaling close to $5.4 billion at the time of acquisition. This small fraction of total merger activity, including acquisitions within the group of the 200 largest firms in this period (when measured by the assets involved), is close to the total capitalizations recorded in the first wave. In addition, there were over fifty-eight hundred other acquisitions in this second wave.

On the basis of the available evidence, it appears that this late-1920s merger movement was substantial. Even allowing for price level adjustments and the growth of assets in the mining and manufacturing sector of the economy, the real relative volume of activity was substantial.[2]

Merger Forms and Types

The merger-acquisition replaced the merger-consolidation during this period, and thus the second wave was not as spectacular as the first wave. Nelson reported the demise of the consolidation form as follows: "The huge turn-of-the-century merger wave was probably unique in the overwhelming importance of the consolidation form of merger. In neither the 1905–1914 decade of very low activity nor the 1915–1920 period of reviving merger activity did the consolidation resume this dominant role."[3]

Most of the mergers in this wave were piecemeal and were much less comprehensive than the consolidations in the first wave. One of the principal causes mentioned in the literature for the decline in importance of the consolidation was the Northern Securities decision in 1904.[4]

The late-1920s wave was also characterized by the decline in importance of the horizontal merger, which perhaps is to be expected since the consolidation form had become less significant. This second merger wave witnessed the increased use of the vertical and circular types of merger. McKenna provides some rationale for this development as follows:

> The vertical merger was much more common during the period of the twenties. Such mergers extended the industrial firm backward to its sources of supply, or forward to include its distribution facilities. Although such mergers often aroused the same emotional opposition as the horizontal mergers, they are in a much different class economically. In the first phase, they are more apt to lead to technological economies. As the new doctrine of scientific management developed, it became clear that one difficulty was the control of movement of goods through the production process. Vertical integration, by bringing several stages under unified control, permits closer scheduling and more efficient inventory control.[5]

Weston contends that many integrated organizations were established through the use of vertical mergers during this period; he suggests two motivations for this type of behavior: "Apparently, one motive was to achieve technical gains from integration, but more important, to free the expanding firm from dependence on other firms for raw materials. Mergers also took place at this time in order to consolidate sales and distributing organizations. The second objective was to make advertising expenditures more effective."[6]

Horizontal mergers also played a part during this wave; however, they appear to have been consummated principally to preserve and promote the existing oligopolistic structures that prevailed in many industries. The FTC reports on this as follows: "Thus, many of the horizontal mergers were engineered by concerns, which, though not the largest in the industry, were still among its first three or four (e.g., in steel, Bethlehem Steel Corporation and Republic Steel Corporation, and in chemicals, Allied Chemical & Dye)."[7]

Diversification mergers of a geographical type and circular mergers became important during the late 1920s; as Markham has observed: ". . . a large portion of the mergers formed in the 1920's brought together firms producing totally different lines of products, the same products in noncompeting territories, or firms engaged in different stages of fabrication."[8]

A partial contributing factor to the increased use of the geographical extension variety of the horizontal type of merger and the circular merger was the growth and development of national advertising media, particularly the radio, with its national networks. Thus, the consolidation form and the horizontal type of merger were of declining importance during this merger wave, which witnessed the rise of another type and form of merger.

Mergers and Concentration

Since most of the mergers consummated during this period were more of a piecemeal type and less comprehensive than the consolidations formed during the first wave, their impact upon concentration has not been considered as important as the consolidations of the first wave. Certainly many mergers were consummated with the goal of restoring some measure of monopoly or market power which had become diluted in the intervening years between the first two major waves. However, the mergers of this period have been associated more with the desire to achieve or to preserve existing oligopoly positions in many industries.[9] In addition, during this period of relatively prolonged prosperity, there was new entry into many industries, as well as the growth and development of new industries, which tended to offset the disappearances of firms by merger and to soften the impact of mergers in contributing to higher concentration.

The question of concentration in American business received a great deal of attention as a result of study of this time period by Means, which was published in 1931 and which provided the impetus for a number of concentration studies in subsequent years.[10] Means's findings regarding the share of the 100 largest nonfinancial corporations in the total assets of all nonfinancial corporations identified for the first time the topmost group of firms and their place in the economy.

Various students of this late-1920s wave concede that concentration did increase somewhat as a result of the merger wave. Markham observed: "It has been fairly conclusively established that concentration of control of assets increased between 1924 and 1929, the 6-year span that includes most of the merger activity associated with the second merger movement."[11] Adelman was even more positive in his statement that "increased concentration during the 1924–29 period may be regarded as proved, i.e., the estimated change in the share of the top 200 seems to be greater than the reasonable limits of the depression around it."[12] Thus, there appears to be little doubt that the concentration of industry increased during the roaring twenties and that mergers played an important facilitating role.

The Promoters of Mergers

The increased propensity to promote was apparent again during the prosperity of the roaring twenties. The outside professional promoter appeared again during this wave to play a leading role as an initiator of mergers. As Markham observed, ". . . except where mergers were motivated by production and distribution economies . . . they appear to have been largely inspired by the professional promoter. This explains in part why the merger movement followed the pattern it did."[13]

The principal outside promoters during this second merger wave were the investment bankers. Thorp, in his study of the late 1920s discussed the role of investment bankers as promoters of merger and the intensity of their efforts as follows:

> Many mergers, and some acquisitions, involve the flotation of new securities. In periods like 1928 and early 1929, when there is almost an insatiable demand for securities, the merger movement will be certain to flourish. Its most active sponsor is the investment banker. Reputable business houses merely carrying on their business under their existing organization bring a very slight volume of securities for the banker to handle. But if they can be brought together, in a new organization, it may mean a large flotation of stock. During 1928 and 1929 some investment houses employed men on commission who did nothing but search for potential mergers. One business man told me that he regarded it as a loss of standing if he was not approached at least once a week with a merger proposition. A group of business men and financiers in discussing this matter in the summer of 1928 agreed that nine out of ten mergers had the investment banker at the core.[14]

Nadler, another student of the late-1920s merger wave, discusses the role of the investment banker and the businessman in the promotion of mergers and tells about the promoter's profits:

> Both the businessman and the banker find, especially in times when security prices are high and financing can be accomplished

> with ease, that consolidation may be prolific of large financial profits to themselves. . . . From the bankers' viewpoint, there is a powerful financial incentive to promote consolidation. The banker has access to the capital market which is often indispensable to the accomplishment of a business combination. By taking an active part in the working out of the combination—often by assuming the role of the actual promoter of the combine—the banker entitles himself to receive a substantial stock interest in the new company in reward for his services, and also benefits from profits on the sale of securities for the new company, both at the time of its organization and later if the occasion warrants. In fact, many of the largest consolidations have been conceived and carried out by bankers.[15]

During the late-1920s wave, the investment banker had an increased propensity to promote consolidations since the opportunities for rewards were abundant and it was not necessary to provide equity capital or assume much of the risk. In many cases, the shareholders' equity was diluted by the compensation methods employed (i.e., the outright gift of stock in the new firm). Nadler recognized this possibility when he said:

> In arranging the terms of the combination, provision must be made for rewarding bankers and others who have participated in the transaction. Where there are large shareholders in the enterprises involved, they may be satisfied to rely for their compensation upon the future enhancement in earning power of the properties in which they are interested. Frequently, however, especially in the case of consolidations, a block of shares is set aside for the promoters to purchase at an attractive price, or at times such shares are given outright as compensation. Where the bankers carry out new financing in connection with the combination, their reward may come through a large underwriting commission.[16]

The frenzied promotional efforts of these promoters, as well as the feverish speculation of these times, came to an abrupt halt with the crash of the stock market. The public's reaction to this type of promotion became apparent during the Depression years following this wave. "Promotional puffery" was a contributing factor in enticing many people to join the speculative whirl which burst like an explosion, wiping out the financial holdings of many individuals and families. The reaction of the public was not to call for a change in the antitrust laws to bring about a curtailment of merger activity (since this was accomplished automatically with the decline of prosperous times). Instead, a rash of new legislation emerged during the 1930s aimed at the promoters of mergers. This development was recognized by Markham, who observed: "It is not surprising, therefore, that the public's reaction to the merger movement of the 1920's was not more rigid enforcement of the Sherman Act, but the enactment of the Securities Act of 1933, the Securities Exchange Act of 1934, and the Holding Company Act of 1935."[17] Thus the legislation was not designed to curtail mergers per se, but instead it was aimed at some of the abuses of the promoters.

The importance of the investment banker in the merger field diminished with the separation of investment banking functions from the commercial banking functions during the 1930s.[18] It is also important to note that since consolidations are usually more spectacular than acquisitions, they tend to attract the attention of the observers of merger waves. As noted previously, there were a considerable number of acquisitions during this period, in contrast to the consolidations so prominent in the first wave. Since this form of merger is relatively less complicated to consummate than the consolidation, the management groups assumed a larger role in the promotion of mergers relative to their role during the first wave. It appears that the promoters in this wave emphasized a different rationale for the mergers as an aid to their promotional efforts. During the first wave, the large profits expected from increased market control and production economies were emphasized, and they do not appear to have been realized in any significant manner. During the second wave, more emphasis was directed to expected marketing economies than to production economies. Dewing recognized this when he observed:

> In the period before 1929, much more than in the earlier period consolidations were attempted in order to deal better with merchandising problems. Rubber factories and stationery factories were brought together merely because both rubber goods and stationery could be sold in drug stores, washing powder and breakfast foods because both were found on the shelves of grocery stores.[19]

Dewing's views are shared by Thorp, another astute student of the second merger wave, who says the following in regard to the growing importance of marketing in this period:

> The explanation of the rising secular trend is not to be found so much in the fact of production as in the field of marketing. The problem of the present-day businessman is much less to produce his products than to sell them. In many cases it seems to be true that the large concern is more effective in its marketing. It is not necessary to demonstrate that it is more economical. The point rather is that it seems to be better able to win and hold the public than its somewhat smaller competitors. It can use national advertising. It can deal with larger merchandising units. And it can offer a variety of products each of which may support the other. In many lines, marketing effectiveness appears to call for large size even more than productive economy.[20]

Markham tied in this belief of Dewing and Thorp to the promotion of mergers and the behavior of the promoters during the period; he said:

> In some cases the promoter could probably give convincing evidence that merger would be profitable, either because it made for lower buying, production, or distribution costs, or because it furthered product differentiation through national brand advertising, or both. In others, where the advantage of merger was not so evident, he found his product more difficult to sell. In such cases promoters (principally investment bankers) resorted to high-pressure salesmanship.[21]

Mergers and the Growth of Firms

Spectaculars of all sorts characterized the roaring twenties. Means gives some indication of the role of mergers in the growth of some of the large firms during this period; he says:

> The third and more spectacular method of growth of the large corporations is by consolidations or merger. In considering this growth, it is necessary to treat separately mergers between two companies already included in the list of two hundred companies and mergers in which one of these companies absorbs a company not included. In the six-year period under consideration 26 companies included in the list of 200 largest at one time or another during the period were acquired by another large corporation. This concentration of the 200 large companies in 1922 into a smaller group in 1927 required the addition of other companies to take the place of those absorbed if the total of 200 independent companies was to be maintained. The mergers therefore increased the assets of the 200 corporations in the latter year by the amount of the assets of the companies added. Since this involved the addition of smaller companies having average assets in 1927 of approximately $90,000,000, the increase in the assets of the 200 largest in 1927 over the 200 largest in 1922 would amount to roughly $2,340,000,000 (26 times $90,000,000). This is the amount of the increase in assets which should be attributed to mergers between companies already included in the 200 largest.
>
> The addition to the assets of the 200 largest companies through the acquisition of smaller companies is extremely difficult to estimate. It is safe to say, however, that it is large, perhaps involving an addition of as much as $2,000,000,000 for the six-year period.[22]

Thorp, another student of the merger wave during the late 1920s, says that "it is not surprising that the 'expansiveness' of the businessman during periods of prosperity often expresses itself in the merger movement and larger business organizations."[23]

Again, during this second merger wave, merger contributed substantially to the growth of a number of large firms which were using this form of growth as a vehicle to increase their size, in the hope of gaining some scale economies and/or increasing their own power and prestige among other reasons.

The Relative Success of Mergers

This extensive merger wave was followed by the most severe depression in American economic history, during which the economists of the period were busy trying to theorize how the nation could get on the road to recovery. In addition, they must have realized that most of the mergers consummated in the optimistic glow of the roaring twenties were struggling to keep their plants open, rather than having board meetings to attempt to divide the spoils of success. Consequently, we do not have many studies concerned with the relative success of merging firms for the second major merger wave. Comparitively little research was conducted on the mergers during this period, which prompted Markham to observe that "no one has yet written the 'Truth about Mergers' for the 1920's."[24]

The only study made during this period which reveals any pattern of relative success was conducted by the National Industrial Conference Board in 1929.[25] This survey of industrial combinations led to the following conclusion concerning the record of their stock values:

> They are far from being universally successful. Like other enterprises some go down in times of business stress, nor do all profit in equal degree from periods of business prosperity. Whether or not they have been more successful or less successful than enterprises organized upon a different basis there is no satisfactory means of measuring by statistical methods. But it at least seems to be clear that there are no inherent advantages in the consolidated form or organization which insure greater profitableness for the investor than is offered by many non-consolidated enterprises.[26]

In summarizing, the NICB study concluded that mergers had not generally attained a high degree of relative success:

> A study of the business history of a large number of consolidations, based upon published financial statements covering a period from ten to twenty-three years prior to the war, and upon the course of prices of their securities for a longer period, discloses that, by and large, these mergers did not prove exceptionally profitable. Some of them made high profits and grew in size and industrial importance correspondingly. But there were many that failed abso-

> lutely and passed out of existence. The majority did not achieve a conspicuous success as profit-makers . . . [and] the study makes clear that industrial consolidations have not provided a safe, easy, and sure way to business success.[27]

We can only speculate about the relative success of the mergers formed in the late 1920s; however, it would appear that the earnings of these mergers for the following decade were considerably lower than anticipated, since these were the years of the Great Depression. Although it is true that a number of these firms survived and have persisted to the present, it must be remembered that nonmerging firms have also survived, so that the test of survival regarding mergers is inconclusive and not especially persuasive. Certainly it is doubtful that the expected profitability test was passed during this period of economic contraction.

Mergers and Antitrust

Between the end of the first great wave and the beginning of the second wave in the 1920s, two additional antitrust laws were added to the books—the Clayton Act and the Federal Trade Commission Act, which were passed in 1914. Despite these additional weapons in the antitrust arsenal, another wave of merger activity became a historical fact during the prosperous twenties.

As noted previously, the predominant type of merger changed from the many-at-once consolidation to the acquisition of individual firms which were generally smaller in size than the acquiring firm. This development suggests that the mergers of the period were not necessarily designed to create monopolies, but rather (in many cases) to establish or reinforce oligopolistic positions. Stigler attributes this change to the existence of the Sherman Antitrust Law (which had failed to halt the first wave); he states that "the Sherman Law seems to have been the fundamental cause for the shift from merger for monopoly to merger for oligopoly."[28] Stigler further states: "Sometimes its workings were obvious, as when Standard Oil was dismembered and when the leading baking mergers were prevented from combining. More often, its workings have been more subtle: The ghost of Senator Sherman is an ex officio member of the board of directors of every large company."[29] Perhaps a more relevant factor was the new interpretation of the law as rendered by the courts. The Sherman Act was on the books during the period when mergers for monopoly were being consummated at the turn of the century.

It is obvious that during the second merger wave in the late 1920s, neither the Sherman Act, the Clayton Act, nor the Federal Trade Commission Act effectively curbed merger activity. These laws *did* have some impact (aided by the Northern Securities decision) on the form of merger. As noted previously, consolidations declined during this period, and there was a corresponding increase in the acquisition form of merger. Perhaps this development can be attributed mainly to the existence of the three antitrust laws and the legal interpretations of the courts. However, I am inclined to believe that another factor (which is not generally acknowledged in the literature) also contributed to this change, that is, the realization by the merger promoters that the early consolidations designed to achieve monopoly did not in fact generally produce either monopoly profits (as per Dewing and Livermore) or the anticipated "quiet life." Mergers and acquisitions for promoting or preserving oligopolies could eliminate actual or potential competitors in pricing, which appears to be the type of "trouble" managers dislike the most.

The emergence of a new generation and the growing prosperity of the roaring twenties caused a change in the public attitude concerning mergers and the concentration of industry during the second merger wave. Thorp recognized this when he said:

> There has been an amazing shift in public attitude towards the concentration of economic activity since the years before the war. Certainly, from 1890 to 1914 it was the prevailing opinion that any such trend as that outlined above was contrary to the interests of the public. *Today the only persons who appear to be disturbed by the announcement of the merger are those directly involved whose jobs or income may be threatened* [italics supplied].[30]

Following the peak of merger activity in 1929, the bottom dropped out of the economy. It is ironic, yet true, that the public (including the legislators) did not attempt to isolate the impact of the merger wave upon the collapse of prosperity. The attention of the public was diverted and directed elsewhere. The reaction after the stock market crash (which signaled an end to prosperity as well as the merger wave) was directed more toward promotional abuses than toward mergers per se. The result was no change in the antitrust laws; yet a rash of new legislation was passed by Congress. As Markham observed: "It is not surprising, therefore, that the public's reaction to the merger movement of the 1920's was not more rigid enforcement of the Sherman Act, but the enactment of the Securities Act of 1933, the Securities Exchange Act of 1934, and the Holding Company Act of 1935."[31]

Thorp, the major student of the second merger wave, collected and analyzed merger data for the period 1919–1930 and concluded that the Supreme Court was a factor in the movement; he said:

> It is a most interesting statistical record. All the things that a statistician glories in, are present. There is a secular trend, a cyclical movement, and a pronounced seasonal fluctuation.
>
> I suppose the first reaction of an individual not familiar with the developments in this field to this statistical display would be to inquire how such a degree of consolidation is possible in the country of the Sherman Anti-Trust Law, the Bureau of Corporations, the Clayton Act, the Federal Trade Commission, the "big stick" of Roosevelt, and thousands of board feet of antitrust plants [*sic*] in party platforms. The truth of the matter is that the Supreme Court has played a practical joke on the legislators.[32]

Many theories have been advanced and many factors cited to help explain the second merger wave, and yet the fact remains that it did take place, despite the existence of antitrust laws regarding merger activity. The antitrust laws did not deter a second merger wave.

The Environment for Mergers

The generally recognized fact that the roaring twenties was a period of relative prosperity and a buoyant stock market should be news to no one; it has been well documented over the years. The second great merger wave was part of this prosperous period. Weston recognized the influence of the buoyant stock market upon the merger wave when he said:

> The factor of overwhelming significance in the merger movement of the 1920's was the great bull market in security prices. Combinations took place to create new securities. Mergers made possible great gains to participating stockholders and promoters. Outside financing required in connection with some mergers was readily obtainable on very favorable terms in the buoyant capital markets. In these ways the extremely high stock-market prices stimulated the mergers of the late 1920's.[33]

Nelson also documented the important role of the stock market during this period; he said: "Since merger activity generally tends to follow business conditions rather than to move opposite to them, this finding suggests that, in years of peak merger activity, movements in stock prices may be more important than those in industrial production."[34] In a footnote to this statement, Nelson says: "The experience in the late 1920's also tends to support this hypothesis. Stock prices rose

150 percent from 1926 to 1929, merger activity rose 165 percent, and industrial production rose only 25 percent."[35]

Thorp, one of the leading students of the merger wave of the twenties, interrelated the role of the capital markets, prosperity, and mergers as follows:

> One important element which stimulates the merger movement in time of prosperity is the condition of the money market. Many mergers, and some acquisitions, involve the flotation of new securities. In periods like 1928 and early 1929, when there is almost an insatiable demand for securities, the merger movement will be certain to flourish. . . . The fact that the public will take the securities makes possible a sharing of the increased capitalization between the banker and the original owners and makes the owners willing to join the merger even when they can see little technical advantage to be gained from the new organization. This is undoubtedly the explanation for many of the larger mergers during periods of prosperity.[36]

Thorp has made a number of other interesting observations related to the second merger wave which seem to have almost universal application to merger waves of any period. Regarding mergers and prosperity, he said:

> I have already suggested that the timing of the data is not to be regarded as exact. Nevertheless one cannot help but be struck by the degree to which the merger movement corresponds to the business cycle. Industrial concentration appears to proceed most rapidly in periods of prosperity and to show a marked decline during depression.[37]

Discussing prosperity and the resulting increased cash flows and their impact upon the "expansiveness" of businessmen, Thorp said:

> A more significant factor is undoubtedly the large profits which many concerns have made during the period of prosperity, combined with the decision to use them for expansion rather than to distribute them to stockholders. . . . It is not surprising that the "expansiveness" of the businessman during periods of prosperity often expresses itself in the merger movement and larger business organizations.[38]

Thorp also made the following interesting observation relating the desire for increased control over pricing to periods of relative prosperity:

> A monopoly is most significant in times of prosperity. As some one said not long ago, "Who cares whether the price of copper is eight cents or twelve cents if no one is buying copper?" Price control is important when there is a volume of business. Price control is

desirable in a sellers' market. It is in times of prosperity that the elimination of competition is most profitable.[39]

Thus, two important environmental factors were present during the twenties; it was a period of (1) relatively prolonged prosperity and (2) a buoyant stock market, accompanied by the second great merger wave in our economic history.

Mergers and the Economy

Much as was the case in the first wave, both merger activity and stock prices led the peak of the business cycle during the late 1920s. Anticipation of large profits again contributed to high price-earnings ratios in 1929. However, investors become uncertain about the profit performance of many of the firms engaging in merger activity during the period, and prices tumbled late in the year. The only study for this period which is comparable to the Dewing study was the one made by the NICB in 1929. As mentioned previously this study demonstrated that merging firms did not demonstrate any superiority in profit performance, which again could have contributed to the new discounting undertaken by investors.

Business investment was a key factor in the economy during this period also, and except for a few minor differences, my analysis of this aspect of demand during the late 1920s is similar to my analysis of it during the first wave. Remember that the majority of mergers were of a different form during the second wave, with the acquisition rather than the consolidation dominating the merger activity. Thus, the mergers were less comprehensive and generally followed the pattern of a larger acquiring firm buying a smaller firm. The acquiring firms were also expanding by internal growth methods, and thus new investment spending was taking place simultaneously with the formation of mergers. The result was that new capacity was being added to industries as well as to individual firms, and this fact—that the relatively smaller acquisitions were being digested into the acquiring firms at the same time that they were building new capacity through internal growth and contributing to aggregate demand and prosperity—may explain the differences in longevity between the first two waves. The eventual decline resulted when profit expectations were not realized by the merging firms; this was similar to the situation during the first merger wave. However, the decline was delayed as a result of internal growth expenditures on new plant and equipment, which helped contribute cost savings and consequently offset the lower profits realized from the older assets acquired in the mergers.

Mergers and the Economist

The fact that the mergers of this period were less spectacular than the large consolidations of the previous period may have been one of the reasons why the profession was less concerned about this second merger wave. History repeated itself, since economists again did not recognize the vast merger activity until it was an accomplished fact. Some economists were still analyzing the effects of the first wave while the second wave was in progress. Whatever the cause, the output of research was small relative to that of the first wave. As Markham observed: "For the most part, the small body of literature on the movement that does exist is cast in fairly dispassionate tones."[40]

In a paper presented to the American Economic Association in 1930, Thorp summed up the attitudes of the profession and the public when he said:

> There has been an amazing shift in public attitude towards the concentration of economic activity since the years before the war. Certainly, from 1890 to 1914 it was the prevailing opinion that any such trend as that outlined above was contrary to the interests of the public. Today the only persons who appear to be disturbed by the announcement of the merger are those directly involved whose jobs or income may be threatened.
>
> It is difficult to determine whether economists have shared in this conversion or not. Our teaching and writing in this field are still so obsessed with the scandals of the nineteenth century and the finer points of the position taken by each supreme court justice in the various cases that we have said little about the significance of the present merger movement. The present movement raises certain new problems. For example, businessmen are asking for relief from the antitrust laws that they may stabilize their industries. In general, by this they mean stabilize prices. And by this they mean eliminate downward price movements.[41]

Stigler's analysis of the changing role of merger following the first wave was discussed previously. He believed that the merger movement underwent a great change: the creation or preservation of oligopoly rather than monopoly. In discussing the importance of this change as it related to the economics profession, he stated:

> It is true, no doubt, that oligopoly is a weaker form of monopolization than the single firm, but it is not so weak a form that it can be left to its own devices. If this view—which is almost universally held by modern economists—is correct, then our chief task in the field of antitrust policy is to demonstrate beyond judicial doubt the social undesirability of permitting oligopoly by merger (or by other methods) in large American industries.[42]

The essence of Stigler's statement is a call for economists to help frame public policy designed to restore a less concentrated industrial structure. His plea has, for the most part, fallen upon deaf and uninterested ears.

Another method of determining the interest and concern of the economics profession is to examine the contents of their major journal and the programs of their annual conventions. Their major journal, the *American Economic Review* (published by the American Economic Association), did not contain a single article about the late-1920s merger wave until it had subsided. One of the topics at the forty-third annual meeting, held from December 29 to December 31, 1930, was "The Modern Merger Movement," and the papers presented were published in the March, 1931, supplement of the *American Economic Review.*[43] Again, economists lagged and waited for the peak of the merger wave to be attained and passed before displaying any interest in the development. Even from a historical point of view, this second wave received scant attention from economists, who most likely were more concerned with the deep and prolonged Depression of the 1930s. Even the books which appeared during the 1920s by Seager and Gulick, Jones, Watkins, the NICB and others were concerned mainly with the problems of trusts or the first merger wave.[44]

Looking back upon the merger wave of the late 1920s, one observes that this wave was not as spectacular as its predecessor at the turn of the century, yet it was of sufficient magnitude to have deserved more attention than it has received. All the excesses, economic and otherwise, of this prosperous and speculative era were soon dissipated in the dismal depression years of the 1930s when many current managers were born or growing up. Newer generations are currently involved in another merger surge, which is the subject of the next chapter. It appears that different generations of management react in a similar manner when prosperity is achieved, as evidenced by the gay nineties, the roaring twenties, and the current period.

NOTES

[1] See Gardiner C. Means, "The Growth in the Relative Importance of the Large Corporation in American Economic Life," *American Economic Review,* vol. 21, no. 1, p. 31, table 7, March, 1931.

[2] The wholesale price level index was 52.2 in 1899 and 56.1 in 1900, as compared with 100.0 in 1926. See U.S. Bureau of the Census, *Historical Statistics of the United States: Colonial Times to 1957,* 1960, p. 117.

[3] Ralph L. Nelson, *Merger Movements in American Industry: 1895–1956,* Princeton, N.J.: Princeton University Press, 1959, p. 64.

[4] See, for example, Jesse W. Markham, "Survey of the Evidence and Findings

on Mergers," in National Bureau of Economic Research, Inc., *Business Concentration and Price Policy,* Princeton, N.J.: Princeton University Press, 1955, p. 167; Willard L. Thorp, "The Persistence of the Merger Movement," *American Economic Review,* supplement, vol. 21, no. 1, p. 79, March, 1931; and George J. Stigler, "Monopoly and Oligopoly by Merger," *American Economic Review,* vol. 40, no. 2, p. 31, May, 1950. This development will be discussed in more detail in Chap. 8 of this book.

[5] Joseph P. McKenna, "The Current Merger Movement," *Review of Social Economy,* vol. 16, no. 1, pp. 12–13, March, 1958.

[6] J. Fred Weston, *The Role of Mergers in the Growth of Large Firms,* Berkeley, Calif.: University of California Press, 1953, p. 83. While a forward vertical merger may give a firm control of facilities at the wholesale and/or retail level, it would appear that circular mergers are basically for marketing economies since costs could be spread over a larger product line.

[7] Federal Trade Commission, *Report on the Merger Movement,* 1948, p. 24.

[8] Markham, *op. cit.,* p. 171.

[9] See Stigler, *op. cit.*

[10] An article by Means is credited with having inaugurated the systematic study of concentration; see Means, *op. cit.,* pp. 10–42. Means's findings were included in a widely quoted book which appeared the next year and of which A. A. Berle was coauthor, entitled *The Modern Corporation and Private Property,* New York: The Macmillan Company, 1932. Their findings were elaborated some years later in a study entitled *The Structure of the American Economy,* Washington, D.C.: National Resources Committee, 1939, vol. I. See especially appendixes 10 and 11.

[11] Markham, *op. cit.,* p. 171, footnote.

[12] M. A. Adelman, "The Measurement of Industrial Concentration," *Review of Economics and Statistics,* vol. 33, no. 4, p. 285, November, 1951.

[13] Markham, *op. cit.,* p. 172.

[14] Thorp, *op. cit.,* pp. 85–86.

[15] Marcus Nadler, *Corporate Consolidations and Reorganizations,* New York: Alexander Hamilton Institute, 1930, pp. 12–13.

[16] *Ibid.,* pp. 168–169.

[17] Markham, *op. cit.,* p. 173.

[18] Nadler recognized the facilitating promotional role assumed by other groups in the late-1920s wave; he said: "In recent years lawyers and at times accountants have frequently acted as promoters in arranging a merger or consolidation. They may gain in the regular course of their business, considerable knowledge about individual firms and general conditions in an industry. They also can thus gain the confidence of individual executives, and a wide acquaintanceship in the trade which may greatly facilitate merger negotiations. Many recent chain store and manufacturing mergers have been arranged at the initiation of such promoters." This statement appeared in Nadler, *op. cit.,* p. 122.

[19] Arthur S. Dewing, *The Financial Policy of Corporations,* 4th ed., New York: The Ronald Press Company, 1941, p. 929. Dewing's description of these mergers is similar to the description of the concentric type of merger given by H. Igor Ansoff and J. Fred Weston in their article "Merger Objectives and Organizational Structure," *The Quarterly Review of Economics and Business,* vol. 2, no. 3, August, 1962.

[20] Thorp, *op. cit.*, p. 87.

[21] Markham, *loc. cit.*

[22] Means, *op. cit.*, pp. 30–32. He lists the firms that, at some time during the period 1922–1929, were acquired by other firms on the list; his total is forty-seven, or twenty-one more than mentioned for the period 1922–1927 (p. 31, table 7).

[23] Thorp, *op. cit.*, p. 86.

[24] Markham, *op. cit.*, p. 167.

[25] *Mergers in Industry: A Study of Certain Economic Aspects of Industrial Consolidation,* New York: National Industrial Conference Board, Inc., 1929.

[26] *Ibid.*, pp. 85–86.

[27] *Ibid.*, pp. 170–171.

[28] Stigler, *op. cit.*, p. 32.

[29] *Ibid.*

[30] Thorp, *op. cit.*, p. 88.

[31] Markham, *op. cit.*, p. 173.

[32] Thorp, *op. cit.*, p. 78.

[33] Weston, *loc. cit.*

[34] Nelson, *op. cit.*, p. 96. The word "follow" as used by Nelson gives the impression that merger activity is a lagging indicator. Actually, in his more recent research Nelson suggests that merger activity is a leading indicator, which is what one would expect if it correlates so well with stock prices. Nelson is really pointing out that mergers increase during periods of prosperity rather than in depressed times. See Ralph L. Nelson, "Business Cycle Factors in the Choice between Internal and External Growth," in William W. Alberts and Joel E. Segall (eds.), *The Corporate Merger,* Chicago: The University of Chicago Press, 1966, pp. 52–66.

[35] Nelson, *Merger Movements in American Industry: 1895–1956,* p. 96, footnote.

[36] Thorp, *op. cit.*, pp. 85–86.

[37] *Ibid.*, p. 85.

[38] *Ibid.*, p. 86.

[39] *Ibid.*, pp. 86–87.

[40] Markham, *op. cit.*, p. 167.

[41] Thorp, *op. cit.*, pp. 88–89.

[42] Stigler, *op. cit.*, pp. 32–33. Unfortunately, economists have not done much in a practical way to aid the courts and the regulatory agencies in their decision making.

[43] One of the papers presented at the convention was Thorp, *op. cit.;* the other paper was Myron W. Watkins, "Trustification and Economic Theory," *American Economic Review,* supplement, vol. 21, no. 1, pp. 54–76, March, 1931. Those taking part in the discussion were Charles A. Gulick, Jr., Chester W. Wright, William Orton, Ben W. Lewis, and Abraham Berglund.

[44] Henry R. Seager and Charles A. Gulick, Jr., *Trust and Corporation Problems,* New York: Harper & Brothers, 1929; Eliot Jones, *The Trust Problem in the United States,* New York: The Macmillan Company, 1921; Myron W. Watkins, *Industrial Combinations and Public Policy: A Study of Combination, Competition and Common Welfare,* Boston: Houghton Mifflin Company, 1927; and National Industrial Conference Board, Inc., *op. cit.*

5

The Current Merger Wave

There was relatively little merger activity during the Great Depression of the 1930s. As a matter of fact, the smallest amount of reported activity in the past fifty years occurred in 1939, when only eighty-seven mergers were entered on the record. An upswing was noticeable during the early forties, reaching a small peak in the immediate postwar years of 1946 and 1947. This ripple of merger activity prior to the current wave included slightly over two thousand mergers in the period 1940–1947, involving an estimated $5 billion in assets.

The current wave began in 1955 and has continued on a relatively high plateau since then, and the end is not yet in sight. This wave has been the most persistent of the major waves and has already displayed similarities to the previous waves, as well as some distinctively unique characteristics. The following examination of each of the merger facets should aid in a better understanding of this economic phenomenon and contribute to the development of a theory of merger.

The Magnitude of the Movement

Not only has the current merger wave (which shows no signs of abating) been the most persistent wave in our economic history, but it also has set a number of new records in the process. During the period 1955–1966, a total of 9,834 mergers were recorded, and if the estimated number of 1,400 for 1967 is included, the total will exceed 11,000 mergers. On the basis of numbers alone as an indicator, the movement is considerably larger than that of the period 1898–1902, when 2,653 mergers were reported, and also larger than the movement of the period 1925–1931, when there were 5,846 reported mergers. Considering that the ongoing current wave appears to be an open-end movement at this stage, the eventual record should be substantial in quantitative terms.

The other measure developed to indicate the amount of assets involved in the movement also presents an interesting picture. Using the estimates presented in Table 2.3 as an approximation, about $67 billion of assets have been involved in merger activity since 1955. Compared with the total manufacturing assets of corporations, partnerships, and proprietorships in 1963 of $290.3 billion,[1] the relative amount of assets involved in mergers is substantial. While the economy has changed considerably since the turn of the century, which makes any relative comparison subject to numerous qualifications, it appears on balance that the current ongoing merger wave either has become or is in the process of becoming the largest merger wave in American economic history. During the first ten months of 1967, an estimated $12 billion was spent on mergers, which is more (in absolute terms) than the aggregate total of assets involved in the turn-of-the-century wave.[2]

Merger Forms and Types

The merger-acquisition remains the dominant form of merger in the current wave. The pattern during the 1950s and 1960s is similar to that of the late 1920s; that is, most of the mergers have been made by large firms which are acquiring smaller firms and absorbing them into an existing organization. While there are occasional consolidations, they make up only a minor part of the total reported mergers in this current period.

The most striking characteristic of the current wave is that the merger-acquisitions have become more circular and conglomerate than either of the two previous waves. Keezer and his associates noted this change when they observed that the mergers are "aimed primarily at diversification, in which a firm switches from single to multiple products, often in an entirely new line of business."[3] In commenting upon the importance of this development, Keezer and Associates made the following interesting observation:

> This new type of merger may work a significant change in the evolution of American business. It may mean that business corporations, once established, see themselves as having a durability extending beyond their commitment to any particular line or lines of business. Such firms, often endowed with a real *esprit de corps* among employees and stockholders, will not willingly shut up shop even if there is nothing further for them to do in their original field or fields. With a pool of management, techniques, equipment, and capital—which is too valuable to scrap or not to use to full capacity—the company will seek new worlds to conquer.[4]

Despite the rapid growth of circular and conglomerate mergers, the horizontal merger has remained a contributor to the large number of recorded mergers during this wave, particularly in the initial years. Two studies completed during the early phase of the current wave support this conclusion.[5] The FTC studied the time period from January 1, 1951, to July 31, 1954, and noted that "the advantage most frequently identified among acquisitions recorded by the Commission is an increase in the acquirer's capacity to supply a market it was already serving. An estimated 804 of the 2,091 acquisitions contained this feature."[6] The remainder achieved some measure of diversification for the acquiring firm.

I also did a study which included a sample of firms engaging in ninety-one mergers consummated during the period 1950–1959. Using questionnaires and personal interviews, I found that twenty-eight of the ninety-one mergers were for the purpose of acquiring additional capacity to supply existing markets, twenty-nine were for capacity to supply new markets, and fourteen were for a lengthened product line.[7]

While the horizontal merger is still a factor in the current wave, the most unique characteristic of this wave is the large increase in the use of circular and conglomerate mergers, in contrast to the earlier major waves. Data for three periods during the 1948–1964 time span are presented in Table 5.1. It is becoming obvious that large firms have been diversifying across industry and product or service lines.[8] The conglomerate mergers are classified by the definitions used previously, that is, by the combination of unrelated firms in both production and marketing functions. There has been a tendency in recent years to label mergers as "conglomerate" if they do not fit into either the horizontal or the vertical category. This is an inaccurate practice and only tends to confuse

TABLE 5.1 Distribution of Large Manufacturing and Mining Acquisitions by Type and Period of Acquisition

Type of Merger	*1948–1953* No.	*1948–1953* %	*1954–1959* No.	*1954–1959* %	*1960–1964* No.	*1960–1964* %
Horizontal:*						
Pure	18	31.0	78	24.8	42	12.0
Geographic market Extension	4	6.9	20	6.4	24	6.9
Vertical	6	10.3	43	13.7	59	17.0
Circular	27	46.6	145	46.2	184	52.9
Conglomerate	3	5.2	28	8.9	39	11.2
Total	58	100.0	314	100.0	348	100.0

*The pure horizontal merger is one in which the merging firms produce one or more closely related products in the same geographical market. The geographical market extension mergers are those in which the acquiring and acquired firms manufacture the same products, but sell them in different geographical markets. The totals are the same in the revised table above and the FTC table; however, the classifications are different because of the FTC method of classifying horizontal geographical market extension and circular mergers in the conglomerate category.

Source: Adapted from Committee on the Judiciary, Senate Subcommittee on Antitrust and Monopoly, *Economic Concentration,* 89th Cong., 1st Sess., 1965, testimony of W. F. Mueller, Table 5, p. 516.

the analysis of the conglomeration movement. There has also been an attempt to relate conglomerate mergers to the so-called synergistic benefits commonly associated with "concentric" mergers, which is also obviously incorrect because of the unrelated characteristics of the firms involved.

As a result of the increasing use of conglomerate mergers, many firms and industries are losing their distinctive characteristics and are changing their names to reflect this development. Examples abound, such as U.S. Rubber Company, which has become Uniroyal; American Brake Shoe, which has become Abex Corporation; and the former Pressed Steel Car Company, which has adopted the all-encompassing name of U.S. Industries, to name but a few. These firms are abruptly reversing a hallowed concept that firms should specialize, and they are breaking down traditional industry boundaries by moving into products, services, and markets that are quite different from, and sometimes unrelated to, their "normal" activities. Reynolds Tobacco, commonly associated with cigarettes, sells poultry, catsup, canned soups, and soft drinks. Hershey Chocolate is now in the macaroni business, and a leading dairy firm, Borden, is heavily engaged in chemicals.

In addition to the growing number of firms that "dabble" in conglomeration, there are the "real pros" of diversification. Firms such as Textron, FMC, Litton, Gulf & Western, W. R. Grace & Company, and IT&T are examples. Textron now comprises twenty-eight wholly separate firms making everything from helicopters to sunglasses and fountain pens. FMC makes chemicals and fibers, as well as its original products in the food and agricultural machinery line. Gulf & Western varies from auto parts to zinc and motion pictures, while Litton consists of forty divisions making everything from meat market showcases to computers and various learning devices. W. R. Grace & Company, the shipping and South American operator, has become engaged in chemicals and consumer foods. IT&T has an assortment of enterprises besides the telephone such as furnaces, finance companies, life insurance, films and phonograph records, parking lots, and the No. 2 auto rental service, which claims to "try harder." The No. 1 auto rental service firm recently put one of the biggest electronics firms in the driver's seat by exchanging their shares for $185 million of RCA stock.

The foregoing examples illustrate the compelling rush into conglomeration by some large American business firms which have discovered that mergers of this type are not likely to be challenged by the government on antitrust grounds. The plain truth is that the government has not figured out a method of preventing mergers of this type under the antitrust laws. The legislative bodies have not changed the laws, so that the lack of legislation coupled with a lackadaisical enforcement of existing laws by the administration have provided an environmental factor contributing in part to the current merger wave. It is reasonable to predict that Congress will continue to grapple with the problem and perhaps will eventually pass some legislation. In the meantime, the Senate and House hearings will continue, as the legislators go through the motions of attempting to arrive at a consensus solution. Simultaneously, American business will continue its rush toward conglomeration. Eventually, a government document may contain testimony similar to the following example:

SCENE: WASHINGTON, D.C.—SENATE OFFICE BUILDING

A Senate subcommittee has invited a witness to testify about the conglomerate movement, and in the midst of cameras, bright lights, staff assistants, and bottles (filled with water), the senator in charge gavels the hearing to order:

Committee chairman: Our first witness today is Mr. Roger M. Plow, the chairman of RSK Corporation, which you will all remember as the former

Railway Machine Corporation. That was prior to their merger with Swan Dixie Cup Company, when the name of the firm was changed to Railway Cup Company. The present name was adopted following the acquisition of Sala Spaghetti Company, Pan-Southern Airways, Knott Clothing Company, and, I believe, the Minnesota Mustang Professional Sports Corporation. I have also heard that their latest acquisition is the Electronic Furthburner Company. I'm not sure what a furthburner is—perhaps you can enlighten us, Mr. Plow?

Mr. Plow: Thank you, Senator. It's a pleasure to be here today. Before I answer your question, Senator, perhaps it would be appropriate to correct the record to include my new title of "Doctor."

Chairman: Excuse me, Mr. Plow, I was not aware that you were an M.D.

Mr. Plow: I am now a D.M., Senator, a doctor of management. The degree was conferred last week when I gave the commencement address at one of our colleges. Your committee has overlooked another of our new divisions—the education division. Our vice-president of that division invited me to talk with the customers, rather than the students, and the topic I chose should interest you, "The Preservation of a Free Enterprise System." Our young people need more talks on that subject, with all this growth of power in the government. This is one of my real concerns, and this is precisely why we bought the colleges. I think students should know the kind of economics and discipline that I know. We teach them about Adam Smith and about law and order. There are no demonstrations or anything like that in our colleges. We insist that the students stay in line—you know what I mean, Senator. None of that long hair and "go-go" stuff in *our* colleges.

Chairman: Thank you for correcting the record and for that interesting statement Mr., or rather "Dr.," Plow. Since you have refreshed my memory, I do recall reading about your talk in the California papers.

Mr. Plow: Oh yes, they gave me a good spread. We own those papers now, you know. We decided we needed a news division because of our rapidly growing sports division. They tell me that this kind of acquisition helps our synergy position.

Chairman: I'm not sure I understand, Mr. Plow.

Mr. Plow: Synergy—the "two-plus-two-equals-five" effect. That's why we bought the airlines also; it helps with our travel problems. And besides, since all the rail mergers, it's virtually impossible to use the train to travel anymore. Besides, our executives like it, and we get plenty of goodwill. You probably have your free pass by now, Senator, since we send them to all the important people. It's good business and a tax write-off—that's important.

Chairman: Thank you, Mr. Plow. Now about this synergy—I have heard about that. Can you tell us more about what it means?

Mr. Plow: I don't know exactly, Senator, but it's not important anyway because I know intuitively that it's beneficial to our firm and to society. We think about the public and the community in every merger we make.
Chairman: Well, I'm sure that what you and your firm do is good for the economy. I know that you are very interested in our economy, Mr. Plow, since you serve on the President's Business-Government Advisory and Policy Committee. I know that committee is in close contact with the President on matters such as national defense, education, and taxes. However, I'm not sure if we ever found out what a furthburner is?
Mr. Plow: Excuse me, Senator, I'm not sure myself, but it does sound good, doesn't it? Our financial vice-president thought it would help our stock prices so . . .
Chairman: Has it helped your stock prices?
Mr. Plow: Well, I'm not sure. I've been busy and haven't checked those prices lately—in the last few months, that is. You know how it is when you get busy, you . . .
Chairman: Well, Mr. Plow, can you briefly give us your analysis of diversification?
Mr. Plow: It's great!
Chairman: How do your stockholders feel about diversification and conglomeration?
Mr. Plow: Stockholders? Pardon me, Senator, but . . .
Chairman: Yes, you know—have all these mergers helped your earnings per share?
Mr. Plow: Earnings per share—well, Senator, that's old-fashioned. Nowadays—well, we don't discuss that very much anymore.
Chairman: Well just for old times' sake, tell us about your earnings record for the past few years.
Mr. Plow: I'm sorry, Senator, I don't remember and I don't have that data.
Chairman: What about your annual report?
Mr. Plow: Annual report. Oh yes—well, Senator, we used to publish one; however, we decided to send out a catalog instead. It has a lot of good pictures in it, and it gives our stockholders a chance to use their stamps.
Chairman: Stamps? I don't understand.
Mr. Plow: In order to conserve cash we decided to give the stockholders stamp dividends instead of money. You see, our stamp division . . .
Chairman: What do your stockholders think of this?
Mr. Plow: Well, if they don't like it, they can sell their stock—actually those people are better off with stamps than money anyway.
Chairman: What do you mean?
Mr. Plow: We make a lot of products, and they can redeem their stamps for everything we make, like rail cars, clothes, food, drugs, pool tables,

furthburners, guns, butter, a college education, or retraining if they wish. Also, our sports division has tickets, and our airlines and vacation divisions are popular also.

Chairman: You mean they can get guns *and* butter as well as all those other things?

Mr. Plow: Yes, sir, if they have enough stamps.

Chairman: Thank you, Mr. Plow, for your enlightening testimony, and I know the President will be interested to know that you can get both guns *and* butter. Perhaps we should run our economy like you run your firm.

Mr. Plow: Thank you for the plug, Senator. Actually, I have been thinking about public office myself for some time now. Since you need so much capital to get into politics, I sold all my stock a few years ago (before the stamp plan) and put it into real estate and government bonds—the tax-free kind, of course. Let me know if you need any advice, Senator.

While this fictitious example may be an overexaggeration, it does illustrate the point that a growing number of American firms are rapidly becoming "general stores of business."

Another type of acquisition which is becoming increasingly important is the "partial acquisition," which occurs when a firm buys a division or other part of a firm or when a firm purchases a block of stock of another firm either as a pure investment or with an eye to future takeover possibilities.[9] Although this cannot be considered a new development, it has been happening with increasing frequency in recent years. This could be the natural result not only of increased merger activity in general but of the growth of the conglomerate type as well. The conglomerates can be expected to carry out some "corporate pruning" activities, which will show up in the partial acquisition figures.

In summary, the merger-acquisition is the dominant form of merger in the current wave, while the most striking characteristic of this wave is the growing utilization of the circular and conglomerate merger types. Diversification (both product and geographical), rather than strictly monopolistic power per se has caught the fancy of the professional managers of big business firms.

Mergers and Concentration

In order to determine whether the current merger wave has had an impact upon concentration, the discussion will be confined to the most recent studies covering approximately the time period under consideration. These recent studies indicate that there has been a definite increase in the share of the largest business firms since the stable or deconcentration period of World War II, when merger activity was at a relatively low ebb.[10]

Among the most recent studies is that of the period 1950–1962 made by the FTC and referred to by Mueller in his statement before the Senate Subcommittee on Antitrust and Monopoly; he testified:

> To sum up, the Commission's earlier studies in the area of aggregate concentration indicate that there has been a sizable increase in concentration for manufacturing as a whole. Between 1950 and 1962 the share of manufacturing assets held by the 200 largest corporations increased from 46.7 to 54.6 percent and the share held by the 100 largest corporations grew from 38.6 to 45 percent. Hence, by 1962 the share held by the 100 largest firms was almost as great as the share held by the 200 largest in 1950 . . . [and] the 200 largest manufacturing firms alone acquired over 2,000 concerns with combined assets of about 17.5 billion. . . . In other words, the acquisition activity of the top 200 was sufficient to more than wipe out the equivalent of the second tier of 1,000 corporations in manufacturing.[11]

In another study, Kottke pointed out that between December 31, 1950, and September, 1959, 138 of the 1,001 largest manufacturing firms as of the starting date disappeared by merger, and over 75 percent of the firms were acquired by firms among the largest 500.[12] Kottke concluded that "mergers of the last eight years have increased significantly already existing disparities in size among the largest manufacturing companies."[13] Admittedly, changes in the size differentials of individual firms may or may not have an impact on concentration levels; however, they can be a contributing cause and should be examined. In view of the other available evidence that is relevant to the recent wave, one can safely infer that the levels are rising. *Fortune* recently reported that 68 of the original 500 largest firms (included on their first list, published in 1955) have disappeared by merger in the last decade.[14]

The evidence confirming the trend toward increasing concentration during the current wave of mergers continues to pile up. The most comprehensive examination concerning the current concentration question has been conducted by the Senate Subcommittee on Antitrust and Monopoly through a series of hearings extending over the past few years.[15] The chairman of this subcommittee, Senator Philip A. Hart of Michigan, made the following observation during the hearings:

> For too long we have kept our heads in the sand and refused to recognize what I think most responsible businessmen long have known, that our economy is becoming increasingly concentrated.

> We had hearings last July and September, and at those first hearings we established that whatever measuring stick we might use, overall concentration has increased significantly since 1947.
>
> One example: Since 1947 the 100 largest manufacturing corporations increased their share of total assets of all manufacturing firms from 39.3 to 48.1. During the same time, their share of net capital assets (land, buildings, and equipment) rose from 45.8 to 56.9. We learned that mergers and acquisitions played a prominent role in this increase in overall concentration.[16]

Shepherd made an interesting concentration study of the period 1947–1958.[17] He found that "overall concentration" had increased more rapidly in this period than "intraindustry concentration." The rising tide of conglomerate mergers was advanced as a partial explanation; he stated:

> It appears then, that large firm conglomerate diversification (through merger and innovation) has played some role in keeping intra-industry concentration about constant while the over-all share of the largest firms has been increasing. This lends some support to the rising concern among some economists and policy makers about large firm diversification in American industry.[18]

The increased utilization of conglomerate mergers by large firms in the United States during recent years supports the economic logic of examining the role of the 100 or 200 largest firms in the economy. Since large firms view the probabilities of acceptance by antitrusters as higher for conglomeration mergers, they are tending to move more in this direction. The important additional factor of continuity of the firm through diversification is also undoubtedly present. Customer-supplier-competitor relationships are becoming increasingly blurred in the process.

Shepherd has also provided a most interesting study concerning trends of concentration in oligopolistic industries, which was prompted by the differing opinions of Stigler and Bain. Stigler has suggested (in an analysis of oligopoly pricing) that in "open" oligopoly, the dominant firms will often deliberately give up part of their market share over time, as a side effect of their long-run profit maximizing, thus leading to the prediction that concentration will decline over time.[19] In contrast, Bain suggests that oligopolists will try to forestall entry in order to maintain or increase their market shares.[20] Oligopolists then adopt "limit pricing" as one of a number of barriers to new competition to protect their market positions. Shepherd analyzes the differences of opinion between Stigler and Bain as follows:

> Bain's conclusions evidently differ from Stigler's chiefly because of differences in the implied assumptions about the time discount

rate with which oligopolists weight future profit streams, as compared to the oligopolist's natural desire to maintain or increase his absolute and relative market size *per se*. Yet Stigler's analysis clearly predicts declining concentration, whereas Bain's would predict no change, and possibly an increase in concentration in oligopolistic industries.[21]

Shepherd tested these alternative hypotheses to determine whether there had been a general decrease, an approximate constancy, or an increase in concentration in oligopolistic industries during the period 1947–1958. His findings were:

> One concludes that declining concentration simply has not been the prevailing pattern for "oligopolies" in postwar American industry. On the contrary, the 35 "oligopolies" show a greater tendency for concentration to increase, and less for it to fall, than does the entire population of 4-digit industries. This is in accord with Lanzillotti's evidence that an important objective of large firms is to maintain their market shares.[22]

Another concern related to the concentration question is the role of new entry, since increased entry may offset some of the loss resulting from increased merger activity. One method of determining this is to examine changes in the business population; these changes for the period 1952–1962 are presented in Table 5.2. It is interesting to note that the manufacturing sector was the only area which declined during this time period. These results suggest that the current merger wave is having an adverse impact upon the structure of American manufacturing.

TABLE 5.2 Recent Changes in Business Population

	January 1			
Industry	*1952**	*1962**	*Change, 1952–1962**	*Average Annual Rate of Change, 1952–1962, %*
All industries	4,118	4,752	634	1.5
Retail trade	1,831	2,022	191	1.0
Wholesale trade	276	326	50	1.8
Services	740	917	177	2.4
Manufacturing	328	318	—10	—0.3
Contract construction	387	473	86	2.2
Mining, transportation, and finance	557	696	139	2.5

* In thousands.

Source: U.S. Department of Commerce.

A government document has cautioned: "Thus, it is clear that disappearances of independent enterprises are not easily offset by new entrants. Indeed, it is in the expansion and growth of enterprises that have already weathered risks of the early years that the greatest 'entry' challenge to dominant firms lies, and these are likely to be the very firms that disappear through mergers."[23]

Current Concentration, Bigness, and Innovation

This examination of the impact of merger waves upon the concentration of industry leads to the inescapable and rather disconcerting conclusion that concentration has increased during each of these periods of time. The lack of public and professional concern about this development is disturbing and yet partially understandable. Increasing concentration is viewed in many circles as a potential benefit since it is assumed that it leads to innovative practices, which are believed to be synonymous with increasing monopoly and/or size. Much of this pseudoconsolation stems from the Schumpeterian hypothesis expounded over twenty-five years ago.[24] This hypothesis asserts that the possession of accumulated monopoly rewards, the anticipation of additional rewards in the future, and the security which accrues from market power are prerequisites to the assumption of risks and the uncertainties of pursuing innovational activities. The innovations, as defined by Schumpeter, were broad enough to include mergers, new organization, new advertising campaigns, new products, and new processes. It certainly would not be appropriate to assign equal weights to each innovational activity. Value judgments obviously will determine the relative importance of each; however, it appears that the latter two (new products and new processes) would be the result of research and development expenditures. Some people assume that R & D expenditures are a function of size of firm and that since mergers contribute to increased size, they are *ceteris paribus* beneficial.

Recent empirical research by Hamberg, Scherer, Mansfield, Schmookler, Worley, and others suggests that unqualified acceptance of the Schumpeterian hypothesis (and newer interpretations of it) would indeed be a serious mistake.[25] Regarding the assumed compatibility of bigness rather than smallness with inventive output, Scherer finds that ". . . the data suggest that smallness is not necessarily an impediment to the creation of patentable inventions and may well be an advantage."[26] In specific reference to the concentration question, Scherer states that his results imply "that technological output should tend to increase with concentration up to a point, but that it may decline if too much of an industry's output becomes concentrated in the hands of a single dominant seller."[27] This finding would tend to lend support to the proponents of diversification or conglomeration; however, Scherer finds that ". . . diversification was not per se a structural condition necessarily favorable to patentable invention."[28] Scherer concludes: "These findings among other things raise doubts whether the big, monopolistic, conglomerate corporation is as efficient an engine of technological change as disciples of Schumpeter (including myself) have supposed it to be. Perhaps a bevy of fact-mechanics can still rescue the Schumpeterian engine from disgrace, but at present the outlook seems pessimistic."[29]

It appears that much of the apathy concerning merger waves and concentration is being dispelled as a result of a bevy of empirical research findings. It is possible that constructive policy considerations will eventually emerge; however, since merger waves occur during relatively prosperous periods, the possibility and probability of change are lessened.

Interwave Concentration Studies

Other studies have been made using different time periods and were designed principally to determine whether concentration has been increasing since the turn of the century. A number of these studies were concluded just prior to the beginning of the current wave. Some of the studies indicate that concentration within individual industries appears to have declined slightly, or at least not to have risen, during the first half of this century.[30] Others have found that overall concentration appears to have remained approximately constant or to have increased slightly during the first half of the century, although there was some reduction in the top firms' share during World War II, when mergers were relatively less important.[31] Since these studies had terminal dates prior to the current wave and beginning dates in proximity to the conclusion of major waves of merger activity (which increase concentration levels), the results should be discounted accordingly when considering the impact of waves of merger activity upon concentration. Adelman, for example, studied the period 1909–1947 and summarized his research as follows: "(1) The American economy is highly concentrated. (2) Concentration is highly uneven. (3) The extent of concentration shows no tendency to grow, and it may possibly be declining. Any tendency either way, if it does exist, must be at the pace of a glacial drift."[32]

Thus Adelman believed that concentration was remaining relatively stable, using the base year 1909 and the terminal year 1947, which was prior to the beginning of the current wave. As discussed above,

Shepherd found that overall concentration increased between 1947 and 1958, a period which includes the initial part of the current wave. Collins and Preston used the same base year as Adelman, 1909, and the terminal year used by Shepherd, 1958, and they found that ". . . the share of the 100 largest firms in the assets of all industrial corporations has increased from something under 25 percent (perhaps from under 18 percent) in 1909 to nearly 30 percent in 1958."[33] The evidence strongly supports the contention that the current wave has contributed to increased concentration since the late forties.

A more recent study by Adelman contends that the share of the 100 largest industrials was virtually the same in 1931 and 1961.[34] However, these findings must be discounted since Adelman advanced the base year in the study from 1909 to 1931. Thus his results reflect the increased concentration which resulted during the second merger wave of the 1920s. The fact that Adelman advanced the base year is subject to question since he has acknowledged that concentration increased during the 1920s (as cited previously).[35] The interwave concentration studies are interesting and have been accorded a considerable amount of attention (perhaps more than they deserve). The fact remains that if we wish to know the impact of merger waves upon concentration, a more enlightened approach would be to study the time periods when they occur.

In summary, the studies which have been designed to measure changes in overall concentration during the current merger wave affirm that the share of the largest firms is increasing. Mergers have played an important role in this trend toward a more highly concentrated economy. The growing utilization of circular and conglomerate mergers has tended to hold intraindustry concentration relatively stable, since ownership changes of this type do not necessarily affect concentration levels within particular industries in a narrowly defined sense.

The Promoters of Mergers

The principal promotion efforts during the current wave have been generated by the managers of the acquiring firms. Recognition of this fact is found in most of the emerging literature concerned with the current wave.[36] For example, the following statement appeared in an article in the "Keeping Informed" section of the *Harvard Business Review:* "A review of these listings indicates that acquisitions are now running at the rate of some 1,200 per year. . . . If you add to this the large number of companies that are looking for attractive acquisitions but have not made one, it becomes apparent that this activity is engaging the attention of a substantial proportion of top management in industry."[37]

"Growthmanship" has emerged in recent years as a major corporate preoccupation, a game with wide appeal in business circles. It has become evident that the mania for growth is not the exclusive property (as commonly believed) of government bureaucrats. This intense preoccupation with growthmanship by top executives in many firms has naturally revived interest in the use of merger and acquisition since this is a valued tool in the growthmanship kit. In their management-oriented book concerning mergers, Mace and Montgomery recognize that the responsibility for growth is at the top level of the firm; they state: "The basic responsibility for charting corporate growth is an inseparable part of the chief operating executive's job. It is he who must set short- and long-term goals and outline plans for obtaining them. He may draw upon advice and counsel of the company's line and staff officers but the ultimate responsibility is his."[38] They further state that ". . . in every company in which there was a successful acquisition program, the chief operating executive was personally involved. There were no exceptions."[39] It appears evident that top management is assuming a dominant role in current merger promotion.

This emerging and leading promotional role played by management in the current wave is summed up succinctly in the following statement by a businessman, which appeared in a report published by the American Management Association: "The present phase might well be called the period of management-oriented mergers. In general, the basic purpose is not to monopolize or to pyramid financial structures, but rather, to create and bring together logical industrial and operational empires—business entities of power, commercial position, stability, improved sales and earnings, and greater likelihood of growth and longevity of existence."[40]

Kaplan, a student of the early part of the current merger wave, recognized the increased participation of management when he stated: "In this current movement, not only does the initiative come primarily from management rather than outside financiers, but there is a very definite focusing on the managerial problems of the growing enterprise."[41]

The FTC examined the activities of the various promoters of mergers in their study of the early phase in the current wave and concluded: "On the basis of available materials, it appears that by far the most important type of promotion is that which is carried on by the acquiring company. In such acquisitions the operating executives of the acquiring firm initiate a plan to purchase stock or assets or in some manner take the lead in working out a procedure designed to effect a combination of interests."[42]

In the only study available on the current wave which contains some quantitative data, I found that management was involved in the promotion of approximately 90 percent of the mergers in the sample analyzed for the period 1950–1959, and that about two-thirds were initiated by the acquiring firm's management.[43]

A number of firms have set up new staff positions whose principal function is to search out merger and acquisition opportunities. It is not uncommon to find ads in the employment section of newspapers for personnel to fill positions with such titles as "Director of Acquisitions," "Director of Corporate Development," and so forth. In addition, management or the other promoters need a considerable amount of facilitating effort to consummate a large merger. Management is offered the special services set up by law firms, accounting firms, management consultants, investment brokers, bankers, and the increasing number of business brokers who are entering the field. As one might expect, these outside groups will become more numerous as the merger wave develops into a high tide which spurs more activity as long as business conditions are relatively prosperous and the stock market buoyant. There are groups with vested interests, in addition to management, that can benefit substantially from a sustained merger wave, since it is possible to share in the promoters' profits. An FTC report observed: "Various methods are used in compensating promotional helpers for their assistance. A common practice is to pay a professional promoter a cash retainer fee to cover his immediate expenses and to assign him a block of stock if the acquisition or merger is consummated."[44]

When management receives the assistance of various outside parties in the consummation of a merger, the question of fees to be paid can be a problem. This situation was emphasized in a *Harvard Business Review* article in which it was stated: "These fees can amount to very substantial sums for doing what may seem to be a very small amount of work. Unfortunately, there are always some unscrupulous parties active as business brokers who seek opportunities to demand a fee even in situations where logic would suggest that they are not entitled to one."[45]

The FTC report sums up the situation in the current wave, in which management is playing a more important promotional role than in the prior merger waves and, in the process, is being assisted by a diverse group of outside firms or individuals:

> While most of today's corporate acquisitions are promoted by the operating executives inside the industries involved, the importance

of outside assistance in their initiation and development should be fully recognized. Many outstanding law firms have attorneys who specialize in the various questions of Federal, State, and other laws involved in corporate development. A well-known firm of research engineers in the Boston area has a department set up solely to assist its industrial clients in selecting desirable prospects for mergers or acquisitions. A New York firm of industrial engineers specializes in promoting corporate acquisitions; a firm of economic consultants in the same city specializes in the same activity; and many like firms provide a broad list of such services. A leading bank in Chicago has a vice president who runs a clearing house and brokerage firms in several cities make studies for determining values of companies which may be acquired, and propose deals themselves. In many instances, of course, the outside agency is brought in by an inside industrialist who has spotted an opportunity for an advantageous acquisition or merger.[46]

One final word about the promotion of mergers during the current wave: While the major emphasis in this study of merger waves has been on the industrial side, we shall be examining bank mergers later in Part 2 of this book. Many managers of industrial firms which have been active in the current wave are also members of the boards of directors of commerical banks. While I have no empirical data, I have had discussions with a limited number of bank managers, and my impression is that some of these bank directors from industrial firms recommend and support the use of merger as a form of bank growth at board meetings. It is perhaps paradoxical that during the late-1920s wave a large share of industrial merger activity was promoted by bankers, while currently it could be that the reverse is true to some extent, that is, that many bank mergers are encouraged by industrial managers who are board members of commercial banks.

The most striking development in the current wave is the increased intensity of managerial effort applied to the promotion of merger activity. The role of professional managers has grown from a rather passive one in the first wave to one of active involvement in recent years. It is also interesting to note the increased promotion of conglomerate mergers. The rationale behind this type of merger is not necessarily production economies, marketing economies, or direct market control. Continuity of the firm and stabilized earnings are the main advantages generally cited for the conglomerate merger. In some cases, the promoters also cite expected financial economies, as some industrial firms are beginning to appear more like investment trusts than manufacturers. The implication is that manager-investors can make better investment decisions than stockholders.

In summary, the current merger wave is being promoted for the most part by management groups with the assistance of many service organizations. The role of top management in the promotion of mergers has grown consistently during each of the major waves, to the point where top management is currently the most active of the promotional groups, in contrast to their relatively passive role at the turn of the century. While many of the circular mergers in the current wave are promoted with the expectation of marketing and research economies, the increased use of the conglomerate type is based on quite different considerations. The merging of completely unrelated firms is promoted more for continuity of the enterprise and stability of earnings than for expected economies from operations. In addition, the fusion of large firms with unrelated products and service activities can instantaneously create business entities of considerable size, increasing the role of management in resource allocation and thus enhancing management's power and prestige. A new type of managerial revolution of considerable magnitude is under way in the American economy.

Mergers and the Growth of Firms

Merger is also proving to be a powerful method of growth for many large firms during the current merger wave. As noted previously, Kottke pointed out that between December 31, 1950, and September, 1959, 138 of the 1,001 largest manufacturing firms as of the starting date disappeared by merger, which led Kottke to conclude that "mergers of the last eight years have increased significantly already existing disparities in size among the largest manufacturing companies."[47]

In a later chapter, I shall present the results of a study which suggests that firms using merger as a means of growth have increased the size-related variables of assets, sales, and employees considerably more than nonmerging firms. Additional evidence is presented in a *Fortune* article related to the publication of their list of the 500 largest industrial firms in 1965. In discussing the role of mergers in the growth of these large firms during the current wave of mergers, Loomis stated:

> Since the companies that transformed themselves through mergers and acquisitions so often grew from bases that were small in 1955, they tend to dominate any list of heavy gainers in percentage sales growth. In fact, that list of the twenty leaders consists entirely of companies that were not big enough to appear on the 500 list in 1955. *What's more, the only company on this list which can claim that almost all of its growth has been internally generated is Xerox* [italics supplied].[48]

A report of another interesting development (which can be compared with the earlier statement by Means concerning the merger activity of large firms during the late 1920s) appeared in this issue of *Fortune:*

> A fair number of the acquisitions made by the companies in this directory have been substantial enough to involve other companies that had themselves been listed in earlier directories. Of those on the 1955 list, no fewer than sixty-eight have since had their businesses acquired, in one way or another, by other companies—most of them on the current list. The largest company to "vanish" was Pure Oil, whose sales were over the $600-million level when it was merged into Union Oil last year. The next largest was Philco, which was doing some $400 million in sales when Ford acquired it in 1961.[49]

These 500 largest industrial firms, which represent only one-fourth of 1 percent of all industrials, account for about 60 percent of sales and 70 percent of profits.[50] In 1965 the largest 500's combined sales ($298 billion) comfortably exceeded the totals for all American industrials only ten years before.[51] The fifty largest of this group hold over half of the 500's assets and invested capital and have truly become "big" big business. Merger has played a role in the growth of the vast majority of these firms, since *Fortune* concluded that only fourteen companies on the 1965 list did not participate in at least one merger during the period 1955–1965.[52]

In summary, many large industrial firms have rapidly increased their size through the use of external expansion (merger), in addition to their normal internal investment in new plant and equipment for replacement or expansion purposes.

The Relative Success of Mergers

I made the first extensive study (prior to those reported in this book) of the relative success of firms engaging in acquisitions during the current wave. This study compared the performance of merging and nonmerging firms for the period 1950–1959.[53] Included were sixty-six firms representing a variety of industries. Each firm was rated, in comparison with the "average" firm in the industry in which its major operations were conducted, on the growth variables of assets, sales, and profits. In addition, the firms were compared in terms of growth in market price of common stock and earnings per share with Moody's 125 Industrials for the period. A rating system was used, and in each case half of the acquiring and half of the nonacquiring firms were in the "successful" category. The highest percentage of "very successful" firms was in the group *not* involved with acquisitions.[54]

A more limited study of firms engaging in different types of mergers during the early part of the current wave was made by Ansoff and Weston.[55] Two small groups of firms were used in the study, one consisting of five firms engaged in concentric mergers,[56] and the other consisting of seven firms engaged in conglomerate mergers.

In testing for stability of sales and profits for the recession of 1957–1958, they found that the decline in these variables was substantially smaller for the firms following the concentric strategy.[57] The concentric firms also performed better than the conglomerate firms for the period 1952–1959 in growth of earnings per share and in market price per share.[58] Because of the small sample size used to test this interesting hypothesis, the findings can be considered only suggestive.[59] In addition, merging firms were not compared with nonmerging firms to determine the relative success of firms relying upon external growth and those relying upon pure internal growth.

A recently published book presents some additional evidence concerning the results of mergers.[60] The book is composed of a group of papers presented at a seminar at the Graduate School of Business of the University of Chicago in September, 1963, and includes some of the interesting discussions that followed the presentation of the papers. In one of these discussions, Joel Segall made the following statement concerning an unpublished study he had made:

> I can give you some fairly casual data. I looked at the stock price and earnings behavior of New York Stock Exchange—listed firms that acquired other listed firms during the years 1956 through 1958. On average, the stock prices of the acquiring firms either rose less or fell more than the Dow-Jones stocks. The same was true for earnings per share. Where possible, I compared these data with data for the industry of the acquiring companies; again, the acquiring companies performed somewhat worse than the average for the industry.[61]

At another point in the discussion, as reported in *The Corporate Merger,* Milton Lauenstein replied as follows to a statement by Weston in which he cited the advantages and profit opportunities to be had from diversification:

> But, as a comment on your position, Joel Segall and I—about eighteen months ago—looked at outstanding examples of large companies that had tried new combinations through acquisitions. Of the fifteen or twenty we looked at we were able to find only two that had a record that looked attractive over a ten-year period. Of those two, one was Brunswick, which even then was beginning to show signs of weakness. The other was Litton. Maybe Litton is the

> example that shows how recombinations can be successful, but it is such an exception that I am tempted to think of it as an accident.[62]

Certainly Litton is a prime example (as this time) of a successful merging conglomerate firm. However, as I testified before the Senate Subcommittee on Antitrust and Monopoly, we shall have to watch its progress closely since it is a relatively young firm (founded in the mid-1950). To date, Litton has not paid out cash dividends or had to weather economic storms. It was spawned in, and has been nurtured by, the longest period of sustained prosperity in memory. During the course of this research, a number of firms were mentioned to me as examples of successful acquiring companies, most of which tumbled in a few years, even during relatively prosperous times. We should learn from history, for a similar situation prevailed during the previous period of prolonged prosperity in the United States, as reported in the NICB study published in 1929:

> But the study makes clear that industrial consolidations have not provided a safe, easy, and sure way to business success. In the popular mind the notable profit records of single large consolidations tend to be magnified. Such companies stand out as the striking examples of what consolidation can accomplish. What is commonly overlooked is the fact that concerns like these represent the exceptions rather than the rule among consolidations.[63]

Additional studies (besides those reported in Chapters 8 to 11 in this book) have been made concerning the question of the relative success of merging firms during the current period. Kelly, in his doctoral dissertation, examined two groups of firms. Group A was composed of twenty firms which had over 20 percent increase in sales due to merger activity, and group B was composed of twenty firms which had less than 5 percent increase in sales due to mergers.[64] He then paired group A companies and group B companies according to similarity in product lines and computed averages for a five-year period prior to a merger and five years after the merger for market price of stock and rate of return. In these nonparametric tests of matched pairs, Kelly found that half of the firms in each group led in the increase of market price of common stock. The nonmerging firms led in rate of return, 55 to 45 percent; earnings per share, 57 to 43 percent; and profit margin, 57 to 43 percent. The merging firms led in price-earnings ratio, 60 to 40 percent, and "capital turnover" (which is net sales per share of common stock), 67 to 33 percent. The only variable which was statistically significant in his study was capital turnover (sales per share); this tends to support the results of our earlier research, which suggests that merging firms tend to maximize *sales* per share rather than *earnings* per share.

Another study by Johan Bjorksten,[65] a management adviser of Madison, Wisconsin, was not very scientific, but is nevertheless revealing. This study consisted of a survey of published articles about more than five thousand mergers during the period 1955–1965. He concluded that 17 percent of the mergers, or about one out of every six, were known failures. Mergers were classified as failures if any of the following occurred: (1) The acquired firm did not make a profit within three years; (2) acquired products or processes had to be radically changed in terms of materials or engineering; or (3) the acquired firm was later sold or liquidated. The interesting aspect of this study is the large percentage of known failures that it revealed. The overwhelming majority of failures are most likely never heard of; they are quietly tucked away in a consolidated financial statement, where the better divisions help to offset the performance of the "lemons."

In an unpublished study of 120 acquisitions made during the period 1960–1965, Booz, Allen and Hamilton, Inc., a management consulting firm, found that 11 percent were later sold or liquidated and that another 25 percent were judged by management to have been of doubtful worth.[66] *Forbes* reported on this study as follows: " 'We asked executives what seems to me to be the one meaningful question,' explained Conrad Jones, who heads up the New York office for Booz, Allen and Hamilton. 'We asked them, "If you had a chance, would you do it again?" In only 64% of the cases was the answer, "Yes." ' "[67]

It appears that history is again repeating itself during the current wave. Even if mergers were found to be (on the average) a very profitable method of growth, a number of important public policy questions would remain. It is ironic that we still face the important public policy problems and that at the same time, a considerable body of evidence exists which suggests that mergers (on the average) are a suboptimal method of allocating resources.

It is important to realize that there is a general lack of empirical research demonstrating that mergers, either consolidations or acquisitions, have ever been (on the average) a profitable (successful) method of growth.

Studies of the performance of acquiring firms during various time periods in the current wave again cast doubt on the widely held belief that merger is the best method of corporate growth. There are indications (as will be shown in greater detail later) that the interests of the stockholders of merging firms have not been well served (on the average), when compared with the situation in nonmerging firms. One can only speculate on whether the promoters of mergers would have carried them through to consummation if they had known that the probabilities of success (on the average) were 0.5 or less, as revealed by the empirical tests over the years since the first wave. The common thread revealed in an examination of the relative success of mergers is that they have been less successful than "conventional wisdom" would lead one to believe. This important fact is not widely recognized by the various groups interested in the outcome of merger activity. The highly publicized success of a few mergers tends to obscure the more important empirical findings.

Mergers and Antitrust

In 1950, following the ripple of merger activity in the early post–World War II period, Congress passed legislation designed to plug the loophole that existed in Section 7 of the Clayton Act concerning the purchase of assets. The passage of the Celler-Kefauver amendment (referred to as the "antimerger amendment") coincided with the beginning of the third great merger wave, which is still in progress. Again, a major piece of legislation designed to curb merger activity was passed prior to the beginning of a wave of mergers.

It is clear that the American public has been misled in its belief that the antitrust laws will curtail mergers. A glance at Table 2.1 should convince even the most skeptical that the laws have failed in this respect. The public is not alone in this belief, however; for example, in the following statement, which appeared in an article in the *Harvard Business Review* well after the current wave had gotten under way, the author is commenting on the anticipated impact of the so-called antimerger amendment passed in 1950:

> It is highly unlikely that mergers can be used to increase the competitive effectiveness of a financially sound company—either by expanding the company's relative size in the market for a single product or by expanding the coverage of a product line. Similarly, expansion into new geographical regions by merger is likely to be illegal if there has been any overlap of selling areas in the past.[68]

Again, a glance at the record of mergers since 1959, when this article appeared, suggests that many top executives have not heeded this advice of a Harvard Business School professor concerning the use of merger in the corporate growth process. Very few firms have been hindered in their growth plans by the passage of the so-called antimerger amendment. Rather than concentrating on horizontal or vertical mergers, many firms have utilized diversification mergers in the growth process. Actually, it is a case of business managers finding another loophole in the so-called antimerger amendment, since merger per se has obviously been an important method of expansion for many large firms. Some may argue that the antitrust laws were not designed to curb merger waves (which they have *not* done); yet the public and the legislators in the past have expressed concern about rising concentration and power in the economy.

At this late stage in the history of antitrust legislation and enforcement, the American public is entitled to know the reasons why these laws have not curbed merger waves. I accept the fact that they may have altered the characteristics of merger waves and prevented them from being even more serious in their consequences. Yet an examination of the data reveals that they have not been effective in curbing waves of mergers. Since this is a fact of economic and legal life, the time has come to face squarely the issues surrounding the merger problem. Are mergers opposed only because they have the usually expected anticompetitive effects associated with horizontal or vertical expansion? If conglomerate and circular mergers contribute to overall concentration, is this development in the public interest? What type of industrial structure does this country desire, and what kind of ground rules and policies are needed to achieve this structure? These and related questions must be explored.

Several factors have contributed (in part) to the development of the current merger wave and also explain why the existing laws have not been changed. The first of these is the existence of very powerful and affluent special interest groups. These groups maintain active lobbyists in government halls at the national and state levels. The things they can accomplish are truly amazing and should be recognized by the public. For example, lobbyists representing banking interests succeeded in getting Congress to overrule the Supreme Court regarding bank mergers. Never underestimate the power of any group which can reverse the rulings of the highest court in the land. Some congressmen willingly cooperate with and actively help these vested interest groups. The pressures that lobbyists can apply and the temptations that they dangle before public officials and others (including some academic people) are not to be underestimated or dismissed lightly.

Another reason why merger waves have not been curbed is that it is difficult to get Congress or any legislators to act in the absence of a crisis (unless prodded by vested interest groups). There is a considerable amount of evidence available which suggests that Congress and the executive branch are not really committed to the proposition that the antitrust laws should be vigorously enforced or made more effective.[69] An examination of the appropriations and the appointments made to the government agencies responsible for enforcement activities makes this readily apparent. The following statement, which appeared in a government report, is indicative of the problem. Notice the meager amounts of manpower and funds devoted to the merger problem:

> In the Department of Justice, the Legislation and Clearance Section of the Antitrust Division has primary responsibility for merger investigations. That section has duties in other areas as well including investigation of interlocking directorates, preparing views on legislative proposals, Government surplus property disposals, alien property matters, activities under the Defense Production Act, supervision of cases under various agricultural acts, and Federal Trade Commission penalty proceedings. Of the 16 attorneys assigned to this Section, *6 spend from 80 to 95 percent of their time on merger work; 3 from 50 to 60 percent of their time.* In addition, 3 attorneys from other sections and 5 economists are utilized on a part-time basis.
>
> The Federal Trade Commission's merger activities, on the other hand, are now being handled by a special 12-man task force of attorneys and economists which was established on April 6, 1955, for the single purpose of working on mergers and developing means of speeding their investigation. . . . Between July 1, 1954, the date of the reorganization of the Federal Trade Commission, and February 11, 1955, for example, *total funds expended by the Commission for field investigations of merger cases amounted to $90,640,* which included the cost of project attorneys, accountants, economists, and statisticians in Washington, as well as attorneys in field offices. *Trial of merger cases during this period consumed $33,861.* In short, of the Commission's total appropriation of $4,178,000 for the fiscal year 1955, *$124,501 was expended on merger activity in the 7-month period* beginning July, 1, 1954 [italics supplied].[70]

These two factors combined—the influence of powerful special interest groups and the problem of congressional appropriations—were responsible for the fact that what promised to be one of the most important and revealing studies ever attempted concerning American business was never completed. This was the ill-fated "1,000-firm" study proposed by the Bureau of Economics of the FTC in 1962. Dr. Stanley E. Boyle was a prime mover in attempting to initiate this important study, which would have provided invaluable information to researchers, government officials, businessmen, and other interested parties. The purpose of the study was to determine the merger activity and the web of intercorporate relations between large firms. The study was halted because of the pressure brought to bear by certain members of Congress who were influenced by powerful lobbyists. Boyle and the FTC received numerous telephone calls from members of Congress and various threats, including that of withholding the funds necessary to operate the FTC. This latter threat was the tactic which caused the FTC to cave in and abandon the study. This fact was revealed in the recent Senate hearings on economic concentration; the discussion was as follows:

Senator Hart:

In the development of this information you have several times commented that the Commission lacks certain facts with respect to mergers, not alone the breaking down of the assets of merger, but whether or not mergers in fact occur.

Now, under Section 6 I think it is of your act, you have authority to obtain this information. Why is it not at hand?

Dr. Mueller:

Section 6 of the Federal Trade Commission Act does permit us to require special reports of corporations, and we have used this quite extensively in getting merger information in some industries. But we have never, although we have the legal authority to get information, we have not had, in the Bureau of Economics at least, the resources to undertake the kind of continuing inquiry into the merger activity going on in the economy.

Senator Hart:

In other words, there is an appropriation limitation problem?

Dr. Mueller:

I think this is part of it. The whole question arises as to whether it would be desirable to require corporations to provide this kind of information on a continuing basis.

As you well know, there has been legislation proposed in the two chambers which would require companies to provide information on their contemplated mergers, and this would, of course, provide us with such information.

Senator Hart:

Do you know whether the Commission has ever sought the means to obtain this fuller body of information?

Dr. Mueller:

Yes, we did make an effort in 1962 to initiate an economic inquiry which would have given us this kind of information. The study, so-called intercorporate relations among American manufacturing companies, would have required that the largest companies—those with assets of about $25 million or so—would have supplied to the Commission the history of their merger activity since 1950.

Senator Hart:

What happened to that?

Dr. Mueller:

The Appropriations Committees of the two Houses deleted that study from our budget.

Senator Hart:

> Up to this point I would think that a study like that would be of great value.
>
> My statement was based on an ex parte presentation of the need for it. It was not my conclusion.[71]

This is an example of how the legislative branch or a small number of men in this branch of government can and do operate for certain special interest groups using the ultimate weapon—congressional control over appropriations.

Appointments can also be an effective method of reducing the force with which the antitrust laws are applied. Much depends upon the degree of dedication and tenacity which the people in these responsible positions bring to their jobs. Even with insufficient appropriations, there has been a great variance in the manner in which those responsible for antitrust enforcement have performed. The attitudes of the executive branch of government concerning the importance of the antitrust laws to the structure and performance of the economy will be reflected in the appointments made to these agencies. As would be expected, over the years the individuals in these government posts have ranged from hard-hitting, practical men concerned with the problems of concentrated industry to passive theorists who attempt to formulate merger guidelines while merger waves burn larger totals into the record book.

The antitrust laws are important in a capitalist economy and have been a particularly unique American contribution to the Western economic world. In discussing the uniqueness of these laws as an American phenomenon, McKenna observed:

> The Sherman Act of 1890 made such combinations and monopolization illegal. Although it was many years before the Act was made effective, it showed an increased awareness of the problem. It was also, as we sometimes forget, a unique answer to the problem. *For the first time in history, a government faced with growing monopoly power, chose to fight the power itself rather than concede the inevitability of concentration and regulate its effects* [italics supplied].[72]

It is indeed unfortunate that the desires of the legislators of the late 1800s were not fulfilled, since within a decade following the passage of the Sherman Act, America had a highly concentrated industry, which persists to the present. This development has resulted in a number of laws and other proposals designed to regulate the effects of concentration rather than attack its roots. For example, the recent wage-price guidelines proposed by the Federal government have been manhandled by both labor and management, as have the numerous voluntary controls on banking and foreign investment, which have been far from satisfactory solutions to the complex problems which arise when concentration increases to the point where it produces powerful economic units. It appears to me that we have conceded the inevitability of concentration and that we are uncertain how to regulate the effects, and even more uncertain whether we should.

One industry or group after another has been exempted from the provisions of the antitrust laws. An inquiry into the price behavior of numerous goods and services inevitably produces the reply that the prices or commissions are set by the realtors' association, the dairymen's association, or the barbershop association, etc. Each of these groups is beyond the provisions of the Sherman Act. The result is that a large portion of an individual's or a family's expenditures is made in areas where there is little or no hope for price competition. Even in the areas that have not been exempted, the enforcement has been considerably less than aggressive, as illustrated by the data presented in Table 5.3. It is surprising how few cases related to merger have actually been instituted by the government's antitrust enforcement agencies. The data reveal that the Justice Department and the FTC have initiated and tried only 143 cases under Section 7 of the Clayton Act during the forty-nine-year period from 1914 to 1962, when almost twenty thousand mergers were reported. A partial explanation for the small number of cases initiated prior to 1950 is the wording of the legislation and the courts' interpretation of it, which eliminated cases involving the purchase of assets. The original Clayton Act was aimed primarily at monopolistic controls obtained through stock manipulations and interlocking directorships. Since the Celler-Kefauver amendment of 1950, the law specifically includes the acquisition of properties and thus closes this loophole. Yet the absolute number of cases initiated by the government is still relatively small when viewed against the profile of merger activity. More distressing than the numbers is the lack of action on many mergers involving large firms in the same or related industries, Recommendations for a new approach to this problem will be presented in Part 3, which deals with public policy.

In summary, an examination of the record leads to the inevitable conclusion that the antitrust laws have been ineffective in curbing major waves of merger activity, despite the fact that they may have influenced the size and shape of the waves. Ironically, a major piece of legislation designed to curb mergers and the practices which may arise from them was passed prior to each wave. The Sherman Act was passed in 1890, preceding the first great wave at the turn of the century; the Clayton Act and the Federal Trade Commission Act were passed in 1914, following the first wave and prior to the late-1920s merger wave; and the so-

TABLE 5.3 Numbers of Reported Mergers and Merger Cases Instituted and Tried by the Department of Justice and the Federal Trade Commission under Section 7 of the Clayton Act between 1914 and January 1, 1963

Cases Initiated				*Cases Initiated*			
Year	*No. of Mergers*	*DJ*	*FTC*	*Year*	*No. of Mergers*	*DJ*	*FTC*
1914	39	—	—	1939	87	—	—
1915	71			1940	140	1	—
1916	117	—	—	1941	111	2	—
1917	195	1	—	1942	118	1	—
1918	71	—	1	1943	213	—	—
1919	438	—	4	1944	324	—	—
1920	760	—	—	1945	333	1	—
1921	487	—	2	1946	419	—	—
1922	309	—	—	1947	404	—	—
1923	311	—	1	1948	223	—	—
1924	368	—	—	1949	126	2	—
1925	554	—	—	1950	219	—	—
1926	856	3	—	1951	235	—	—
1927	870	1	1	1952	288	—	1
1928	1,058	—	2	1953	295	—	—
1929	1,245	2	1	1954	387	—	2
1930	799	—	—	1955	683	5	3
1931	464	—	—	1956	673	6	12
1932	203	—	—	1957	585	1	6
1933	120	—	1	1958	589	5	3
1934	101	—	—	1959	835	10	3
1935	130	2	—	1960	844	11	13
1936	126	—	—	1961	954	18	2
1937	124	—	—	1962	853	12	1
1938	110	—	—				
Total					19,865	84	59*

* In addition to these fifty-nine reported cases, another fifty-three were brought before the FTC and were dismissed without opinion between 1918 and 1947.

Sources: Merger data are from the Federal Trade Commission. The data on Section 7 cases are from American Bar Association, *Section 7 of Antitrust Law, Merger Case Digest,* Chicago: American Bar Association, 1963, pp. 3–4 and 269–270.

called antimerger amendment to the Clayton Act became law in 1950, prior to the current wave of merger activity.

Over the years, Congress has exempted numerous industries from the provisions of these acts, while the nonexempt industries have escaped their provisions relatively unharmed. There are numerous reasons for this state of affairs, among them the following: the existence of powerful lobbies which represent various vested interests and exert strong and effective powers upon legislators; enforcement laxities due to insufficient personnel and appropriations; the lack of interest among professional economists in providing effective and convincing analyses as a basis for policy and judicial decision; the courts' interpretation of the intent of Congress when the laws were passed; and the domination by lawyers of the enforcement agencies.[73] There is considerable interaction among these factors, which adds to the confused and ineffective policy which exists in America regarding merger movements.

The Environment for Mergers

The current wave of merger activity has also been taking place during a period of relative prosperity and a relatively buoyant stock market. This fact is apparent from an examination of the data presented in Table 5.4, which includes the number of reported mergers and other selected economic indicators for the period 1950–1966. A graphic presentation is available in Chart 5.1. It is readily evident, after an examination of the data, that the economic environment during the current merger wave has been quite favorable, with the twin factors of relative prosperity and a buoyant stock market being major contributing factors to the economic climate suitable for a major merger wave.

The fact that past merger waves (as well as the current one) have been so closely related to prosperity, with a growing supply of money and buoyant stock prices, is an important fact which should command more attention. It is a phenomenon which has not been sufficiently recognized by either the monetary authorities or the fiscal policy advocates in this country. Recognition of the close association between these factors has important ramifications for public policy considerations concerning mergers. Both monetary and fiscal policy exert an important influence upon the aggregate role of merger activity. Since changes in the money supply generally lead to changes in stock prices,[74] the Board of Governors of the Federal Reserve System is in the unique position of being able to exert a powerful influence over the economic environment in which merger waves are sustained. Yet the rate of industrial merger activity is not a major concern of the Federal Reserve System, and even if it was to notify the FTC or the Antitrust Division of the Justice Department of monetary policy objectives, it is doubtful that the information would be (or could be) used to advantage. It is becoming apparent that prolonged periods of prosperity in this country will solve some economic problems, as well as create new problems which we had better begin to recognize.

TABLE 5.4 Merger Activity (Industrial and Mining) and Selected Economic Indicators, 1950–1966

Year	*No. of Mergers*	*Standard & Poor's Industrial Stock Price Index*	*Money Supply**	*Time Deposits**	*Money Supply plus Time Deposits**	*Industrial Production ('57 — '59 = 100)*	*Gross National Product (Actual)**	*Mfg. Plant and Equipment Expenditures**	*Estimated Merger Expenditures**
1950	219	18.33	116.2	36.7	148.9	74.9	285.1	7.49	0.80
1951	235	22.68	122.7	38.2	160.9	81.3	328.2	10.85	0.88
1952	288	24.78	127.5	41.1	168.6	84.3	345.4	11.63	1.15
1953	295	24.84	128.1	44.7	172.8	91.3	363.2	11.91	1.49
1954	387	30.25	131.8	48.5	180.3	85.8	360.7	11.04	2.50
1955	683	42.40	135.2	50.2	185.4	96.6	390.9	11.44	4.00
1956	673	49.80	136.9	52.1	189.0	99.9	419.2	14.95	3.91
1957	585	47.63	135.9	57.4	193.3	100.7	441.1	15.96	3.07
1958	589	49.36	141.1	65.4	206.5	93.7	447.3	11.43	2.77
1959	835	61.45	142.1	67.4	209.5	105.6	483.7	12.07	4.26
1960	844	59.43	141.1	72.9	214.0	108.7	503.7	14.48	4.05
1961	954	69.99	145.5	82.7	228.2	109.7	520.1	13.68	4.83
1962	853	65.54	147.5	97.8	245.3	118.3	560.3	14.68	4.53
1963	861	73.39	153.1	112.2	265.3	124.3	590.5	15.69	5.18
1964	854	86.19	159.7	126.6	286.3	132.3	631.7	18.58	5.18
1965	1,008	93.48	167.2	146.9	314.1	143.4	681.2	22.45	6.59
1966	995	91.09	170.3	158.0	328.3	156.3	739.6	26.99	6.70

* In billions of dollars.

Sources: Federal Trade Commission, Board of Governors of the Federal Reserve System, Council of Economic Advisers, and the estimated merger expenditures from Table 2.3 in Chap. 2 of this book.

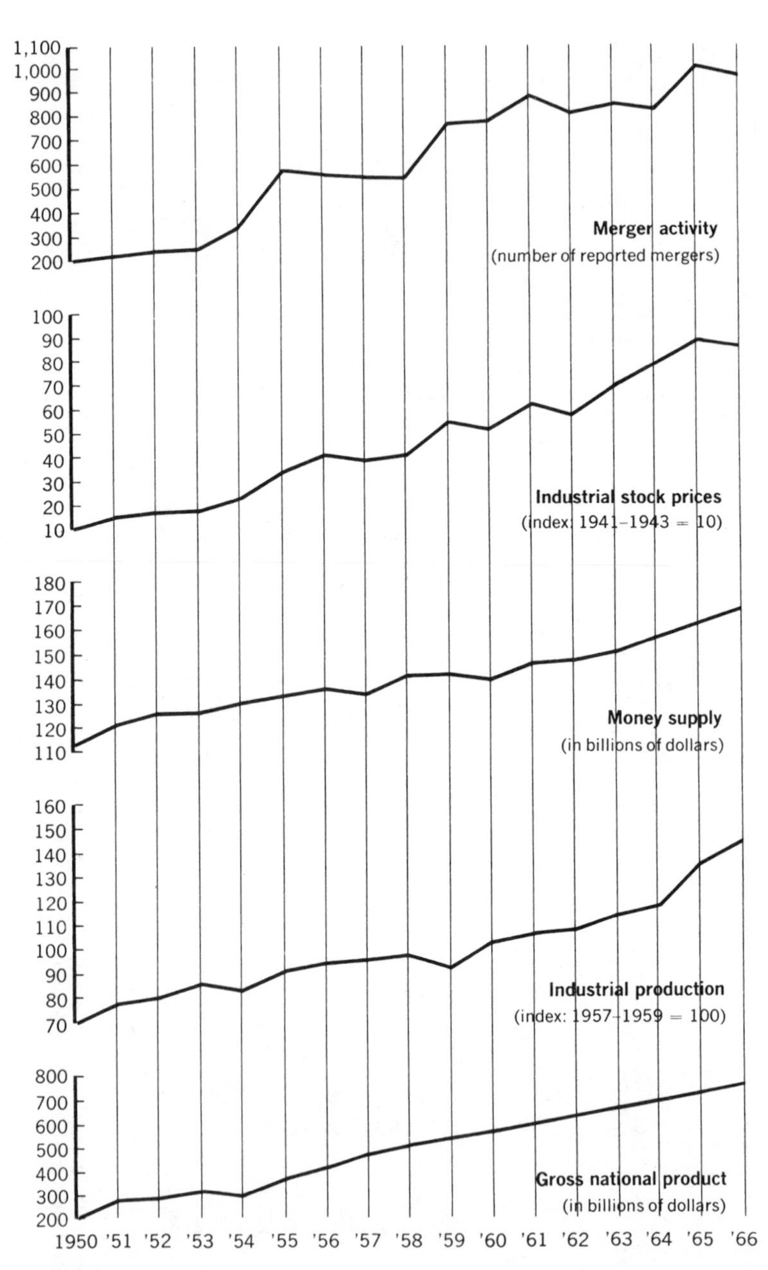

CHART 5.1 Merger activity and selected economic indicators, 1950–1966. *Sources:* **Data on merger activity are from the FTC series; other indicators are from Council of Economic Advisers,** *Economic Indicators.*

Many economists and others have overlooked the aggregate economic environment and its relationship with merger activity. Instead, they have continued to place great emphasis upon the industrial retardation thesis. They believe that mergers take place because of declining industries and/or firms. Certainly some isolated mergers do occur because of retardation problems; however, the data do not lend much support to this hypothesis. Table 5.5 shows the merger activity of various

TABLE 5.5 Reported Mergers and Acquisitions by Manufacturing Industry Group of Acquiring Firm, 1948–1965

Industry Group of Acquiring Firm	*1948–1956*	*Rank*	*1957–1965*	*Rank*
Total, manufacturing	2,735	—	6,263	—
Machinery, nonelectrical	437	1	725	2
Food and kindred products	374	2	572	4
Chemicals	271	3	712	3
Fabricated metals	237	4	421	7
Electrical machinery	227	5	893	1
Transportation equipment	223	6	486	5
Textiles and apparel	201	7	451	6
Primary metals	147	8	300	9
Paper and allied products	113	9	263	10
Stone, glass, and clay	105	10	207	12
Professional and scientific instruments	88	11	305	8
Lumber and furniture	69	12	173	14
Petroleum and coal products	65	13	143	15
Miscellaneous manufacturers	49	14	181	13
Printing and publishing	44	15	232	11
Rubber products	39	16	115	16
Leather products	33	17	46	17
Tobacco manufacturers	13	18	38	18

Sources: Federal Trade Commission, *Report on Corporate Mergers and Acquisitions,* 1955; and FTC news releases.

industry groups for the periods 1948–1956 and 1957–1965. It is interesting to note that the same seven industries had the largest amount of mergers in each period, although their relative rankings changed somewhat. An examination of these industries fails to reveal any major retardation, particularly during the relatively prosperous period of the current merger wave. An analysis of the basic industry membership of conglomerate firms, which is presented in Chapter 9, reveals that these firms originate in a cross section of industries and are not concentrated in any particular subgroup of industrials. Economists have frequently asked the unanswerable question concerning the probable fate of firms if they had not merged. No one can answer this type of question; however, in times of prosperity and rising aggregate demand, one can only speculate that large firms could survive and, with internal growth in new modern capacity, become effective competitors as well as profitable firms.

The merger-prosperity hypothesis (which has been discussed in this chapter) appears to be gaining more advocates. After this chapter was initially written, the following statement appeared in a magazine devoted exclusively to mergers: "Easier money at the banks, coupled with rising stock prices helped to sustain a fast pace in activity during April . . . [and] total dollar volume of April's transactions was more than $900 million."[75] The merger pace quickened and expanded during 1967 with close to $4 billion of reported activity in September and October alone. It should be obvious that the current wave is steadily achieving gigantic proportions.[76]

An examination of the economic environment during each of the three major merger waves has revealed a pattern which cannot be ignored. Hopefully, the monetary and fiscal authorities will become aware of these environmental factors and recognize that prosperity not only solves but also causes special problems in the economy.

Mergers and the Economy

No one has yet attempted specifically to measure the impact of merger spending upon the economy. In the two previous chapters, it was pointed out that either a recession or a depression occurred immediately following each of the first two merger waves. In both these periods, business investment spending for *new* plant and equipment and consumer spending were the major components of aggregate demand. A decline in expenditures of either or both of these groups could trigger a decline in the economy. The situation in the current period is considerably different since government spending (state, local, and Federal) plays such an important role in total aggregate demand.

Since the Full Employment Act of 1946, the maintenance of relative prosperity has been a responsibility of the President and the Federal government. Thus, prolonged prosperity promoted by the government can add a number of new dimensions to the current merger wave, particularly since the government has done little to curb merger activity (at the same time that it is promoting prosperity), which contributes to the environment necessary for a wave of mergers to develop.

It is entirely possible that history may repeat itself again in a more muted way; that is, the current prolonged prosperity, accompanied by the current merger wave, may eventually cause problems in the economy. This could happen in the following way: Assume that large firms are expanding during the current relative prosperity, using both internal growth and acquisition as a means of growth. The internal segment of spending is *new* investment and provides increased capacity to firms as well as new industry capacity. This new investment provides these firms with more productive capacity, enabling them to maintain relatively stable prices and at the same time to increase profits as a result of the increased productivity of the new plant and equipment. The pressure to raise prices is relieved in this situation since total capacity is expanding just ahead of growing aggregate demand. The impact of unprofitable acquisitions is swamped by the generally prosperous times since profits in other lines or divisions may be increasing because of increased demand. Thus, the poor performance of a merger may be offset and go unnoticed in the consolidated statements of merging firms.

Yet there are several factors which could eventually cause havoc in what may appear to be a relatively placid and profitable period. First, some firms may grow rapidly by merger without a corresponding growth in profitability, or earnings per share. This will cause readjustments in investors' behavior since the market has an aversion to uncertainty and does not know what products or divisions are contributing earnings or losses to a firm. The consolidated statements issued by "conglomerates," for example, cover up these operating results. There was evidence of this during the summer of 1966, when the well-known conglomerates were selling at price-earnings ratios below the average for the market.[77] Again, if expected profits are not realized or if a considerable amount of dilution has taken place, we can expect an eventual decline in stock prices. The extent of the decline will depend upon expectations about future aggregate demand and the expanded role of government as a spender, which differentiates the current wave from the previous waves. For example, the first half of the 1960s was a period similar to that in the example discussed earlier, that is, one of increasing demand and capacity expansion (as well as mergers), accompanied by relative price stability and growing profitability. Then the government stepped up its expenditures because of the military escalation in Southeast Asia. Almost simultaneously, the government expanded expenditures on the domestic scene. This resulted in an unexpected strain on productive capacity, causing a round of price increases and a rise in the cost of doing business and the cost of living, which put pressure on costs again at the labor bargaining table. The resulting inflationary pressures cause uncertainty, which is a disrupting influence on the stock market (as in

1966). If the amount spent on mergers during the period 1960–1965 (an estimated $30.4 billion) had instead been spent on additional modern capacity, it is entirely possible that the pressures resulting in price increases could have been somewhat minimized.

If we examine the potential impact of mergers on the accomplishment of our national economic goals, an interesting pattern emerges. The impact of spending by a business firm on a merger may contribute nothing to the economic growth objective since the spending is for *existing* capacity and will not show up in the national income accounts as business investment spending. This is particularly true if the merger is consummated by an exchange of securities (as in the case of most large mergers). An acquisition for cash may have a different effect, depending upon the spending pattern of the recipient(s) of the cash.[78]

The contribution of merger activity to the accomplishment of the reasonable price stability objective is, of course, difficult to measure. Prices generally tend to rise when capacity utilization rates are high and/or when market structures become highly concentrated. Since mergers do not add new capacity to an industry, it is likely that during periods of strong aggregate demand the capacity constraints will eventually become a factor causing prices to rise. Since horizontal mergers add capacity to the firm (although not to the industry), the pressure to raise prices may be postponed until the impact of rising demand manifests itself on an industry-wide basis. Since a merger results in the acquisition of existing capacity (which is in various stages of obsolescence), the relative costs of operation may also be higher than if a similar expenditure had been made on new, modern capacity with the increased probabilities of realizing productivity gains. Increased productivity gains are particularly important during periods of rising labor costs, and the most logical method of achieving these benefits is through replacement and expansion investments in *new* plant and equipment. Perhaps the most pragmatic method of examining the role of mergers upon the price stability objective is to examine the record of price levels during the current merger wave. If the expected efficiencies and economies of scale (generally associated with merger activity) are being realized, these economic events should be contributing to eventual price declines and/or quality improvements, increased profits, and other benefits to the general public. The consumer price index stood at 103.1 in 1960 and advanced to 117.1 in September of 1967. Wholesale prices were 100.7 in 1960 and rose to 106.5 midway in 1967, and the outlook is for further price increases in the period ahead.

While there are a number of variables which affect the level of prices, there is no evidence that mergers per se lead to greater efficiencies and lower prices. Following the first wave (when monopoly power was the objective in many of the mergers), wholesale prices followed an upward movement until the 1920s. The impact of the increased demand resulting from World War I, both during the war and in the immediate postwar period, caused the greatest increase in prices. Prices declined sharply in the early 1920s just prior to the second merger wave and were relatively stable or slightly lower until the Depression of the 1930s. Prices crept upward in the early phase of the current wave, and wholesale prices remained relatively stable in the early 1960s prior to the Vietnam conflict. Military escalation has contributed to increased government spending, and the resulting strain on capacity has led to sharp price increases since 1965.[79] The best hope for eventual price stability, economic growth, and the creation of employment opportunities lies in convincing managers, legislators, and government officials that the qualitative as well as the quantitative aspects of capacity are important.

The act of merger alone does not contribute to the full employment objective in the economy since the employees involved remain with the same firm or with the new owners. In other words, new jobs are not created by the merger act per se. Actually, the much-stated efficiency objective of merger suggests that some jobs will be eliminated in the process. The ultimate effect of a merger upon employment creation depends upon the relative success and the eventual internal expansion of the combination. The fact that the number of employees in merging firms generally increases faster than that in nonmerging firms does not indicate that more jobs have been created by merging firms. An acquiring firm instantly adds size dimensions, including the employees of the acquired firm, and does not change aggregate employment with the merger.

It has not been my intention to oversimplify a complex question; however, it is difficult to understand just how mergers (in general) can contribute substantially (or even moderately) to the accomplishment of our national economic goals. It certainly appears that the economic environment influences the rate of merger activity, and it is possible that mergers in turn may have an influence upon the economy in various ways. It is also entirely possible that there are differential effects generated by the various types of mergers. For example, a horizontal merger represents an expenditure for existing capacity in the same industry, rather than for new capacity, and the degree of control in the particular industry is generally increased. A conglomerate merger represents an expenditure for existing capacity also, and there is a substitution effect on the number of competitors in the particular industry. If the firm following the conglomerate strategy relies on pure internal growth for the acquired firm or division in the postmerger period, new productive capacity will result, and the probabilities of realizing increased profitability through lower costs will be enhanced. It appears that the "successful" conglomerates are following precisely this type of policy, although this is difficult to determine because of the consolidated method of financial reporting. The ultimate success of the newer conglomerates appears to be closely related to business conditions, specifically the need for continued and prolonged prosperity.

A paper by Nelson contains a relevant observation concerning business cycle factors and mergers; he states:

> Arthur Stone Dewing once made a study of the financial record of several large consolidations created at the turn of the century, during the frenzied years of trust-building. His frequently quoted conclusion was that "the trusts turned out ill." What he described was essentially a record of overcapitalization and the wholesale issuance of stock, actions which led many mergers to painful reorganizations. With today's economy in mind, we can correctly say that Dewing wrote about another time, long past, and that nothing as extreme is likely to recur. Yet many contemporary developments may be muted repetitions of the more flamboyant past. Their consequences also may be muted, but nonetheless worth considering.[80]

Both the "new economics" group and the "money supply" school of economists have devoted a vast amount of time and effort developing theories of growth and prosperity; yet they have exhibited little or no concern about the structural changes resulting from growth and prosperity or about the impact these structural changes may have on growth and prosperity. The realized benefits of government-promoted prosperity are recognized, and yet the costs may be higher than we now realize and should be considered in policy formulations. If this circular effect of prosperity plus a buoyant stock market contributes to the environment for mergers and the resulting mergers contribute eventually to a relative decline in the economy, it may well be that merger waves are self-destructive. This theory must be tempered in the present wave by the realization of the fact that the Federal government has the responsibility by law to promote prosperity. Certainly the current wave has persisted for a longer period of time than any other merger wave in American economic history (see Table 2.1 and Chart 2.1). An expanding money supply as well as increased cash flows within business firms resulting from prosperous periods are fuel cells which can ignite a merger thrust, a development which should be given more recognition and analysis in policy formulation and research.

Mergers and the Economist

In the two previous chapters, I noted the lagging professional interest of economists in the first two merger waves. On the basis of the available evidence, it appears that economists (in general) have again virtually ignored the current wave of mergers. It is particularly surprising that the profession has ignored this wave when one considers the longevity of the activity as well as the magnitude of the mergers in this current period. Actually, the relatively minor increase in mergers during the period, 1940–1947 which was a ripple compared with the activity of the 1950s and 1960s, received more attention from economists.[81]

The official publication of the American Economic Association, the *American Economic Review,* published only one article on the subject of mergers during the period 1954–1966. The one article is related to the Brown Shoe Company case as decided by the Supreme Court.[82] Another article appeared in the *Papers and Proceedings Supplement* concerning mergers in the transportation field,[83] and there was a session on "Antitrust Problems" at the seventy-third annual meeting of the American Economic Association in St. Louis, December 28 to December 30, 1960.[84] History is again repeating itself, as evidenced by this scant concern of economists about current merger activity.

Economists publish articles in many other journals, and if I had examined only the *American Economic Review,* I might have been accused of not doing the profession justice. Consequently, I examined volumes V and VI of the *Index of Economic Journals,* which list all the major articles related to economics that appeared in a wide variety of journals during the period 1954–1963.[85] Twenty-six articles on the subject of combination mergers were listed in these two volumes.[86] The journal with the largest number of articles was the *Journal of Farm Economics,* with such titles as "Integration in Theory with an Application to Hogs," "Farm Tenure Perspective of Vertical Integration," and "Coordination and Vertical Expansion in Marketing Cooperatives." The *Harvard Business Review* contained an article entitled "A Conjecture about Fashion and Vertical Process Integration." In addition, other journals published articles concerning mergers in Australia and Japan, and there was one note on Zaibatsu combines. When one sifts through the current literature, the list is substantially less than impressive, and the index of "concern" of the economics profession is small indeed.[87]

The subject of bank mergers has received considerably more attention in the last few years; however, the same effort has not been put forth by economists in relation to the other segments of American industry. The profession has looked the other way and has virtually ignored the important economic phenomenon which is a current happening.

The government has shown its traditional concern for the merger problem during this period, at least as measured by the output of studies and hearings. The FTC published a report on the period 1948–1955.[88] The Antitrust Subcommittee of the House has published a report,[89] as has the Select Committee of the House on Small Business,[90] and hearings were conducted before the Subcommittee on Antitrust and Monopoly of the Senate Judiciary Committee in 1965 and 1966.[91]

Most of the publications concerning the current wave have been generated by either management people or those closely associated with them. At least one book was published by the American Management Association;[92] another was written by an executive and an investment banker;[93] a partner in an accounting firm produced a book;[94] a partner in a law firm also wrote a merger book;[95] and another book was written by a group of management consultants.[96] Thus it is easy to demonstrate that the principal concern during the current wave is centered on the management problems of merger activity. Perhaps this result should be expected since this is the management-oriented wave of mergers. In the only books produced by academic people, the emphasis is again on the management problems of merger.[97] In the foreword to one book, the dean of a leading graduate school of business states: "Despite the many mergers in postwar years, investigations into the characteristics of the merger phenomenon have lagged. The present work thus represents a contribution to scholarship in an important and developing area underlying business management."[98] Two other studies designed basically for businessmen were published by the National Industrial Conference Board.[99]

The only conclusion that can be drawn from an examination of the professional literature and other works published during the current merger wave is that economists have again displayed a lagging interest in the wave of merger activity which surrounds them. Most of the recent literature concerned with mergers has been oriented more toward the management problems resulting from mergers than toward the effects of mergers upon concentration, competition, and structure.

Although perhaps it is ironic, it seems appropriate at this point to paraphrase Stigler's statement, quoted earlier, concerning the passive attitude of economists toward the mergers at the turn of the century: One must regretfully record that in this period the late Estes Kefauver and Emanuel Celler have done more than the American Economic Association to foster the policy of competition. Stigler is a former president of the American Economic Association.

No doubt, my criticism of the profession will not be especially appreciated by many of its members. However, if by exposing a consistently lagging professional interest in an important economic problem I can stimulate a more aggressive and intelligent search for the many necessary answers to the numerous merger hypotheses, their understandable resentment should be minimized. Pragmatic answers to pragmatic problems are within the scope of the economists' contributions to public policy. I am reminded of the statement made by Ben W. Lewis concerning the Supreme Court decisions regarding industrial consolidations at the American Economic Association meetings in 1930; he said:

> The Court in all its inadequacy is here speaking for the experts of the country. It has been plunged headlong into the whirlpool by the incapacity of Congress or the desire of that body to escape responsibility. We on the shore, from whom expert assistance might have been expected, have given no assistance. We have been mightily amused or perturbed at the Court's efforts, but the lines we have thrown have not been life lines. Till our economic and social theories and aims come to be crystallized into a policy to which men conversant with the situation are willing to lend substantial support, it must be recognized that the Supreme Court in all its fumbling is performing the difficult task of deciding specific controversies with very little help from the social sciences. Until we know what we want, it becomes us to blame the Court for not giving it to us.[100]

It is ironic that at the height of the current prolonged period of merger activity in the United States not *one* paper on the subject was presented at the annual meeting of the American Economic Association, held in Washington, D.C., during late December of 1967. Attempts to discuss the subject at professional meetings are rebuffed with the excuse that too many papers are on the program, yet a glance at the titles of many papers suggests a substantial degree of frivolity.

In summary, it again appears that the professional economists (in general) have demonstrated the same lagging interest in the current merger wave that they did in the previous waves. While the social science of economics has contributed much in many areas of economic life, one of the problems—the merger wave—remains relatively neglected, despite the fact that there are many more economists today than there were at the turn of the century. Membership in the American Economic Association has grown from 182 in 1886 to over 10,000 in the 1960s.[101]

NOTES

[1] See U.S. Treasury, Internal Revenue Service, *Statistics of Income: 1963*, 1967, p. 160.

[2] The figures on monthly merger expenditures are published in *Mergers and Acquisitions Monthly.* Acquired firms with assets of $700,000 or less are generally excluded.

[3] Dexter Merriman Keezer and Associates, *New Forces in American Business,* New York: McGraw-Hill Book Company, 1959, p. 171.

[4] *Ibid.* The implication here is that firms will not abandon their original line of business; however, rather than expanding in this field, they purchase firms in unrelated fields and become conglomerate corporations. A seldom-used alternative is to sell out the existing business (maintaining the existing corporate structure of the firm) and enter a completely new field. Two firms that have done this are the Magic Chef Company and ACF-Brill Motors. Each sold its manufacturing business and entered the retail food business. The original Magic Chef Company became Food Giant supermarkets in California, and Brill became ACF-Wrigley, which now has a large share of the retail food market in Detroit and has expanded into other markets as well.

[5] Federal Trade Commission, *Report on Corporate Mergers and Acquisitions,* 1955; and Samuel Richardson Reid, *Corporate Mergers and Acquisitions Involving Firms in Missouri, 1950–1959: Some Economic Results and Administrative Policies and Procedures,* Ann Arbor, Mich.: University Microfilms, 1962.

[6] Federal Trade Commission, *op. cit.,* pp. 50–51.

[7] Reid, *op. cit.,* pp. 96–97.

[8] See, for example, studies by Michael Gort, *Diversification and Integration in American Industry,* Princeton, N.J.: Princeton University Press, 1962; and Select Committee on Small Business, House of Representatives, *Mergers and Superconcentration: Acquisitions of 500 Largest Industrial and 50 Largest Merchandising Firms,* 87th Cong., 2d Sess., 1962.

[9] In addition to takeover possibilities, some firms purchase stock in other firms in order to obtain leverage which can be used on a supplier or customer to attain certain objectives. One famous case that was recently settled in the courts involved General Motors and du Pont. McKenna commented on this relationship as follows: "Since Du Pont receives the entire additional profit in the paint and shares only 23% of the relative loss on the automobiles, it pays to force GM to buy, even if the price differences are substantial. In a case such as this, partial ownership serves as a device for bleeding the remaining holders of GM stock for the benefit of Du Pont, and leads to lesser efficiency of production in the bargain." Joseph P. McKenna, "The Current Merger Movement," *Review of Social Economy,* vol. 16, no. 1, p. 16, March, 1958.

[10] See N. R. Collins and L. E. Preston, "The Size Structure of the Largest Industrial Firms: 1909–1958," *American Economic Review,* vol. 51, no. 5, pp. 968–1011, December, 1961, especially pp. 987–990; *Concentration Ratios in Manufacturing Industry: 1958,* 87th Cong., 2d Sess., 1962, especially tables 1-A to 1-G; Select Committee on Small Business, House of Representatives, *op. cit.,* p. 45; and P. Sylos-Tabini, *Oligopoly and Technical Progress,* Cambridge, Mass.: Harvard University Press, 1962, pp. 191–194.

[11] Committee on the Judiciary, Senate Subcommittee on Antitrust and Monopoly, *Economic Concentration,* 89th Cong., 1st Sess., 1965, part 2, p. 519.

[12] Frank J. Kottke, "Mergers of Large Manufacturing Companies: 1951 to 1959," *Review of Economics and Statistics,* vol. 41, no. 4, p. 431, November, 1959.

[13] *Ibid.,* p. 433.

[14] See Carol J. Loomis, "The 500: A Decade of Growth," *Fortune,* July 15, 1966, p. 214. It was also reported in this article (p. 213) that "in each year during the 1955–1965 period the 500 accounted for at least 56 percent of total sales of all industrial companies. . . . last year their share was 60 percent." It is important to note that other large firms (in addition to the 68 from the 1955 list of 500) were acquired; a number of firms that were added to the list during the decade were subsequently acquired and thus disappeared from the list.

[15] For a variety of studies and views on the concentration question, see Committee on the Judiciary, Senate Subcommittee on Antitrust and Monopoly, *op. cit.,* parts 1–5.

[16] *Ibid.,* part 2, p. 499.

[17] William G. Shepherd, "Trends of Concentration in American Manufacturing Industries: 1947–1958," *Review of Economics and Statistics,* vol. 46, no. 2, pp. 200–212, May, 1964.

[18] *Ibid.,* pp. 202–203.

[19] See G. J. Stigler, "The Theory of Oligopoly," in *The Theory of Price,* rev. ed., New York: The Macmillan Company, 1952, chap. 13.

[20] See J. S. Bain, "A Note on Pricing and Monopoly and Oligopoly," *American Economic Review,* vol. 39, no. 1, pp. 448–464, March, 1949.

[21] Shepherd, *op. cit.,* pp. 209–210.

[22] *Ibid.,* p. 212. Similar results are obtained in Chaps. 10 and 11, in which commercial banking is discussed in more detail.

[23] Select Committee on Small Business, House of Representatives, *op. cit.,* p. 8.

[24] See Joseph A. Schumpeter, *Capitalism, Socialism and Democracy,* New York: Harper & Row, Publishers, Incorporated, 1942. See especially chap. 7.

[25] See, for example, D. Hamberg, "Size of Firm, Oligopoly, and Research: The Evidence," *Canadian Journal of Economics and Political Science,* vol. 30, no. 1, pp. 62–75, February, 1964; Frederic M. Scherer, "Firm Size, Market Structure, Opportunity, and the Output of Patented Inventions," *American Economic Review,* vol. 55, no. 5, pp. 1097–1126, December, 1965; Edwin Mansfield, "Size of Firm, Market Structure, and Innovation," *Journal of Political Economy,* vol. 71, no. 6, pp. 556–576, December, 1963; Jacob Schmookler, "Bigness, Fewness, and Research," *Journal of Political Economy,* vol. 67, no. 6, pp. 628–635, December, 1959; and James S. Worley, "Industrial Research and the New Competition," *Journal of Political Economy,* vol. 69, no. 2, pp. 183–186, April, 1961.

[26] Scherer, *op. cit.,* p. 1105.

[27] *Ibid.,* p. 1117.

[28] *Ibid.,* p. 1116.

[29] *Ibid.,* p. 1122.

[30] See especially M. A. Adelman, "The Measurement of Industrial Concentration," *Review of Economics and Statistics,* vol. 33, no. 4, November, 1951; S. Fabricant, "Is Monopoly Increasing?" *Journal of Economic History*, vol. 13, no. 1, pp. 89–94, winter, 1953; and G. Warren Nutter, "Is Competition Decreasing in Our Economy?" *Journal of Farm Economics,* vol. 36, no. 5, pp. 751–759, December, 1954.

[31] For example, see Norman R. Collins and L. E. Preston, "The Size Structure of the Largest Industrial Firms: 1909–1958," *American Economic Review,* vol. 51, no. 5, pp. 968–1011, December, 1961.

[32] Adelman, *op. cit.,* p. 295. In measuring the growth or decline in concentration over time, the extent of concentration in the initial year is a critical factor. The American economy was highly concentrated in 1909 as a result of the first merger wave. In 1914, for example, 3.4 percent of the manufacturing firms employed over half the wage earners.

[33] Collins and Preston, *op. cit.,* p. 987.

[34] M. A. Adelman, "Monopoly and Concentration: Comparisons in Time and Space," *Revista Internationale di Scienze Economiche e Commerciali,* August, 1965.

[35] If the base year is chosen after a merger wave, such as 1909 or 1931, the level of concentration is high. It would be interesting, as well as pertinent, if Adelman would use either 1909 or 1947 (or both) as the base year and a more recent year to determine changes in concentration. All the available evidence suggests that he would find overall concentration rising during the current merger wave.

[36] This literature will be listed and discussed in more detail later in this Chapter.

[37] B. R. Wakefield, "Mergers and Acquisitions," *Harvard Business Review,* vol. 43, no. 5, p. 6, September–October, 1965.

[38] Myles L. Mace and George G. Montgomery, Jr., *Management Problems of Corporate Acquisitions,* Cambridge, Mass.: Harvard University Press, 1962, p. 57.

[39] *Ibid.,* p. 75.

[40] Robert G. Dettmer, "Reasons for Mergers and Acquisitions," *Corporate Growth through Merger and Acquisition*, American Management Association, Management Report No. 75, New York, 1963, p. 29.

[41] A. D. H. Kaplan, "The Current Merger Movement Analyzed," *Harvard Business Review,* vol. 33, no. 3, p. 95, May–June, 1955.

[42] Federal Trade Commission, *op. cit.,* p. 73.

[43] Reid, *op. cit.,* pp. 187–188.

[44] Federal Trade Commission, *op. cit.,* p. 84. As part of a comprehensive research project currently under way at Carnegie-Mellon University, Professors H. Igor Ansoff and R. G. Brandenburg and I are attempting to determine the relative costs to merging firms of the "do-or-buy" policy concerning merger search activities. One of the objectives of this research is to determine whether such activities can be accomplished more successfully and at a lower cost by outside agencies or by the firm itself.

[45] Wakefield, *op. cit.,* p. 7. Fees charged probably vary considerably in amount. A management consulting firm which specializes in mergers makes the following statement concerning fees in its brochure: "For our services, our clients pay a commission that is a small percentage of the principal amount of each completed transaction. All the services incident to a merger as outlined in this brochure, as well as any other advisory assistance that may be required, are covered by this fee. There are no additional charges. There are usually no charges if the merger is not consummated."

[46] Federal Trade Commission, *op. cit.,* p. 84. Advertisements in the financial press have contained the names of new business brokers who have emerged during the current rising tide of mergers.

[47] Kottke, *op. cit.,* p. 433.

[48] Loomis, *loc. cit.* p. 214.

[49] *Ibid.*

[50] *Ibid.*, p. 213.

[51] *Ibid.* Certainly some type of price level adjustments would have to be made for comparisons of "real" growth, taking into account the fact that price increases do not affect all firms uniformly; that is, some prices actually declined, such as those for products like tires, appliances, television sets, and so forth. Other prices remained relatively stable, such as those for industrial chemicals, petroleum products, lumber, and cotton goods, while other major product groups rose considerably in price, with gains of 20 percent or more in iron and steel, shoes, and agricultural and construction equipment. The *average* price increase for this decade for manufactured goods was 11.3 percent; thus discounting for this factor, the sales increase would be 66 rather than 84.7 percent, or a "real" sales increase on an annual basis of 5.2 rather than 6.3 percent not adjusted. It is a substantial increase measured either way. See *ibid.*, pp. 213–214.

[52] *Ibid.*

[53] Reid, *op. cit.*

[54] *Ibid.*, p. 234.

[55] H. Igor Ansoff and J. Fred Weston, "Merger Objectives and Organizational Structure," *The Quarterly Review of Economics and Business*, vol. 2, no. 3, pp. 49–58, August, 1962.

[56] As discussed previously, concentric mergers involve a common thread in the relationships between firms; conglomerate mergers combine unrelated product lines. *Ibid.*, pp. 51–52.

[57] *Ibid.*, p. 53.

[58] *Ibid.*

[59] As stated previously, empirical tests of this hypothesis and others developed in my earlier study are currently being conducted at Carnegie-Mellon University by Professors Ansoff and Brandenburg and me under a grant from the McKinsey Foundation.

[60] William W. Alberts and Joel E. Segall (eds.), *The Corporate Merger*, Chicago: The University of Chicago Press, 1966.

[61] *Ibid.*, p. 45.

[62] *Ibid.*, p. 51.

[63] *Mergers in Industry: A Study of Certain Economic Aspects of Industrial Consolidation*, New York: National Industrial Conference Board, Inc., 1929, p. 171.

[64] Eamon M. Kelly, *Profitability of Growth through Mergers*, University Park, Pa.: The Pennsylvania State University, 1967.

[65] Johan Bjorksten, "Merger Lemons," *Mergers and Acquisitions: The Journal of Corporate Venture*, vol. 1, no. 1, pp. 36–41, Fall, 1965.

[66] See "Diversification's Marriage Brokers," *Forbes*, Feb. 15, 1967, p. 38. The article further states that ". . . the pages of *Forbes* frequently tell of still other mergers which obviously have gone sour, even though management still defends them."

[67] *Ibid.*

[68] Paul W. Cook, Jr., "Thinking Ahead: Trends in Merger Activity," *Harvard Business Review*, vol. 37, no. 2, p. 16, March–April, 1959.

[69] President Johnson, in his long State of the Union address and in the budget message that followed, did *not* mention antitrust during this current period of merger activity and growing concentration.

[70] Committee on the Judiciary, House of Representatives, *Corporate and Bank*

Mergers: Interim Report of the Antitrust Subcommittee, 84th Cong., 1st Sess., 1955, p. 17. Increased appropriations to the antitrust agencies do not necessarily mean increased effectiveness. The budgets of these agencies have generally been increasing during the 1960s, while their formal case loads have declined. For example, the FTC has a budget of $14 million, which is up from the $8-million budget of fiscal 1961 and the $4.2-million budget of fiscal 1955.

[71] Committee on the Judiciary, Senate Subcommittee on Antitrust and Monopoly, *Economic Concentration,* 89th Cong., 1st Sess., 1965, pp. 520–521.

[72] Joseph P. McKenna, "The Current Merger Movement," *Review of Social Economy,* vol. 16, no. 1, p. 12, March, 1958.

[73] For an interesting study of the relations between lawyers and economists, see Mark S. Massel, *Competition and Monopoly: Legal and Economic Issues,* Garden City, N.Y.: Doubleday & Company, Inc., 1964. The substitution of economists for lawyers in the top posts of antitrust agencies would not necessarily be an improvement; however, change for the sake of change may be a benefit in this case. Since economists have usually lacked positions of prime responsibility over the years, it has been difficult to attract highly competent personnel in these agencies. Many lawyers have used their government experience in antitrust as a stepping-stone to a more lucrative private practice defending corporate clients. Even the private legal firms have complained about the lack of activity in recent years.

[74] See Beryl W. Sprinkel, *Money and Stock Prices,* Homewood, Ill: Richard D. Irwin, Inc., 1964.

[75] "April Brings Merger Shower as Deals Exceed $900,000,000," *Mergers and Acquisitions Monthly,* vol. 1, no. 5, p. 1, May 31, 1967.

[76] See "Merger Activity during May Breaks All Monthly Records," *Mergers and Acquisitions Monthly,* vol. 1, no. 6, p. 1, June 30, 1967, for a report of merger activity during the spring of 1967. It appears almost certain that 1967 will be a record year for merger activity in the American economy.

[77] "Looking for a New Yardstick," *Business Week,* Aug. 20, 1966, p. 199. It appears that the conglomerates are making a concerted effort to develop a new image, with the help of the news media and some financial analysts. *Mergers and Acquisitions Monthly,* for example, has begun publishing a monthly comparison of what the publication calls the "conglomerate averages" with the Dow-Jones Industrials and the New York Stock Exchange index for all listed stocks. The only firms comprising the conglomerate index are Litton, Textron, and Gulf & Western Industries, which is hardly a representative sampling of the conglomerate firms. A more reliable indicator would be a comparison of the performance of the conglomerates listed in the July, 1967, issue of *Fortune* with that of other groups of firms following different kinds of growth strategies.

[78] An entrepreneur, for example, may invest the proceeds by beginning a new business, which would have a positive effect. However, in many cases the acquiring firm hires the former managers and/or entrepreneurs to continue running the acquired firm and to keep them from becoming actual or potential competitors.

[79] It appears paradoxical to me that the government would attempt to control inflation (i.e., during 1966 and 1967) by suspending the tax credit for business spending on new plant and equipment. This short-range move tends to

discourage expenditures for the capacity necessary to satisfy increasing aggregate demand. See my comments on this subject in Committee on the Judiciary, Senate Subcommittee on Antitrust and Monopoly, *op. cit.*, part 5, p. 1930. Recent developments in the economy lend support to this position since the suspension did *not* appear to halt inflation, and the need for more productive capacity is readily apparent in many sectors in 1968.

[80] Ralph L. Nelson, "Business Cycle Factors in the Choice between Internal and External Growth," in William W. Alberts and Joel E. Segall (eds.), *The Corporate Merger,* Chicago: The University of Chicago Press, 1966, pp. 65–66.

[81] In addition to the articles concerning this period, there were two widely quoted studies: J. Keith Butters, John Lintner, and William L. Cary, *Effects of Taxation: Corporate Mergers,* Cambridge, Mass.: Harvard University Press, 1951; and Federal Trade Commission, *The Merger Movement,* 1948.

[82] David D. Martin, "The Brown Shoe Case and the New Antitrust Policy," *American Economic Review,* vol. 53, no. 3, pp. 340–358, June, 1963.

[83] Kent T. Healy, "The Merger Movement in Transportation," *American Economic Review,* supplement, vol. 52, no. 2, pp. 436–444, May, 1962.

[84] The three papers presented were M. A. Adelman, "The Antimerger Act: 1950–1960"; Almarin Phillips, "Policy Implications of the Theory of Interfirm Organization"; and Donald Dewey, "Mergers and Cartels: Some Reservations about Policy." The discussants were James W. McKie, Reuben E. Slisinger, and Jerome B. Cohen.

[85] These volumes were published under the auspices of the American Economic Association by Richard D. Irwin, Inc., Homewood, Ill. Volume V covers the period 1954–1959 and was published in 1962, and vol. VI, published in 1965, covers the period 1960–1963.

[86] A number of other articles deal with subjects such as concentration, monopoly, oligopoly, etc., that can be linked in some way with mergers. However, I am referring to articles related *directly* to mergers and the current wave of merger activity.

[87] It is entirely possible that individual economists may be personally "concerned" about the merger problem; however, my main interest is in the amount of demonstrated research effort. A handful of economists have testified in congressional hearings, and a few government economists have been active, such as Dr. Willard F. Mueller of the FTC who has attempted to alert the legislative and executive branches to the problem. A number of other economists have received handsome fees to testify for big business lobbies or particular firms.

[88] Federal Trade Commission, *Report on Corporate Mergers and Acquisitions.*

[89] Committee on the Judiciary, House of Representatives, *op. cit.*

[90] Select Committee on Small Business, House of Representatives, *op. cit.*

[91] Committee on the Judiciary, Senate Subcommittee on Antitrust and Monopoly, *op. cit.,* part 2.

[92] *Corporate Growth through Merger and Acquisition,* American Management Association, Management Report No. 75, New York, 1963.

[93] Mace and Montgomery, *op. cit.*

[94] George D. McCarthy, *Acquisitions and Mergers,* New York: The Ronald Press Company, 1963.

[95] Charles A. Scharf, *Techniques for Buying, Selling, and Merging Businesses,* Englewood Cliffs, N.J.: Prentice-Hall, Inc., 1964.

[96] Clarence I. Drayton, Jr., Craig Emerson, and John D. Griswold, under the direction of G. Richard Young, *Mergers and Acquisitions: Planning and Action,* New York: Financial Executives Research Foundation, Inc., 1963.

[97] This book (Alberts and Segall, *op. cit.*) is a collection of papers, including the discussion following them, presented at a seminar held at the University of Chicago in September, 1963. Academics, business consultants, a lawyer, and businessmen attended.

[98] *Ibid.,* pp. v. and vi., foreword by George P. Schultz, dean of the Graduate School of Business, University of Chicago.

[99] Both studies were by Betty Bock; they are entitled *Mergers and Markets: A Guide to Economic Analysis of Case Law,* 3d ed., New York: National Industrial Conference Board, Inc., 1964; and *Mergers and Markets: An Economic Analysis of the 1964 Supreme Court Merger Decisions,* 4th ed., New York: National Industrial Conference Board, Inc., 1965.

[100] Ben W. Lewis, "The Modern Merger Movement: Discussion," *American Economic Review,* supplement, vol. 21, no. 1, p. 101, March, 1931.

[101] See John B. Parrish, "Rise of Economics as an Academic Discipline: The Formative Years to 1900," *Southern Economic Journal,* vol. 34, no. 1, p. 12, July, 1967.

6

A Merger Mosaic

Each of the previous chapters in this part has been designed to isolate various facets of the merger problem and to determine the impact of each merger wave upon that facet, or vice versa. In other words, the objective has been to attempt to determine the factors that have been common to each merger wave as well as the factors that have operated with different force and effect during these waves. This collection of homogeneous and heterogeneous facets provides a framework for the construction of a "theory of merger." This chapter will be devoted to developing a *merger mosaic* consisting of these various facets, with the purpose of contributing to an improved understanding of the merger phenomenon.

The dictionary defines a mosaic image as that "formed by a compound eye . . . in which each visual facet receives independently a small portion of the image and the total visual impression is a composite of the various unit images."[1] In developing this mosaic image concerning mergers, I shall begin by isolating the homogeneous facets apparent in each of the major merger waves. Following this exposition the heterogeneous facets will be examined, and then an economic and behavioral theory of merger will be presented.

Homogeneous Facets

The "common threads" that have been apparent during each of the three major merger waves are discussed below.

Data Problems

The problem of accurately recording all consummated mergers has persisted throughout American economic history, which naturally includes the three major waves of merger activity. A related problem is that associated with the reporting of financial results in consolidated form by business firms. This latter problem has assumed added significance in the current merger wave, during which many conglomerate firms have emerged as a result of the growing use of this type of merger. The persistent lack of data has hampered research efforts and complicated and delayed an appraisal by the financial community concerning the performance of mergers and merging firms. A separate (but related) problem is that of the analysis of the conglomerate firm and its role in the economy. Data problems have been common in each period of merger activity.

Concentration

Increased overall industrial concentration has resulted from merger activity during each of the three merger waves. The highest degree of interindustry concentration resulted from the turn-of-the-century merger wave—the classical era of consolidation—when most of the mergers were comprehensive and horizontal. Since mergers result in a change of control over existing assets rather than in an expenditure for new, additional capacity, they increase the probability of increasing levels of concentration. Most of the dilution of concentration in American industry has been attained in the periods between the major merger waves.

The Role of Mergers in the Growth of Firms

Since most mergers result in an immediate increase in the variables related to size (i.e., sales, assets, number of employees, etc.), it is reasonable to expect that firms which use this method of growth will become larger during periods of intense merger activity. Merger has been a vital force in the growth of many individual firms, particularly during periods of increased merger activity.

Relative Success of Merging Firms

Each of the major studies designed to measure the relative success of firms engaging in mergers during each wave of activity has failed to reveal a pattern of relative success. Despite these less-than-favorable results, firms continue to utilize this vehicle of institutional and capacity growth. The history of unsuccessful mergers continues to repeat itself during the current period in American economic history.

Promotion of Merger Activity

Initiators of merger activity have been present during each wave of merger activity. These promoters have sought personal gain and have felt little or no concern about other groups or individuals affected by the mergers. This is an important fact of economic life on the industrial and financial scene and should not be passed over or dismissed lightly. The uneven distribution of costs and benefits arising from merger activity is an important problem which deserves more attention than it has received in the past. Self-seeking promoters have been apparent in each major merger wave.

The Legal and Political Environment

A major piece of legislation designed to curb merger activity was passed prior to each merger wave. The Sherman Antitrust Law was passed in 1890, prior to the first merger wave; the Clayton Act and the Federal Trade Commission Act were passed in 1914, prior to the second merger wave; and the Cellar-Kefauver antimerger amendment was passed in 1950, prior to the current merger wave. These laws have had an effect upon the forms and types of combination activity during each wave, and yet the record demonstrates their ineffectiveness in curbing merger activity. A universal lack of concern about the merger problem at high levels of government (with the resultant lack of enforcement of the laws) has also been a contributing factor to this aspect of the environment.

The Economic Environment

A period of relative prosperity accompanied by a buoyant stock market has been in evidence during each merger wave. Similarly, periods of declining economic conditions have witnessed a decline in merger activity. The economic environment of realized or anticipated prosperity as evidenced by security prices has been a contributing factor to increased merger activity. Depressed stock prices and economic conditions have been more of a deterrent to merger activity than the antitrust laws.

Professional Interest

The professional group which one would expect to have the most interest in the merger phenomenon—the economists—has had a consistently lagging interest in the merger problem. This has been apparent during each merger wave. This lack of interest is the result of a combination of factors, and yet it is a fact of economic life and should be acknowledged as such. A lax and laggard leadership is of little help to the general public and the other groups in society which are interested in preserving and promoting a more effective free enterprise, competitive system. The "monetary school" and the "fiscal school" have made substantial contributions in the last few decades; yet neither group has evidenced much concern for the structure of industry which would result from their policy recommendations. An important variable has been omitted, and this fact should be recognized and corrected in an expedient manner. Economists have consistently avoided the merger problem until the wave of activity has subsided.

Post-merger-wave Economic Conditions

Depressed economic conditions in the form of a recession and/or depression followed the peaks of merger activity in both the turn-of-the-century merger wave and the late-1920s merger wave. Since the peak of the current wave has not as yet been determined, it is not possible to make any meaningful observation at present. The increased role of government in the promotion of growth and prosperity has to be considered. Prolonged prosperity (promoted by the government) intensifies the need for recognition of the merger problem. The common thread is that a recession and/or depression has followed each of the previous merger waves.

Public Concern

A lack of demonstrated public concern has been apparent during each of the merger waves. Perhaps this is natural, since merger waves occur during periods of prosperity, when unemployment is lower and personal incomes are higher and the basic economic conditions are thus conducive to a general public apathy. In addition, it would be surprising to see public concern manifest itself during periods when the professional groups, which should be concerned, are lethargic and quiet.

Heterogeneous Facets

While there are a number of common threads apparent in each of the major merger waves, some facets of the merger phenomenon have changed over the years. Recognition of these changes and an examination of some of the reasons for them should aid our understanding of these economic events.

Change in Merger Form

One of the major areas of change involves the predominant form of merger during each period. The consolidation, which dominated merger activity in the first wave, gave way during the 1920s to the acquisition, which is the predominant form in the current wave. This shift from the many-at-once form to the one-at-a-time form is the result of several factors. The change in the public and legal attitude following the first merger wave, as manifested in the Northern Securities decision and the trust-busting of the Theodore Roosevelt administration at the beginning of the century, contributed importantly to this development. Another contributing factor was the lack of success of the early consolidations, which increased the difficulty of promoting this form of merger activity in the subsequent period. Increasing dispersal of ownership was also a complicating factor to those who would have liked to utilize the consolidation form of merger. While both forms of merger have been used during each of the major waves of merger activity, the acquisition form has dominated since the early years of the century.

Change in Merger Type

Along with the decline in the consolidation form of merger there has been a shift away from the use of horizontal mergers as the main type of merger. The use of vertical mergers increased during the late-1920s merger wave, which also witnessed a gain in the use of circular mergers. The dominant type of merger in the current wave is the circular merger, with the conglomerate merger gaining in importance as the current wave swells.

The factors responsible for the change in the merger form utilized also partially explain the change in the dominant merger types. These changes also suggest a decline in the importance of economic reasoning concerning the mergers. The first merger wave was the era of consolidations, which were mainly horizontal and could be rationalized on the basis of attempts to achieve market control through creation of a single or dominant firm and/or production economies of scale. Since a large number of these mergers did not achieve the success expected of them, a new rationale had to be utilized. The backward vertical merger prominent during the second wave represented another attempt to rationalize the use of merger in gaining production efficiency through controlled sources of supply. The circular merger grew in importance since it could be promoted on the expectation of achieving marketing economies during a period of growing national markets and media. The continued and increasing use of circular mergers during the current wave is also rationalized on the same grounds, as well as on the grounds of the alleged synergistic benefits resulting from economies in R&D expenditures and managerial utilization. The current dramatic rise in the conglomerate category is difficult to explain by economic reasoning. Traditional market control and economies-of-scale arguments do not fit into the picture, except perhaps in the area of anticipated financial economies. A behavioral theory related to the desire of management for a continuity of control and the resulting benefits to them seems to be a more plausible general explanation for the increased use of this merger type. Diversification and stability appear to be more in the interests of management desiring continuity than of stockholders, since the latter group can, if they wish, accomplish this objective through portfolio changes.

Changes in the Role of the Promoter

Each merger wave has witnessed a change in the kind of promoters dominant in the merger activity. The outside professional promoter played a major role during the era of consolidations at the turn of the century. During the late 1920s, the investment banker moved into the forefront of merger activity. The current wave is dominated by the professional managers of the firms involved in merger activity. This is the most striking development during the current wave and is partially accounted for by the increased freedom of management from stockholder control. The majority of mergers during the current wave are consummated without stockholder approval, since management may use cash generated through retained earnings or shares of unissued stock.

Change Related to Market Control

A large number of the mergers during the first wave were consummated to achieve a high degree of market control. The change during the second merger wave was more toward the preservation of oligopoly positions through the acquisition of the "competitive fringe," as well as firms with related but different products. It is difficult to ascertain strict market control objectives during the current wave, when it appears that preservation of oligopoly and diversification are so dominant. This development complicates the work of the antitrust agencies, where traditionally concern has been centered on narrowly defined market control problems.

Concluding Comment

It should not be necessary to remind the reader that in each wave there have been consolidations as well as acquisitions, that management has promoted mergers in each wave, and that increased market control has been an objective. The main emphasis in this chapter has been on the general patterns of change observable during each of the waves. My purpose has been to demonstrate the homogeneous and the heterogeneous facets of merger waves, which, when taken together, form a merger mosaic.

An Economic and Behavioral Theory of Merger

Since a merger can be viewed as an exchange and combination of property, this type of economic activity can be expected to take place at any time (unless there are specific laws designed to prevent it). Major waves of merger activity (periods of time characterized by large increases in activity across broad lines of commerce and industry) develop when the economic, legal, and political environment is conducive to the consummation of mergers. A period of relative prosperity, accompanied by a buoyant securities market, constitutes a favorable economic environment. A favorable legal environment results from vaguely written laws and a confused interpretation and lax enforcement policy of them. The necessary political environment is characterized by a permissive attitude by the administration (the executive branch) and a lack of concern by the legislative branch (particularly in the absence of an economic crisis, coupled with pressures from powerful lobbies). Decreases in overall concentration cannot be expected to occur during these periods of heightened merger activity, and many of the mergers will be less than conspicuously "successful." When the environmental factors are favorable the promoters of merger activity are better able to achieve their primary goal of personal gain because during such relatively prosperous periods, mergers are comparatively easy to consummate; the fear of "image damage," which could result from legal action is reduced; it is difficult to determine results presented in consolidated form; and there is a general lack of public concern.

A merger is an investment decision that will generally be rationalized on economic grounds, promoted to serve narrow self-interests, and consummated for a variety of noneconomic factors in addition to the usual economic ones. Since the use of merger in the growth process is a hypertonic method of increasing the size of firms, some merging firms will grow faster in size than in profitability. Many firms that have a large percentage of merger-induced growth follow a program of "conspicuous investment" (or expansion) which may have differential effects upon the interests of the various groups involved in these economic events and in the allocation of resources.

NOTES

[1] *Webster's Third New International Dictionary,* Springfield, Mass: G. & C. Merriam Company, 1961, p. 1473.

Part Two ۞

Mergers, Growth, and Profitability

7

Mergers for Whom?[1]

It should be evident that a corporate merger is a multifaceted economic event which has an impact upon a number of interested individuals and groups. The relative impact of the costs and benefits resulting from a merger may not be evenly distributed among these interested groups. This rather basic fact seems to have been generally ignored in merger research and the merger literature. The fact that the important question "Mergers for whom?" is bypassed in most of the discussions of mergers implies a rather naïve belief that all interested parties share proportionately in the costs and benefits of mergers. At a minimum, there seems to be an assumption that the interests of the groups are complementary rather than independent or perhaps conflicting.

The fact that the owners and the management of large publicly held corporations may have different interests has been recognized and discussed, particularly since the publication of the Berle and Means classic over thirty years ago.[2] This study appeared following the second merger wave, during the depths of the Depression in the United States.

Three striking propositions were contained in this study which have since received considerable attention. The first asserted an increasing concentration in the economic and financial structure of the American economy. The second Berle and Means proposition emphasized progressive separation of control from ownership and foresaw a growing independence of management from stockholder influence and classical market constraints. The third proposition related this growing independence to changing managerial behavior and performance.

The concentration question was discussed in Part 1, and there is no need to deal with it again here. It does appear that prosperity and the accompanying waves of merger activity contribute to increased concentration or at a minimum do not contribute to deconcentration. Berle and Means were observing the prosperous 1920s when they wrote their book, and they had witnessed the effects of the second merger wave. The fact that neither merger activity nor economic conditions were buoyant during the 1930s or the war years in the 1940s no doubt has delayed realization of the first Berle and Means proposition. More recent research, updating the effect of time upon the second Berle and Means proposition, indicates that they were indeed correct in their earlier observations. Larner summarized his study on this topic by concluding: ". . . it would appear that Berle and Means in 1929 were observing a 'managerial revolution' in process. Now 30 years later, that revolution seems close to complete, at least within the range of the 200 largest nonfinancial corporations."[3] Discussion in this chapter will relate merger activity and growth of the firm to the second and third Berle and Means propositions.

Classical Economic and Behavioral Models of the Firm

The entrepreneur in classical economic theory was both an owner and a manager. It was naturally assumed that the decisions made by this owner-manager would be in his self-interest as well as in the interest of those affected by his decisions. The validity of this assumption in the modern world of large, publicly owned corporate entities operated by professional management groups is logically open to question. Fortunately, a new group of academic scholars have been examining this proposition in recent years and are making contributions to an enriched theory of the firm by adding important dimensions to the classical economic model. One locus of this activity is the Graduate School of Industrial Administration at Carnegie-Mellon University; in addition, a number of individuals at other institutions have also made important contributions in this area.

The emerging body of literature devoted to developing a behavioral theory of the firm has contributed much to our understanding of the corporate entity.[4] Even allowing for the extension of classical profit maximization models to take risk and costs of analysis explicitly into account, it has become evident that such models do not adequately reflect the objective functions implicitly used by managers in making decisions.[5] Gordon has claimed: ". . . management's small stockholdings have significantly diminished the strength of the profits incentive among professional business leaders, and this has been accompanied by a strengthening of the various non-financial attractions which the corporation has to offer."[6]

As a result of the addition of nonprofit goals to the objectives of large firms, promotion and protection of stockholders' interests may become secondary to, or intermingled with, promotion and protection of the personal and group goals of top and middle management in the executive ranks. Obviously, profits cannot be entirely disregarded by salaried executives, since at a minimum it is necessary to earn at least enough profits to keep directors and stockholders content. However, there is a great difference between profits being *the* objective and being merely a constraint.

Traditional classical economics tends to be locked into a proprietary concept which perceives the firm as being owned by a sole proprietor, partners, or a group of stockholders. Even in the large, publicly held firm, the stockholders are viewed as making the basic decisions related to hiring, firing, and retaining management; thus they are considered the entrepreneurs.[7] Consequently, in the traditional classical economic model it is unrealistic to consider that professional managers and owners (stockholders) might have different interests. Many economists are strongly biased in this matter since a good part of their economic education and training has been based upon assumptions and models stemming from classical theory. Admittedly, this is a sensitive area, and it is not my intention to offend any group; however, for purposes of analysis a behavioral approach will be introduced, since Part 2 of this book is concerned chiefly with the effects of mergers on the growth process of large publicly held firms. Consequently, the interests of each group will be treated separately. In addition, both economic and behavioral models will be discussed in later sections of this chapter.

The Interests of Managers and Stockholders

Managers' personal and group goals of security, power, prestige, increased personal income, and advancement within the firm may well be identified more with firm growth and size maximization than with classical profit maximization. In addition, stability and continuity of the firm also appear to be emerging as important management interests. Let us examine each of these factors as they relate to management's interests.

Management's Interests: Growth and Size Maximization

In the modern corporation, growth can become an end in itself. Growth is usually measured in terms of increased sales, assets, and/or number of employees. Baumol has suggested that ". . . management's goal may well be to maximize 'sales' (total revenue) subject to a profit constraint."[8] Managements concerned with size maximization can use mergers as an effective vehicle for accelerating the growth of their firms. Edith Penrose, in discussing the role of mergers in the growth process, stated: "in general the inducements to merger are so numerous and so pervasive that the appropriate question perhaps is not, why so much merger? but rather, why not more merger?"[9] She states that managers are vitally interested in growth because individuals ". . . gain prestige, personal satisfaction in the successful growth of the firm with which they are connected, more responsible and better paid positions, and wider scope for their ambitions and abilities."[10]

This desire for rapid growth can explain why the managers of large firms have been utilizing mergers and acquisitions, since absorption of another firm is a quick way to add sales, assets, and employees to the firm. In a report of the American Management Association, an executive wrote:

> The present phase might well be called the period of management-oriented mergers. In general, the basic purpose is not to monopolize or to pyramid financial structures, but, rather, to create and bring together logical industrial and operational empires—business entities of power, commercial position, stability, improved sales and earnings, and greater likelihood of growth and longevity of existence.[11]

It is interesting to note that profit has become only one among many objectives of the management-promoted mergers. This same executive continues: "personal power and personal ownership-control are rarely the long-term goal since, in the long run, most mergers and acquisitions mean the dilution of ownership and an increase in the number of owners."[12] Such dilution is in itself unlikely to be of benefit to the firm's stockholders. However, the managers of these firms may well benefit from increased dilution of ownership and the consequent increased freedom from stockholder control.

The power of merger to accelerate the growth of firms as measured by sales increases was recently recognized in an article in *Fortune;* it was stated:

> Since the companies that transformed themselves through mergers and acquisitions so often grew from bases that were small in 1955, they tend to dominate any list of heavy gainers in percentage sales growth. In fact, that list of the twenty leaders consists entirely of companies that were not big enough to appear on the 500 list in 1955. What's more, the only company on this list which can claim that almost all of its growth has been internally generated is Xerox.
> One large conclusion can be drawn from this list of twenty companies: massive growth in sales does not necessarily guarantee massive benefits to the stockholders. . . . Similarly, we shall see, some of the leaders in earnings growth have had only a moderate growth in sales.[13]

Growthmanship can become a preoccupation of top management; as Baumol has suggested:

> Expansion is a theme which (with some variations) is dinned into the ears of stockholders, is constantly reported in the financial pages and in the journals devoted to business affairs. Indeed, in talking to business executives one may easily come to believe that growth of the firm is the main preoccupation of top management.[14]

Subsequent tests lend support to Baumol's sales maximization hypothesis. McGuire, Chiu, and Elbing conducted a statistical investigation of the correlations between executive incomes, sales, and profits for 45 of the largest 100 industrial corporations in the United States covering the seven-year period 1953–1959. They found that ". . . the evidence presented would seem to support the likelihood that there is a valid relationship between sales and executive incomes as Baumol assumed, but not between profits and executive incomes. . . ."[15] In another study, Roberts found that the relationship between executive compensation and sales appeared to be stronger than the relationship between compensation and profits.[16] Patton, another student of executive compensation, studied 420 companies for the period 1953–1964 and found: "Company size, of course, is the principal determinant of top executive pay. For every doubling of company size, experience shows that the compensation of top management tends to increase about 20%."[17] Regarding the relationships between profits and executive compensation, Patton states: ". . . the profit increases between 1953 and 1964 of the companies with the highest paid chief executives (relative to company size) in 1953 were no better than the profit gains turned in by their lowest paid competitors."[18] In addition, Patton notes that in 1964, 60 percent of the variance in top executive pay was explained by differences in company sales and similarly, that 50.4 percent of the variance in top executive pay in 1953 was explained by differences in company sales.[19] Since sales growth is such an important variable in determining top management income, there is a basis for conflict between the personal interests of top management and the interests of shareholders.[20] This may be particularly true during the current wave of management-promoted mergers. Historically, the promoters of mergers have operated in their own self-interest, and the growing separation of management and ownership in large publicly held firms is contributing to a recurrence of this development.

Management's Interests: Continuity of the Firm

In addition to its preoccupation with size maximization and the accompanying increase in power, prestige, and personal income, management also considers continuity of the firm important. Executives are hired and paid by one firm at a time, and thus their loyalty naturally is to that unit. Management's present and future compensation is intimately bound up with the firm with which they are associated, and consequently continuity assumes importance and becomes a management interest. This fact is becoming increasingly clear during the current merger movement since many firms are using the acquisition route to achieve a conglomerate status. An increasing number of giant firms have utilized the diversification concept to such a degree that it is becoming difficult to classify them by industry membership. These firms are beginning to look more like investment companies or investment trusts than manufacturing firms. The ultimate effect of this attempt to preserve continuity by diversification is to move in the direction of averaging risk and return. Firms engaging in horizontal and vertical mergers are also displaying evidence of management's desire for continuity (as well as for mere survival of the firm in a few cases).

One of the most interesting commentaries on the merger process as it relates to the desire for continuity in big business is contained in a book by Parkinson, *In-laws and Outlaws,* in which this astute student of organization behavior makes the following observation about the ambitious executive:

> An industrial empire such as you aspire to rule is not a mechanical structure in which steel girders rest on concrete blocks. It is rather the result of a biological process in which seed and mating, growth and fertility play the dominant role. The world of business is an

> avenue in which parasites cling to the trees; a garden where weeds spring up among the flowers; an orchard in which bees carry the pollen of management science from one plant to another; a wood in which the branches of economic theory are strictly for the birds. In this wonderland of nature the facts of life are not to be ignored. One such fact is sex and we should be wrong to pretend otherwise. Victorian authors who dealt with the business world were reticent about the sexual aspects although all too prone to smiles of furtive innuendo. Today we have learned to discuss these matters frankly and openly, giving our children illustrated pamphlets about the flowers and the bees and telling each other (perhaps too often) that the mysteries of nature are really very beautiful. We can no longer disguise the fact that the Corporation has Sex.[21]

Parkinson describes the sex characteristics of the male corporation as follows:

> A male corporation is to be identified, first of all, by its rough exterior. It may be fairly tidy but it has made no effort to look attractive. The layout is more practical than pleasing, the machinery unconcealed and paint-work conservative and drab. Combined with this rugged appearance is an assertiveness in advertising, a rather crude claim to offer what is at once the cheapest and the best. The organization is extrovert, outgoing and inquisitive, its representatives more likely to visit another organization than wait to be visited. With this type of company's boastful manner goes a carelessness over details, a failure to check the outgoing mail, a neglect to clean the windows, an omission to test the fire appliance. Added to all this is the male extravagance. Faced with a decline in gross turnover, the male urge is not so much to economize as to seek some other source of income. It has been suggested that the male corporation is polygamous, showing a tendency to form temporary attachments to engage at least in casual flirtations. This theory cannot be accepted without certain reservations but that it has some basis is undeniable. While many or perhaps most male organizations are loyal to their chief business associate, others have a roving tendency and all (it may be) a roving eye. Last of all, the male corporation is apt to treat its male offspring with some severity, telling them to fight their own battles and punishing any whose gambling losses seem excessive.[22]

The sex characteristics of the female firm are described by Parkinson in the following manner:

> The female corporation shows all the opposite characteristics. Its factory buildings are prettily sited and smartly kept, with pastel shades in the paintwork and flower beds near the gate. But with the attractive layout there goes a certain modesty. Some parts of the production process are usually concealed and there may be a certain reticence shown in other ways—as affecting past associations, for example, and even the age of the plant. In the female

> organization there can be too much fuss over details, an insistence on exact procedure and an overemphasis on the appearance (as opposed to the reality) of competence. In general policy the female trend is toward economy and financial caution. Faced with a recession, the female corporation hastens to curtail expenditure and reduce the dividend. In general negotiations this type of company is more introvert, less outgoing. It will receive representatives of another firm but is unlikely to return the visit. There is last of all, a difference in its attitude towards the young. In a female corporation the maternal instinct is highly developed. Towards its offspring there is a protective attitude, a lenience which often goes beyond the bounds of its generally conservative finance.[23]

As part of the "Parkinsey report," Parkinson provides the following advice to aspiring professional managers regarding corporate sex characteristics and merger activity:

> For the present purpose it should suffice to note that mergers occur and that the rising executive should never lose sight of the fact. When a merger takes place the advantage lies normally with the male corporation, which has been acquisitive and active. It is to such a corporation that the rising executive should attach himself, remembering that the reorganization which accompanies the merger will create opportunities for those who look ahead. Executives on the female side are more likely to be displaced and thrust aside. For them the future is indeed pregnant with trouble and they have only themselves to blame. Through ignorance of the facts of life, they have found themselves on the wrong side of the merger. Theirs is a fate which others should seek to avoid. Always be on the male or active side. And when you come to hold high office, maintain at all costs the masculine character of your firm. Merge but never submerge.[24]

Parkinson is widely recognized as an astute observer of the world of big business and organizations. The fact that he recognizes that management's interests are associated with the acquiring firm is of considerable interest. However, since no consideration is given to the interests of the stockholders of the male (acquiring) firm, a corollary to the "Parkinsey report" will be given in the next chapter.

In summary, the managements of merging firms are interested primarily in growth (as measured by the size-related variables of sales, assets, and number of employees) and in the accompanying increase in power and prestige, as well as in the continuity of the firm. Management's interest in the growth of earnings may be secondary to, or intermingled with, other personal and group goals. If the interests of managers are aligned with those of the stockholders in large merging firms, the postmerger performance of these firms should reflect this economic alignment. The empirical studies which were discussed previously are at least suggestive of a potential dichotomous split or an independence of interests.

Stockholders' Interests

Common stockholders are presumably interested in the growth of the market value of their holdings and hence, *ceteris paribus,* in the growth of earnings per share.

In discussing the optimal financing of corporate growth, Lintner has pointed out that managerial decision rules should be such as ". . . to accomplish the same ultimate objective—the greatest satisfaction of common stockholders' preferences."[25] This ultimate objective is not very operational. In Lintner's words: "Moreover, since increased current share valuations *ceteris paribus* obviously increase stockholders' current wealth, which in turn clearly implies greater utility, this criterion of optimizing shareholders' utility has in practice been identified with the maximization of the current market value of the common stock."[26] The two criteria are identical if stockholders can be assumed to be facing perfect capital markets.

The current market price of a stock reflects investors' expectations about a stream of discounted future earnings. If professional managers are making growth decisions including those related to mergers and acquisitions with the objective of optimizing long-run gains to shareholders, this should be reflected in the market price of the stock of these firms. This does not imply that stockholders are not also interested in growth in sales, assets, and/or number of employees, but rather that they expect growth in these variables to be accompanied by improved earnings per share. If, instead, "growth" is accomplished through a dilution in the earnings per share of common stock, this is not in the best interests of the shareholder. Bigness has no intrinsic value if earnings per share are not increased.[27]

Fortune, which annually lists the 500 largest industrials based upon sales size, has finally recognized stockholders' interests in corporate growth. For the first time in a decade (1955–1965), earnings per share is included with the other size-related variables. The following statement concerning this addition appeared in *Fortune*:

> Another way to compare these industry groups is to examine the earnings-per-share growth of the companies in them. In the final analysis the direction of these earnings is the best measure of corporate progress, since no amount of sales growth or of improvement in profit ratios counts for much unless it is translated into gains for the shareholders—*for whose benefit corporations are pre-*

> *sumably run.* It is for this reason that FORTUNE has now added earnings-per-share figures to its 500 list [italics supplied]. . . .[28]

Weston has attacked prudent and legitimate concern about the possible dilution effects of mergers upon earnings per share; he discusses one of the four errors involved in an excessive preoccupation with initial dilution caused by merger as follows:

> The third error is that the analysis fails to recognize that any initial dilution in earnings per share constitutes initial accretion in earnings per share for the acquired company. Furthermore, if the analysis is extended in time it will be seen that, from the point of view of the combined interests of L and M shareholders, there is simply an exchange of earnings dilution and accretion between the two companies. The initial dilution in earnings per share of the acquiring company is offset in total by the initial accretion in total earnings of the acquired company. The subsequent crossover will reverse the two situations.[29]

It seems highly unlikely to me that one group of stockholders would be pleased or willing to subsidize a different group of stockholders if presented with accurate information.[30]

In summary, the stockholders of acquiring firms (or of any firms, for that matter) are generally interested in the firms' property values and profit potential, which are reflected in the earnings per share and the market price of its common stock. Hypertonic growth in size is not necessarily desirable per se unless proportional earnings increments are realized and accompany the rapid expansion.

Complementarity, Independence, and Conflict of Managers' Interests and Stockholders' Interests

The mere suggestion that managers' interests and stockholders' interests are not complementary offends many professional managers as well as some classical economists. Some managers will understandably resent the inference that they may not be serving the best interests of their stockholders when they engage in merger activity to accomplish rapid growth in the size and/or diversification of the firm. In addition, there are a number of economists who will not accept any theories or evidence which may cast doubt upon the validity of the classical profit maximization model. This again is readily understandable since each group finds it less troublesome to look the other way and pretend that the world is the way they would like it to be, rather than subject traditional assumptions to empirical tests.

The implication that certain managers of large publicly held merging firms may have disposed of (or even considered an open break with) the historic position of complete allegiance to the shareholders (owners) is heresy that perhaps rivals the "God is dead" hypothesis in theological circles. Professional managers, including those advocates of the entity concept of the firm, prefer to make pronouncements from a proprietary viewpoint. Donaldson observed this when he said of managers:

> They are apt to argue that their primary duty and intent is to make money for the stockholder and that in the long-run what is best for the corporation and for management is also best for the stockholder. This is all in the time-honored tradition of a society in which private ownership of the means of production has been regarded as a powerful motivating force toward maximum economic growth.
> Whatever the real feelings of professional managers are in this regard (I know from private and public expressions that they are decidedly mixed), the fact is that the objectives of the stockholder as just described may conflict with the objectives of professional management, both in regard to the latter's own personal or selfish interests and in the broader context of management's responsibility to the corporate entity.[31]

Since the alignment or nonalignment of interests of these groups is an important topic in general and is related to merger activity in particular, we shall examine each possibility separately.

Complementary Interests of Managers and Stockholders

If we assume that managers' interests and stockholders' interests are complementary, we would expect management to identify with the owners (stockholders) and a particular type of behavior to result. First, we shall examine this proposition in general and then in particular, as it relates to growth by merger. Discussing this identification of management objectives with stockholder objectives, Donaldson said:

> Under one view, management voluntarily adopts, or by one device or another has imposed on it, an identification with the objectives of the professional stockholder. Supposedly, the device of stock options works in this direction. If this is so, then it may be expected that the pressures of other groups involved in corporate activity—union members, white-collar workers, customers, the government, the general public, competitors—would be resisted and their interests subordinated to the stockholder interest.
> Of course, it is recognized that full maximization of the stockholder interest is a theoretical extreme which is not attained in practice, and could not be even if the goals and related standards of performance were crystal clear (which they are not). However, it can still be an operational concept if the supremacy of the stockholder

> interest is accepted by management, in which case the idea of maximization is in reality a statement of tendency only or of the direction of thrust of financial policy.
>
> Regardless of any misgivings about the desirability or practicality of this view, two things may be said in its favor: (1) it is consistent with the legal traditions of the corporation and the institution of private ownership; and (2) it is relatively simple, objective, and understandable as an operating guide.[32]

If the interests of the managers and those of the owners of firms engaging in merger activity are complementary, we should expect these firms to be growing in relative size *and* market value. It has long been assumed that merging firms can increase their earnings per share through increased profits resulting from either monopoly positions or realized economies of scale. The conventional wisdom places great stress upon the economies-of-scale argument in rationalizing the benefits of merger activity. However, the lack of empirical evidence confirming this assumption about mergers leads one to question the wisdom of accepting this widely held belief. Actually, the opposite view has been held by many of the students of merger activity; Nelson, for example, made the following comments concerning economies of scale and the control of markets during the first wave of merger activity:

> Economies of vertical integration, upon which many merger students have placed great stress, played a relatively small role in the merger movement. . . . It is hard to believe that such a variety of technological developments as would be needed to bring production economies of scale to these diverse industries could have converged in the same short period of time. . . . Emphasis on the control of markets might well have been more important than cost factors in determining firm size. It would be difficult to demonstrate that the most efficient or potentially most efficient firm size from the cost standpoint was systematically related to the size of the market—as would have to be demonstrated if scale economies were to be reconciled with market control.[33]

In observing the cyclical pattern of merger activity (that is, waves of merger activity occurring during periods of prosperity and a buoyant stock market), it is logical to wonder whether mergers are actually consummated to achieve cost reductions per unit of output. Weston observed this development and has made the following comment regarding mergers and their cyclical pattern as they relate to scale economies:

> If mergers occur in cycles, it is necessary to discover the rationale for the periodicity. On logical grounds, it might be inferred that if the dominant reason for mergers was the achievement of economies of operation, the greatest pressure for securing cost reductions would have taken place during cyclical contractions. Hence

> we would expect mergers to exhibit a pattern inverse to that of general business activity. . . . Since mergers do not in fact occur with greatest frequency during business contractions when the pressure for more efficient operations is greatest, the hypothesis that the achievement of economies is a strong motive for mergers remains unsupported.[34]

Stigler has suggested that the economies-of-scale argument (in general) may well be overstressed; he says:

> . . . if a firm of a given size survives, we may infer that its costs are equal to those of other sizes of firms, being neither less . . . nor more.
>
> A combination of this argument and casual observation suggests that the economies of scale are unimportant over a wide range of sizes in most American industries, for we commonly find both small and large firms persisting.[35]

Since mergers take place with increasing frequency during periods of rising demand, it appears somewhat naïve to believe that managements are preoccupied with lowering costs. Perhaps it is more realistic to assume that a period of rising demand is an excellent time to gain rapid control over capacity (even if it is in varying stages of obsolescence) and simultaneously to eliminate either actual or potential competitors or an excellent time to diversify the firm to avoid the risks associated with a particular industry and/or general business conditions. This assumption is considerably broader and perhaps more realistic than the economies-of-scale argument.

In addition, the pattern of mergers in the current wave does not lend much support to the economies-of-scale argument. An increasing amount of reported mergers involve large firms acquiring smaller firms in unrelated lines of business activity. Thus there is little basis in fact for the assumption that the desire for monopoly or scale economies is a motive in the majority of mergers in the current wave. Whether or not managers' interests and stockholders' interests were complementary even when monopoly was the main objective (as it was during the first wave) is debatable.[36]

In some of his more recent writings, Weston has explored an interesting concept based upon the complementarity of managers' and owners' interests, as related to merger activity. In discussing the impact of mergers upon the performance of a firm, Weston refers to the benefits which may be achieved when "synergy" is present in mergers; he says:

> The economic basis for a merger is the prospect of net gains from the transaction. The effects of the merger must be multiplicative

> rather than simply additive; or, put another way, the merger must involve synergy. Synergy is defined as the situation in which the sum of two or more parts is greater than their individual contributions. This has also been referred to as the "2 + 2 = 5" effect.
>
> In a merger in which synergistic effects may be achieved, both parties may gain from the transaction. Or at least in a synergistic merger, the net advantages that accrue to one firm need not come at the expense of the other firm.[37]

While this is an appealing concept, the major difficulty is in determining whether in fact synergy has been realized and, if it has, who benefits from the resulting synergy-induced residual. In discussing the "two-plus-two-equals-five" effect, the variable or variables to which the numbers refer have not been identified. If the managers of merging firms are realizing synergistic profit or earnings-per-share figures, synergy is contributing to stockholder welfare. If instead the numbers refer to size growth (sales, assets, etc.), synergy may be operating to the benefit of management's interest without effecting a proportional, complementary gain for the stockholders.

Unfortunately, no empirical evidence has been presented concerning the realized benefits resulting from mergers that produce synergistic effects. In fact, a principal case study which Weston uses to illustrate synergy involves two large banks in California, the Crocker-Angelo National Bank and the Citizens National Bank.[38] These banks were consolidated in 1963 to form Crocker–Citizens National Bank. At the end of 1966, according to *Fortune,* this bank ranked twelfth in size, while it ranked fortieth in terms of growth in earnings per share for the decade 1956–1966 and its growth in earnings as a percent of capital funds declined relative to the other large commercial banks after the merger.[39] *Moody's Handbook of Common Stocks* summarizes the position of this bank as follows: "The merger has given the bank a state wide branching system serving the rapid growing California area. Its aggregate deposits, loans and earnings have expanded at a fast pace but per share growth has been less impressive. Still, the banks long term outlook is favorable."[40]

It may well be that most of the synergy residual (if realized) accrues to the managers of merging firms rather than to the stockholders, particularly if the mergers are promoted by managers seeking to serve their self-interests. If, in fact, long-term benefits are realized, the time value of money must be considered in appraising the realized benefits. Proponents of the economies-of-scale and synergy concepts could contribute to an improved understanding of the merger process if they subjected these concepts to empirical testing. At present, both concepts are speculative (yet widely held), basically because they fit so neatly into traditional theory concerning mergers and managerial behavior.

Independence of Interests of Owners and Managers

If the growing separation of ownership from control is contributing to changing behavior and performance patterns in some large merging firms, this development will manifest itself in numerous ways. The discussion in this section will be limited to an important facet of the problem, a growing attempt to introduce new goals for the firm.

One such movement (which has been under way for some time in this country) is designed to create a "corporate conscience," that is, to broaden the perspective of the corporation and its managers in terms of seeking and promoting the public good, however defined. The avowed purpose of this movement is to have management improve its image by making the firm responsible to society as a "good neighbor," thus contributing to the cultural, educational, and civic environment. Decision constraints are expected to be expanded beyond the "old-fashioned" rule of concern for the interests of the owners. This development is apparent, as measured by both the number of books which have appeared on the subject and the expanded number of courses on the philosophy of business, business and society, etc., which have appeared in the curriculums of collegiate schools of business.

Friedman, a prominent economist, decries the growing acceptance of the "social responsibility" concept by executives; he says: "Few trends could so thoroughly undermine the very foundations of our free society as the acceptance by corporate officials of a social responsibility other than to make as much money for the stockholder as possible."[41]

The role of managers in this philosophy is viewed as that of trustees responsible to numerous groups other than the owners. Donaldson describes this development in the following manner:

> There has been growing support among professional managers for a second quite different concept often referred to as "management trusteeship." In part, this concept reflects an emphasis on the professional view of management and on the responsibilities of management (with strong support from professional schools of business). More significantly, it has been interpreted as a recognition of the plurality of responsibility in the modern corporation and of the need for an arbitration role for management in balancing conflicting interests. Under the concept of trusteeship in its extreme form the stockholder interest is merely one of several coequal vested interests to be considered when corporate policy is formulated.
>
> This approach is, it seems to me, a natural and predictable evolutionary step in the development of the larger scale corporate enterprise in today's society, though undoubtedly it has not yet

> reached the extreme form just suggested. If there is such a trend, then it is desirable to try to anticipate the effect on decisions in the area of financial policy. If the supremacy of the stockholder interest is abandoned, what takes its place?[42]

Donaldson raises a fundamental question, since a situation in which managers' interests are becoming increasingly independent of stockholders' interests is certainly a step removed from the situation in which the interests of these groups are complementary.

Managers of firms engaging in merger activity may rationalize their actions on the grounds that growth and continuity of the enterprise are more important to the managers than the owners since managers have less freedom to switch allegiances than owners do. A stockholder, whether an individual or an institutional owner, can change investments (not without various costs) more easily than managers can change jobs. As a matter of fact, American business tends to discourage mobility of managerial personnel by a number of devices such as pensions, stock options, deferred compensation, etc., which are all designed to discourage executive job mobility. Loyalty to the firm is also more easily recognized among managers than stockholders since the interests of the latter group may appear crass and impersonal.

These various movements tend to cloud our view of the role and purpose of the business firm and have an effect upon the allocation process. Movements of this type also contribute to a "dilution effect" since the ultimate criterion of profits to the stockholder becomes merely one among a variety of operational objectives. Decisions related to the methods of growth which firms may utilize can be affected by a diminishing conviction concerning the urgency of profitability. An indication of the independence of interests as related to merging firms would be a growth in size-related variables without a corresponding growth in profit-related variables.

The discussion in this section should not be construed as meaning that merging firms which do not display evidence of profitability are operating in this manner because they have developed a particular type of corporate conscience of a certain kind of "trustee" concept. The point is that attempts are constantly being made to submerge the basic objectives of the firm, and there is evidence that some managements have been seduced. While economists design models of, and accept assumptions about, how they believe professional managers should behave, there is no empirical evidence that the majority *do* in fact behave in this manner. Economic models will become more relevant when the assumptions upon which they are constructed have been empirically verified. The result will be a richer and more comprehensive theory of the firm.

Conflicting Interests of Managers and Stockholders

There are a number of potential areas of conflict which may develop between the owners and the professional managers of large, publicly held firms. The discussion will concentrate on only two of these areas, which are particularly pertinent to the merger problem. One potential area of conflict is related to the cost of providing managerial services, and the other is related to the investment decisions made by the managers of a firm.

The former problem is accentuated in merging firms which are growing rapidly in size as a result of mergers and acquisitions. It has been previously acknowledged that executive compensation is more a function of sales size than of profitability. Thus there is a basis of conflict between stockholders desiring to have managerial services provided at the lowest possible cost consistent with efficiency and the professional managers with divergent interests. Dean and Smith recognized this fact of life in the large, growing firm when they observed:

> We will assert that any firm large enough to be listed on the New York Stock Exchange has already exhausted its managerial economies of scale. This merely sharpens a position that has great sanction both in traditional economic analysis and in such modern analyses as those of Stigler and Parkinson. . . . Indeed, for any firm beyond the owner-management stage, it is likely that managerial costs will increase faster than size.[43]

The fact that the interests of managers and stockholders may *not* be aligned is further substantiated by the widespread use of stock option plans for management personnel. The mere existence of these plans is an admission of a potential conflict. They represent a form of "payoff" to management designed to aid managers in aligning their interests with those of the owners. Donaldson recognized this situation regarding stock options when he said:

> One of the key arguments for the stock option is that it serves to identify the professional manager with the interests of the stockholder and thus helps to restore the historic identity of ownership and management. This is a misconception. As previously emphasized, the stockholder is a diversified investor with a multicompany viewpoint and a loyalty which persists only as long as superior investment performance persists. This can never be management's viewpoint. A stock option merely serves to give added strength to the ties which already bind an executive firmly to a single corporate entity and its unique future. The one thing that can be said for a stock option in this regard is that it reminds management that E.P.S. and market price are important considera-

tions. It is unlikely, however, to overcome a primary allegiance to near-term cash flows.[44]

Since stock options represent a direct substitute for incentive cash payments to managers, they do not affect cash flows and are an expense only to the stockholder in the form of dilution of earnings per share and market price growth. This is an interesting situation since the owners of a firm are presumably paying management to administer the firm for their (the owners') benefit, and yet they are asked to provide a separate payoff to facilitate the accomplishment of this primary and basic task of management.

One of the most important areas in which conflicts may arise between the interests of managers and those of owners is in the investment activities of a firm. This is particularly true when the investment alternatives of merger and internal expansion are being considered. If mergers are accomplished through the payment of a large "premium" to the acquired firm (as well as other costs, such as side payments to the management of the acquired firm and fees to those facilitating the transaction), stockholders' interests may be unduly diluted. It is interesting to note that Weston, one of the leading men in the finance field, openly recommends this practice:

> Benjamin Graham has suggested (in discussions with the writer) that, as a broad empirical matter, an acquiring company must pay a 20 percent premium to the company it seeks to acquire. The 20 percent premium must be more than the existing market price of the acquired company's stock if it is to provide an inducement for the acquired company's stockholders to approve the sale. But if a 20 percent premium is to be paid to the sellers, the buyers also will demand a gain. Moreover, if the buyer takes the initiative, one expects him to achieve somewhat more than the seller. Hence it might be concluded that, on a general basis, the buyer receives something like a 30 percent premium. Thus the true value of the acquired company may be on the order of 50 percent more than its current market price.[45]

Weston's logic in this argument is rather difficult to follow, since he presumes that the knowledge of the acquiring firms' managements is superior to that of the marketplace. It reminds one of typical statements made by the promoters of many ill-fated mergers in the previous two merger waves. As stated previously, the assumption that a nebulous concept called "synergy" is present in mergers remains to be proved, particularly as it relates to stockholder interests. Until this concept is empirically tested and substantiated, the dilution effects of mergers must be given serious consideration by management if they do indeed wish to make investment decisions aligned with stockholder interests.

The nonalignment of the interests of these two distinct groups would suggest that many merging firms are engaging in a form of "conspicuous investment" (or expansion) primarily at the expense of the stockholders. This would be particularly true in merging firms which are *actively* attempting to maximize size instead of earnings per share.

The next four chapters are devoted to reporting the results of extensive empirical tests which have been conducted to determine whether the profit-related variables have moved in the same direction as the size-related variables. In other words, do mergers contribute to a complementarity of the interests of owners and managers or to a dichotomy between them? How do the various *types* of mergers contribute to firm growth and profitability and the attainment of the interests of managers and stockholders (as defined)? Do mergers in a partially regulated industry produce different effects from those produced by mergers in unregulated industries? These and related questions will be examined in the remainder of this part.

NOTES

[1] This chapter is an expanded version of the introductory part of a paper which John Bossons of the University of Toronto, Kalman J. Cohen of Carnegie-Mellon University, and I coauthored, entitled "Mergers for Whom: Managers or Stockholders?" I presented this paper to the Senate Subcommittee on Antitrust and Monopoly on Sept. 13, 1966, and the proceedings are published in Committee on the Judiciary, Senate Subcommittee on Antitrust and Monopoly, *Economic Concentration,* 89th Cong., 1st Sess., 1967, part 5, pp. 1914–1939. I also presented a preliminary version of the paper at the Midwest Economic Association meetings in Chicago on Apr. 18, 1964, and later that year at the Finance Workshop of the Graduate School of Business at The University of Chicago.

[2] Adolph A. Berle, Jr., and Gardiner C. Means, *The Modern Corporation and Private Property,* New York: The Macmillan Company, 1932.

[3] Robert J. Larner, "Ownership and Control in the 200 Largest Nonfinancial Corporations: 1929 and 1963," *American Economic Review,* vol. 56, no. 4, part 1, pp. 786–787, September, 1966.

[4] Oliver E. Williamson, for example, has provided some insight into managerial behavior regarding *expense preference,* suggesting: "Subject to loose performance constraints imposed by the capital market (both the stockholders and the firm's creditors), the management is largely free to exercise the monopoly power that the firm possesses at its own discretion." See Oliver E. Williamson, "Managerial Discretion and Business Behavior," *American Economic Review,* vol. 52, no. 5, p. 1054, December, 1963.

[5] For a summary of recent developments of a more behaviorally oriented model, see Herbert A. Simon, "Theories of Decision-making in Economics and Behavioral Science," *American Economic Review,* vol. 69, no. 3, pp. 253–283; June, 1959; Richard M. Cyert and James G. March, *A Behavioral*

Theory of the Firm, Englewood Cliffs, N.J.: Prentice-Hall, Inc., 1963; Oliver E. Williamson, *The Economics of Discretionary Behavior: Managerial Objectives in a Theory of the Firm,* Englewood Cliffs, N.J.: Prentice-Hall, Inc., 1964; and Joseph W. McGuire, *Theories of Business Behavior,* Englewood Cliffs, N.J.: Prentice-Hall, Inc., 1964.

[6] R. A. Gordon, *Business Leadership in the Large Corporation,* Washington, D.C.: The Brookings Institution, 1945, p. 325.

[7] See, for example, John F. Due, *Intermediate Economic Analysis,* Homewood, Ill.: Richard D. Irwin, Inc., 1951, p. 415; and M. M. Bober, *Intermediate Price and Income Theory,* New York: W. W. Norton & Company, Inc., 1955, pp. 425ff. However, Martin Bronfenbrenner, in "A Reformulation of Naive Profit Theory," *Southern Economic Journal,* vol. 27, no. 1, p. 301, July, 1960, writes: ". . . the attempt to locate within a corporate body any 'entrepreneur' with paramount claim to profit is to look in a dark room for a black cat which is not there."

[8] William J. Baumol, "On the Theory of the Expansion of the Firm," *American Economic Review,* vol. 52, no. 5, p. 1085, December, 1962.

[9] Edith Penrose, *The Theory of the Growth of the Firm,* Oxford: Basil Blackwell & Mott, Ltd., 1959, p. 242.

[10] *Ibid.,* p. 28.

[11] R. G. Dettmer, "Reasons for Mergers and Acquisitions," *Corporate Growth through Merger and Acquisition,* American Management Association, Management Report No. 75, New York, 1963, p. 29.

[12] *Ibid.*

[13] Carol J. Loomis, "The 500: A Decade of Growth," *Fortune,* July 15, 1966, p. 214.

[14] Baumol, *op. cit.,* p. 1078.

[15] Joseph W. McGuire, John S. Y. Chiu, and Alvas O. Elbing, "Executive Incomes, Sales and Profits," *American Economic Review,* vol. 52, no. 4, p. 760, September, 1962.

[16] See D. R. Roberts, *Executive Compensation,* New York: The Free Press of Glencoe, 1959.

[17] Arch Patton, "Deterioration in Top Executive Pay," *Harvard Business Review,* vol. 43, no. 6, p. 106, November–December, 1965.

[18] *Ibid.,* p. 114. A Chicago consulting firm, Manplan Associates, conducted a study and found that the median annual salary for chief executives was $45,000 in private firms and $55,000 in public firms, of comparable size, as reported in *The Wall Street Journal,* Feb. 28, 1967, p. 1.

[19] *Ibid.,* p. 113.

[20] For an interesting discussion of the growth and profitability question, see Joel Dean and Winfield Smith, "The Relationships between Profitability Size," in William W. Alberts and Joel E. Segall (eds.), *The Corporate Merger,* Chicago: The University of Chicago Press, 1966, pp. 3–22. The discussion following this paper is also interesting (pp. 22–30).

[21] C. Northcote Parkinson, *In-laws and Outlaws,* Cambridge, Mass.: The Riverside Press, 1962, p. 199.

[22] *Ibid.,* pp. 200–201.

[23] *Ibid.,* p. 201.

[24] *Ibid.,* pp. 203–204.

[25] John Lintner, "The Cost of Capital and Optimal Financing of Corporate Growth," *Journal of Finance,* vol. 18, no. 2, p. 292, May, 1963.

[26] *Ibid.*

[27] Put in other terms, asset growth is of negative value to stockholders if it is accomplished through investments yielding less than the cost of capital to the firm. See Merton H. Miller and Franco Modigliani, "Dividend Policy, Growth and the Valuation of Shares," *Journal of Business,* vol. 34, no. 4, pp. 411–433, October, 1961.

[28] Loomis, *op. cit.,* p. 271.

[29] J. Fred Weston, "The Determination of Share Exchange Ratios in Mergers," in William W. Alberts and Joel E. Segall (eds.), *The Corporate Merger,* Chicago: The University of Chicago Press, 1966, pp. 126–127.

[30] The situation of stockholders in terms of a proposed merger differs, depending upon which side of the merger they are on. Generally the stockholders of the acquired firm are paid a premium in the transaction and thus are "paid off," while the stockholders of the acquiring firm (if given a vote) are usually influenced by management, which obviously favors the transaction. In addition, mergers generally occur during periods of prosperity, when stockholders are usually relatively satisfied and reluctant to upset management.

[31] Gordon Donaldson, "Financial Goals: Management vs. Stockholders," *Harvard Business Review,* vol. 41, no. 3, p. 118, May–June 1963.

[32] *Ibid.*

[33] Ralph L. Nelson, *Merger Movements in American Industry: 1895–1956,* Princeton, N.J.: Princeton University Press, 1959, pp. 103–104.

[34] J. Fred Weston, *The Role of Mergers in the Growth of Large Firms,* Berkeley, Calif.: University of California Press, 1953, pp. 79–81.

[35] George J. Stigler, "Monopoly and Oligopoly by Merger," *American Economic Review,* vol. 40, no. 2, p. 26, May, 1950.

[36] See Arthur S. Dewing, "A Statistical Test of the Success of Consolidations," *Quarterly Journal of Economics,* vol. 36, no. 4, November, 1921.

[37] Weston, *op. cit.,* pp. 130–131.

[38] *Ibid.,* pp. 132–137.

[39] "The 50 Largest Commerical Banks," *Fortune,* June 15, 1967, p. 216.

[40] *Moody's Handbook of Common Stocks,* 2d ed., New York: Moody's Investors Service, 1966, p. 265. The adjusted premerger earnings per share for the bank were $2.26 in 1962; after the merger they were $2.38 in 1963, $2.48 in 1964, and $2.52 in 1965. This is hardly an impressive record when compared with that of other California banks.

[41] Milton Friedman, *Capitalism and Freedom,* Chicago: The University of Chicago Press, 1962, p. 133.

[42] Donaldson, *op. cit.,* pp. 118–119.

[43] Dean and Smith, *op. cit.,* p. 14.

[44] Donaldson, *op. cit.,* p. 123.

[45] Weston, *op. cit.,* pp. 136–137. A number of financial analysts watch for sellout, takeover, and arbitrary opportunities which develop during merger waves and can offer the investor in securities of the acquired firm high rates of return in relatively short periods of time. The following statement appeared in *Market and Business Survey,* New York: E. F. Hutton & Co., Inc., vol. 20, no. 11, p. 1, November–December, 1962: "Specifically, companies in liquidation or in the process of being acquired have offered potential returns of up to 30% this year. Many investors might now welcome the opportunity to escape

from the role of market forecaster and investigate such equities which offer good potential for capital appreciation, and which are somewhat insulated from wide market risk, but rather a speculation on a favorable ruling by the stockholders of companies concerned, and on the approval of the necessary tax and legal authorities where their concurrence is a requirement." Situations of this type should offer opportunities for application of Bayesian statistical techniques to problems of risk and uncertainty, and probabilities of consummation.

8

Some Empirical Tests: The Large Industrials[1]

The empirical tests reported in this chapter were designed to relate merger activity involving large, publicly held industrial firms to the second and third Berle and Means propositions concerning managerial behavior and performance. As discussed in the previous chapter, Berle and Means foresaw a growing *independence* of management from stockholders' influence and classical market constraints. The possibility that there may also be *conflicts* of interests as well as independence of interests regarding merging firms was also discussed. In order to examine this hypothesis in more detail, a number of tests were conducted to determine whether the interests of managers and stockholders of large merging firms were indeed complementary, independent, or conflicting. If the tests demonstrate that the interests of these primary groups are complementary, there is little need to improve upon classical economic theory regarding behavior.

The Underlying Hypothesis

As stated previously, the underlying hypothesis is motivated by the second and third propositions of Berle and Means regarding the separation of control from ownership and changes in corporate behavior and performance stemming from this independence. Stated in operational terms: *The more actively that large, publicly held firms merge, the more they tend to be oriented to furthering managers' interests rather than stockholders' interests.*

Managers' Interest Variables

Previously it was argued that in acquiring firms, managers' interests can be regarded as primarily a desire for growth (as measured by variables related to size, such as sales, assets, and number of employees) together with the accompanying increase in the power and prestige of the firm as well as its continuity. Managers' interest in the growth of earnings per share is at most secondary, serving as a constraint in the attainment of other interests.[2] The following three size-related variables are used in the tests to represent the interests of managers:

(1) $Y^1 = \frac{S_t - S_{t-1}}{S_{t-1}}$ = the relative change in sales from time $t-1$ (the beginning of the period) to time t (the end of the period)[3]

(2) $Y^2 = \frac{A_t - A_{t-1}}{A_{t-1}}$ = the relative change in assets from time $t-1$ to time t

(3) $Y^3 = \frac{E_t - E_{t-1}}{E_{t-1}}$ = the relative change in number of employees from time $t-1$ to time t

Stockholders' Interest Variables

In the previous chapter, owners' (stockholders') interests were identified with the growth of the market value of their holdings and hence, *ceteris paribus*, the growth of earnings per share. The following three variables are used to represent the interests of stockholders in the statistical tests:

(4) $Y^4 = \frac{MP_t - MP_{t-1}}{MP_{t-1}}$ = the relative change in market price per share of common stock (adjusted for stock splits and stock dividends) from time $t-1$ to time t[4]

(5) $Y^5 = \frac{P_t^* - P_{t-1}^*}{A_{t-1}}$ = the increase in the share of profits from time $t-1$ to time t attributable to the stockholders as of time $t-1$,[5] relative to assets at time $t-1$[6]

(6) $Y^6 = \frac{P_t^* - P_{t-1}^*}{S_{t-1}}$ = the same as (5), except relative to sales at time $t-1$

CHART 8.1 A simple graphic presentation of the hypothesis concerning interests of managers and stockholders.

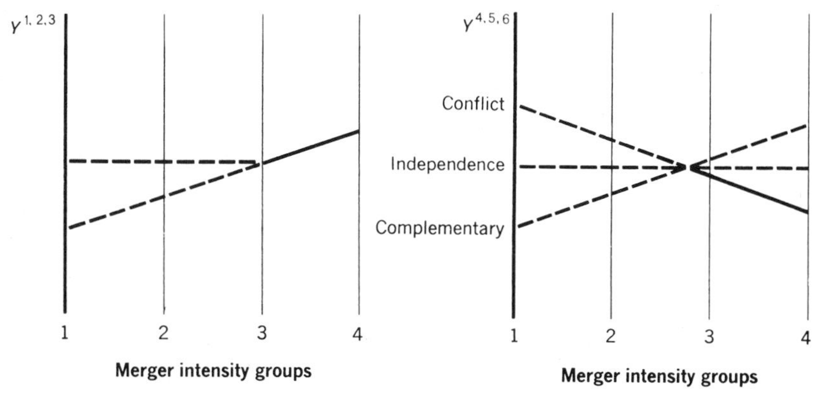

Left: **Sales, assets, and number of employees increase by merger intensity more than otherwise, particularly the group which is active in the process (group 4).** ***Right:*** **Market price per share and profits to stockholders relate to whether interests are complementary, independent, or conflicting. A potential conflict is represented by the solid line in a downward position as merger intensity increases. That is, a dichotomy results from increased merger activity diluting the stockholders' position.**

The Formal Hypothesis

Using the six variables defined above, $Y^1, \ldots, Y^6$, the formal hypothesis tested can be stated in the following manner: The more actively firms have merged during the period, the larger their relative increases in sales, assets, and number of employees tend to be; similarly, there will be a tendency for their relative increases in market price per share and profits attributable to the original stockholders to be smaller.[7] A graphic presentation of this hypothesis is given in Chart 8.1. In this chart, the size-related variables are increasing with intensity of merger activity, which is to be expected (unless there are numerous vertical mergers), while the profit-related variables would move in the same direction if complementarity of interests were present. If the interests are not complementary, they would be as indicated, either flat or mixed (suggesting independence of interests) or downward (indicating a possible conflict of interests). This latter possibility is strong and unexpected, and has been chosen for that reason and because it has behavioral as well as economic implications.

The Evidence

In order to test the above hypothesis, data were obtained pertaining to a sample of 478 large American industrial firms during the period 1951–1961.[8] The firms included in this study acquired over 3,300 firms between 1951 and 1961, more than half of the 6,176 mergers reported by the FTC during this period. The firms were initially separated by the simple dichotomy of no-merging and merging firms. Since our concern is primarily with the intensity of merger activity rather than merger per se, other groupings were made based upon the number of mergers reported for each firm.[9] Since this was the only possible method of measuring intensity, there was no alternative except to utilize the number of mergers as the basis for classification. In addition to the simple dichotomy, three groups of firms were isolated: (1) those firms which did not merge at all during the decade, (2) those firms which had engaged in one to five mergers, and (3) those firms which had six or more mergers during the time period. In addition, a third method of classification was used which attempted to distinguish the more active merging firms. The 478 industrial firms were divided into the following four groups:

Group 1 Pure internal growth firms—firms with no reported mergers, 1951–1961

Group 2 Occasional acquirers—firms with one to five reported mergers, 1951–1961

Group 3 Moderate acquirers—firms with six to ten reported mergers, 1951–1961

Group 4 Active acquirers—firms with eleven or more reported mergers, 1951–1961

Initial Tests

As a first step toward testing the hypothesis, the average (arithmetic mean) values of $Y^1, \ldots, Y^6$ were computed for all 478 firms in the sample, as well as for these same firms divided into merger activity groups. The results, which are shown in Tables 8.1 and 8.2, provide (at least on the surface) striking confirmation of the underlying hypothesis. The three variables representing managers' interests (sales, assets, and number of employees) show a definite positive association with the intensity of merger activity, whereas the three variables representing stockholders' interests (market price, profits to original stockholders scaled by assets, and profits to original stockholders scaled by sales) show a definite negative association with the intensity of merger activity.[10] For each variable, moreover (when merger intensity is introduced), the observed differences between group means are statistically significant; a one-way analysis-of-variance test indicates that it is extremely unlikely that these differences could have arisen as a result of chance.[11] Thus, mergers do matter, and the more actively a firm merges, the more it tends to further the self-interests of managers rather than the interests of stockholders.

Further Tests Holding Industry Constant

By themselves, however, the results of these initial tests are not entirely conclusive. A one-way analysis-of-variance test implicitly assumes that except for the classificatory variable (in this case, the intensity of merger activity), there are no other omitted variables which exert systematic effects upon the dependent variable (i.e., upon $Y^1, \ldots, Y^6$). It is conceivable that this is not the case for this sample of large industrial firms. It could be argued, for example, that the apparent systematic association between the intensity of merger activity and the variables representing managers' and stockholders' interests is spurious and is actually the result of a third variable systematically related to both merger activity and the managers' and stockholders' interest variables. Without employing a type of analysis which holds constant the effects of such a third variable, it is unsafe to conclude that the apparent effects of mergers are their real effects.

TABLE 8.1 Means of the Variables for All Industrial Firms in the Study and by Merger Groups

	Simple Dichotomy				Merger Intensity			
Variable	*All Firms*	*No Mergers*	*Mergers*	F-*ratio**	*No Mergers*	*Low (1–5 Mergers)*	*High (6-plus Mergers)*	F-*ratio**
Size-related:								
Y_1	1.823	1.597	1.848	0.20	1.597	1.206	2.490	*6.84*$^{(0.005)}$
Y_2	2.035	1.636	2.079	0.56	1.640	1.348	2.811	*8.18*$^{(0.005)}$
Y_3	0.943	0.428	1.000	2.18	0.428	0.551	1.450	*7.96*$^{(0.005)}$
Profit-related:								
Y_4	2.916	6.804	2.483	*13.99*$^{(0.005)}$	6.804	2.316	2.649	*7.09*$^{(0.005)}$
Y_5	0.037	0.121	0.027	*14.99*$^{(0.005)}$	0.121	0.032	0.022	*7.67*$^{(0.005)}$
Y_6	0.028	0.109	0.019	*17.45*$^{(0.005)}$	0.109	0.024	0.014	*9.03*$^{(0.005)}$
Number of firms	478	48	430		48	214	216	

* The *F*-ratios shown for each variable are based on one-way analysis-of-variance tests of the significance of the observed differences in group means for that variable. In the middle column, the *F*-ratios are based on a classification of firms into two groups; in the rightmost column, the *F*-ratios are based on a classification of firms into three groups. The italicized *F*-ratios are those for which the probability is less than 0.10 that the observed differences in group means could be the result of chance; in these cases, the significance levels are shown in parentheses as superscripts to the *F*-ratios.

TABLE 8.2 Means of the Variables for All Industrial Firms in the Study and by Merger Group

Variables	*All Firms*	*No Mergers*	*1–5 Mergers*	*6–10 Mergers*	*11-plus Mergers*	F-*ratio**
Size related:						
Y^1	1.823	1.597	1.206	2.005	3.405	$7.03^{(0.005)}$
Y^2	2.035	1.640	1.344	2.227	3.920	$8.80^{(0.005)}$
Y^3	0.943	0.428	0.552	1.120	2.069	$7.64^{(0.005)}$
Profit-related:						
Y^4	2.916	6.804	2.304	2.447	3.066	$4.84^{(0.005)}$
Y^5	0.037	0.121	0.032	0.023	0.022	$5.11^{(0.005)}$
Y^6	0.028	0.109	0.025	0.013	0.014	$6.01^{(0.005)}$
Number of firms	478	48	214	142	74	

* The *F*-ratio shown for each variable is based on a one-way analysis-of-variance test of the significance of the observed differences in group means for that variable. The significance levels are shown in parentheses as superscripts to the *F*-ratios. The italicized *F*-ratios are those for which the probability is less than 0.005 that the observed differences in group means could be the result of chance.

The most obvious variable omitted from the initial tests is the industrial composition of the firms in the sample.[12] There are reasons for believing that mergers occur more frequently in some industries than in others and that the growth in sales, assets, number of employees, market price, and profits differs markedly from one industry to another. In order to determine whether the apparent effects of mergers revealed in Tables 8.1 and 8.2 could be due entirely to interindustry differences that are systematically related to both merger activity groups, further statistical tests were conducted.

The 478 firms in the sample were divided into fourteen industry groupings (based on their principle lines of business and SIC codes).[13] Table 8.3 shows the number of firms in each industry belonging to each of the four merger activity groups. In order to hold interindustry effects constant, the type of analysis reported above in the section headed "Managers' Interest Variables" and in Tables 8.1 and 8.2 was repeated fourteen additional times, each time using only those firms belonging to the same industry. The results for the three variables representing managers' interests are shown in Tables 8.4 to 8.6, while the results for the three variables representing stockholders' interests are shown in Tables 8.7 to 8.9.

When interindustry effects are held constant, the statistical tests still confirm the underlying hypothesis, although not quite as strongly as appeared to be the case on the basis of the original tests (which did not hold interindustry effects constant). The basic difference is that when the effects of merger activity are analyzed within specific industries, mergers do not always have a significant effect. Thus, for the six dependent variables representing managers' and stockholders' interests, $Y^1, \ldots,$ Y^6, out of fourteen industries the numbers of industries for which the observed differences between group means are statistically significant[14] are, respectively, six, six, four, five, eight, and seven.

In examining whether each dependent variable has the hypothesized direction of relationship with merger activity, it is meaningful to consider only those industries for which the effects of mergers on that variable are statistically significant. Tables 8.4 to 8.6 reveal that, except for instruments, in every industry in which the observed differences in merger group means are statistically significant, there is a positive association between the dependent variable representing managers' interests and the intensity of merger activity. In fourteen of the sixteen combinations of managers' interest variable and industry for which mergers mattered, the effects of merger activity were in the hypothesized direction.

TABLE 8.3 Number of Firms in Each Industry and in Each Merger Group

Industry	*All Firms*	*No Mergers*	*1–5 Mergers*	*6–10 Mergers*	*11-plus Mergers*
All Industries	*478*	*48*	*214*	*142*	*74*
Mining	8	2	1	4	1
Food	66	6	30	16	14
Textiles and apparel	21	—	10	6	5
Paper and printing	34	4	12	12	6
Chemicals	58	5	20	26	7
Petroleum	32	4	12	11	5
Stone, glass, and clay	15	1	10	2	2
Primary metals	47	6	26	14	1
Fabricated metals	20	1	9	4	6
Machinery	52	6	30	10	6
Electrical equipment	45	3	20	16	6
Transportation equipment	46	5	19	14	8
Instruments	8	1	5	2	—
Miscellaneous	26	4	10	5	7

TABLE 8.4 Means of Y^1 (Growth in Sales) in Each Industry for All Firms and by Merger Intensity Group

Industry	*All Firms*	*No Mergers*	*1–5 Mergers*	*6–10 Mergers*	*11-plus Mergers*	F-*ratio**
Mining	1.085	0.869	−0.199	1.524	1.043	0.17
Food	1.102	0.334	1.016	1.481	1.185	0.64
Textiles and apparel	0.856	—	0.226	0.625	2.394	*11.22*$^{(0.005)}$
Paper and printing	1.714	0.678	1.032	1.444	4.309	*3.01*$^{(0.05)}$
Chemicals	1.814	1.377	1.982	1.716	2.008	0.16
Petroleum	2.027	0.637	1.277	3.227	2.299	0.57
Stone, glass, and clay	0.954	0.983	0.721	1.441	1.618	1.51
Primary metals	0.547	0.415	0.266	0.997	2.366	*7.39*$^{(0.005)}$
Fabricated metals	2.690	1.495	1.115	1.650	5.946	0.90
Machinery	1.519	4.360	1.095	1.093	1.508	2.09
Electrical equipment	3.161	0.307	1.995	3.092	8.658	*3.82*$^{(0.025)}$
Transportation equipment	3.350	3.505	2.621	4.022	3.807	0.12
Instruments	3.243	9.914	1.891	3.288	—	*4.17*$^{(0.10)}$
Miscellaneous	1.867	0.318	0.204	1.394	5.465	*4.33*$^{(0.025)}$

* The *F*-ratios shown for each variable are based on one-way analysis-of-variance tests (within each industry) of the significance of the observed differences in group means for that variable. The italicized *F*-ratios are those for which the probability is less than 0.10 that the observed differences in group means could be the result of chance; in these cases, the significance levels are shown in parentheses as superscripts to the *F*-ratios. This note applies also to Tables 8.5 to 8.9.

The picture revealed for the variables representing stockholders' interests in Tables 8.7 to 8.9 is slightly less favorable to the underlying hypothesis. In seventeen of the total of twenty combinations of stockholders' interest variable and industry for which mergers mattered, the effects of merger activity were in the negative direction, as hypothesized. The only exceptions are (1) mergers fail to be negatively associated with profits for original stockholders scaled by assets for both the electrical equipment and the miscellaneous industries and (2) mergers fail to be negatively associated with profits for original stockholders scaled by sales for the electrical equipment industry.[15]

On balance, then, when interindustry effects are held constant, the evidence is consistent with the underlying hypothesis. To the extent that mergers have significant effects in particular industries, the more actively a firm merges, the more it tends to further managers' interests rather than stockholders' interests.

TABLE 8.5 Means of Y^2 (Growth in Assets) in Each Industry for All Firms and by Merger Intensity Group

Industry	*All Firms*	*No Mergers*	*1–5 Mergers*	*6–10 Mergers*	*11-plus Mergers*	F-*ratio*
Mining	2.065	1.615	0.333	2.655	2.339	0.14
Food	1.069	0.580	0.981	1.217	1.299	0.44
Textiles and apparel	0.935	—	0.406	0.958	1.969	$7.81^{(0.005)}$
Paper and printing	2.304	0.802	1.429	2.261	5.143	2.21
Chemicals	1.781	1.680	1.823	1.716	1.970	0.05
Petroleum	1.845	1.149	1.545	1.603	3.653	$2.28^{(0.10)}$
Stone, glass, and clay	1.415	1.260	1.179	1.635	2.452	2.18
Primary metals	1.286	1.334	0.832	2.089	1.552	1.51
Fabricated metals	1.740	2.297	1.370	1.436	2.407	0.50
Machinery	2.121	1.821	1.418	1.527	6.924	3.19
Electrical equipment	3.689	0.521	2.111	3.660	10.609	3.83
Transportation equipment	2.959	1.900	1.793	4.629	3.466	0.43
Instruments	4.410	18.000	2.313	2.858	—	$10.75^{(0.025)}$
Miscellaneous	2.353	1.057	0.557	1.675	6.143	$3.48^{(0.05)}$

TABLE 8.6 Means of Y^3 (Growth in Number of Employees) in Each Industry for All Firms and by Merger Intensity Group

Industry	*All Firms*	*No Mergers*	*1–5 Mergers*	*6–10 Mergers*	*11-plus Mergers*	F-*ratio*
Mining	0.361	1.737	−0.489	0.879	−0.485	0.22
Food	0.393	−0.305	0.347	0.514	0.536	0.47
Textiles and apparel	0.413	—	0.030	0.338	1.267	$9.37^{(0.005)}$
Paper and printing	1.628	0.160	0.843	1.270	4.895	$3.53^{(0.005)}$
Chemicals	0.854	0.508	0.708	0.982	1.045	0.43
Petroleum	1.351	0.125	0.688	2.682	0.996	0.57
Stone, glass, and clay	0.236	0.189	0.064	0.417	0.941	2.59
Primary metals	0.131	0.411	0.003	0.222	0.500	2.03
Fabricated metals	1.476	0.786	0.714	1.251	2.885	0.76
Machinery	0.834	0.700	0.601	0.603	2.521	$2.49^{(0.10)}$
Electrical equipment	1.768	0.217	0.787	1.641	6.151	$3.61^{(0.005)}$
Transportation equipment	1.023	0.902	0.389	1.794	1.254	0.58
Instruments	1.427	3.975	0.836	1.632	—	1.63
Miscellaneous	1.710	−0.019	2.285	1.076	2.329	0.30

TABLE 8.7 **Means of Y^4 (Growth in Market Price) in Each Industry for All Firms and by Merger Intensity Group**

Industry	*All Firms*	*No Mergers*	*1–5 Mergers*	*6–10 Mergers*	*11-plus Mergers*	F-*ratio*
Mining	0.935	1.163	2.231	0.204	2.111	2.31
Food	1.741	0.986	1.381	3.073	1.314	0.78
Textiles and apparel	0.668	—	0.260	1.118	0.945	0.59
Paper and printing	2.880	4.171	2.647	2.313	3.621	0.44
Chemicals	4.144	20.031	3.217	2.491	1.583	*3.63*(0.025)
Petroleum	0.973	0.184	1.218	0.794	1.411	1.32
Stone, glass, and clay	2.255	6.083	2.061	2.265	1.304	*4.31*(0.05)
Primary metals	1.328	2.937	0.953	1.444	−0.174	*2.62*(0.10)
Fabricated metals	2.061	15.200	1.981	0.968	0.719	*19.38*(0.05)
Machinery	3.007	5.144	2.740	1.929	3.999	0.90
Electrical equipment	3.920	2.159	3.795	3.980	5.057	0.20
Transportation equipment	2.466	2.416	2.159	3.381	1.627	0.46
Instruments	29.403	105.500	9.387	6.896	—	*17.44*(0.01)
Miscellaneous	5.436	2.481	2.690	3.366	12.526	1.29

TABLE 8.8 **Means of Y^5 (Growth in Profits for Original Stockholders Scaled by Assets) in Each Industry for All Firms and by Merger Intensity Group**

Industry	*All Firms*	*No Mergers*	*1–5 Mergers*	*6–10 Mergers*	*11-plus Mergers*	F-*ratio*
Mining	−0.001	0.105	−0.014	−0.059	−0.015	*5.35*(0.10)
Food	0.033	0.054	0.024	0.062	0.010	0.74
Textiles and apparel	0.016	—	0.007	0.004	0.047	0.88
Paper and printing	0.023	−0.008	0.003	0.030	0.082	0.97
Chemicals	0.085	0.267	0.116	0.047	0.006	*3.31*(0.025)
Petroleum	0.003	−0.021	0.005	−0.010	0.049	1.09
Stone, glass, and clay	0.048	0.186	0.057	−0.004	−0.013	2.53
Primary metals	0.015	0.027	−0.027	−0.006	−0.087	*2.36*(0.10)
Fabricated metals	0.008	0.104	0.044	0.016	−0.068	1.29
Machinery	0.024	0.142	0.010	0.023	−0.024	*3.39*(0.05)
Electrical equipment	0.072	0.058	0.062	0.021	0.251	*2.56*(0.10)
Transportation equipment	0.019	0.096	0.051	0.045	−0.149	*2.39*(0.10)
Instruments	0.367	1.890	0.187	0.056	—	*14.97* 0.01)
Miscellaneous	0.028	0.055	0.004	−0.061	0.111	*5.41*(0.005)

TABLE 8.9 Means of Y^6 (Growth in Profits for Original Stockholders Scaled by Sales) in Each Industry for All Firms and by Merger Intensity Group

Industry	*All Firms*	*No Mergers*	*1–5 Mergers*	*6–10 Mergers*	*11-plus Mergers*	F-*ratio*
Mining	0.017	0.149	−0.013	−0.041	0.014	*12.21*$^{(0.025)}$
Food	0.019	0.027	0.019	0.029	0.002	0.72
Textiles and apparel	0.014	—	0.008	0.004	0.038	0.91
Paper and printing	0.014	−0.011	−0.001	0.013	0.063	1.00
Chemicals	0.066	0.156	0.100	0.038	0.004	*3.33*$^{(0.025)}$
Petroleum	0.014	−0.019	0.009	0.014	0.052	0.40
Stone, glass, and clay	0.043	0.136	0.055	−0.005	−0.011	1.52
Primary metals	−0.017	0.017	−0.021	−0.018	−0.095	*2.36*$^{(0.10)}$
Fabricated metals	−0.027	0.056	0.024	0.020	−0.148	1.19
Machinery	0.050	0.392	0.009	0.004	−0.007	*3.24*$^{(0.05)}$
Electrical equipment	0.040	0.052	0.032	0.013	0.133	*2.40*$^{(0.10)}$
Transportation equipment	0.021	0.056	0.046	0.023	−0.066	*2.23*$^{(0.10)}$
Instruments	0.178	0.874	0.091	0.048	—	*13.50*$^{(0.01)}$
Miscellaneous	0.035	0.039	0.005	−0.042	0.129	1.33

Further Explanations of the Differences among Merger Groups

Only about 10 percent of the 478 largest firms were "pure" internal growth firms.[16] These firms are not concentrated in any particular industry, but are scattered throughout different industries. In the aggregate, it was these firms that best served the interests of their shareholders, as discussed in the section headed "The Evidence."

A logical question to ask is "Why are firms that do not use the merger route to growth more profitable, on the average, for the stockholders?" Perhaps this is best answered by examining the *investment* aspects of the alternative methods of growth. The asset structure of the acquiring firm may be changed considerably by a merger, depending upon the relative size of the acquiring firm and the acquired firm. If the acquired firm is sizable relative to the acquiring firm, this results in a sudden expansion of the acquiring firm that may be less profitable than a step-by-step expansion that is subject to repetitive reexamination of the costs and benefits for each additional increment of growth. In addition, if sales and asset growth is the primary concern of merging firms, one would expect distortion of the cost-benefit analysis to be introduced (at least in terms of shareholder objectives).

If executives of merging firms are interested primarily in growth of sales and assets (subject to some minimum profit constraint), it is reasonable to expect problems in determining a proper price to be paid in an acquisition.[17] In many cases, substantial premiums over market value have been paid for the assets acquired. A survey by W. T. Grimm and Company, a corporate acquisition consulting firm, provides some confirmatory evidence on this point. They reported that buyers paid an average of 113 percent of the price-earnings ratio at which the acquired firms' shares were selling just before the merger announcement. This study was based on those mergers occurring in 1964 for which purchase price and earnings of the acquired firm were disclosed.[18]

In addition to the "premium" being paid by the acquiring firms for a bundle of physical and manpower assets in varying stages of obsolescence, there is the cost of side payments, which is seldom given adequate attention. There is a growing body of evidence supporting the fact that the managers of acquired firms receive payoffs or side payments in return for permitting the firms they are managing to be acquired. Manne recognized this in a recent article when he said:

> The shareholders should ordinarily be willing to accept any offer of a tax-free exchange of new marketable shares worth more than their old shares. But the managers are in a position to claim almost the full market value of control, since they have it in their power to block the merger by voting against it. When we find incumbents recommending a control change, it is generally safe to assume that some side-payment is occurring.
>
> Side-payments are often not simple transactions at law because of the rule that directors and officers may not sell their positions shorn of the share interest necessary to insure a transfer of control. The most obvious kind of side-payment to managers is a position within the new structure either paying a salary or making them privy to valuable market information. This arrangement, easily established with mergers, can look like normal business expediency, since the argument can always be made that the old management provides continuity and a link with the past experience of the corporation.[19]

Further evidence of managerial payoffs appeared in the discussion section of *The Corporate Merger:*

Wallace:

> We have been talking about price a good deal throughout these discussions, and I would like to add another factor. Often there are supplemental financial arrangements with the previous owners or

management. Often these arrangements can amount to a substantial percent of the total sales price. So one can get a misleading picture of the actual price paid for an acquisition if you look only at the number of shares exchanged or the announced sale price.

Bicks:

Pay-off in the kind of terms you have been emphasizing, of insuring continuing challenge and some satisfying work?

Wallace:

No, in dollars—through deferred compensation contracts, stock options, and many other financial devices with important tax savings.

Bicks:

These things are all reflected in the properties registration, though.

Wallace:

They may be reflected there, true, but they may be overlooked when the sale price is analyzed.[20]

Thus, two groups in the *acquired* firm may benefit from an acquisition: the stockholders, who are paid a premium above market price for their holdings, and the top management of the acquired firm. There is growing evidence that middle management in some acquired firms may not fare so well. A national financial daily reported that management placement firms have a surplus of senior marketing and financial executives and that this is attributable basically to merger activity.[21] Parkinson's interesting advice to the ambitious executive, referred to in the previous chapter, should be discounted to the extent that the top management of the acquired firm may benefit from the payoffs resulting from an acquisition.

In addition, we can introduce a corollary to Parkinson's advice to the ambitious executive concerning the plight of the acquired (female) firm; this corollary relates to the interests of stockholders, whom he did not consider since he was addressing his remarks to aspiring administrators. On the basis of evidence from the empirical tests, the other interested group in a merger, the stockholders, would be advised to be on the female side in a merger and reap the benefits of the premiums paid in an acquisition.

There are other costs to some acquiring firms which must be considered in addition to those which have been discussed. Search, negotiation, and closing costs can, in some mergers, amount to a sizable sum.[22] It is relatively easy to identify some of these costs since they are paid in the form of commissions, finder's fees, legal fees, and the like. The problem of determining the costs of top management time spent on merging activity is, of course, more difficult. In some mergers and acquisitions, this element of cost may be substantial and yet not readily apparent or easily detectable.

Other financial aspects of this type of investment decision should also be given proper consideration. If internally generated funds are used to finance growth by merger, the implicit interest rate which manager-investors charge themselves is probably substantially lower than the market cost of capital. If stock is used in the exchange, the ratio of exchange may be set so that it is favorable to the seller, in terms of winning the approval of its managers and/or stockholders, with perhaps little regard shown for the stockholders of the acquiring firm. As Heflebower has pointed out: "The typical merger is affected by use of internal funds or by issuing additional stock of the acquiring company that formally stockholders, but actually management-voted proxies, had authorized earlier, often without reference to a particular use of that stock."[23]

The time value of money should also be given proper consideration, and the relevant factors should be taken into account in the forecasts concerning the timing of returns on the expenditure. It must be remembered that a dollar received by a stockholder today (in earnings per share) has more value than a dollar he (hopefully) expects to receive at some distant point in time. A number of acquiring firms mention time as a key reason for using the external route, since merger quickly supplies capacity and/or market penetration. However, the time factor is an advantage only if it speeds the return of money to the investor, and there is no empirical evidence that this objective is being accomplished by the majority of merging firms. If premiums are paid to acquire time and if additional profits are not realized, such an investment is clearly not in the interests of the stockholders.[24]

Modern capacity provided by new internal investment, with productivity advantages, may well reduce costs for nonmerging firms, thus lowering their "break-even point." This development increases the operating leverage of these firms and enhances their position to realize profit gains in periods of rising demand, as well as strengthening their position during slack periods. The advantages of possessing capacity with a productivity edge on competitors should be apparent to firms and industries as well as nations.[25]

In addition to the valuation problems, another problem that is often understated concerns the need to integrate a formerly independent behavioral system into the parent organization. There are costs involved in the process, and there is some evidence that they are seldom given proper consideration.[26] If the increment of expansion is too large for the acquiring firm to control effectively, diseconomies may result. Geographical scatter may also cause diseconomies to be realized rather than the expected economies. It may be predicted that such losses are least likely to be important for a firm which makes a large number of acquisitions, either because this reflects a smaller average size of acquired firm or because management of the acquiring firm will generally be better organized in such cases to integrate acquired firms into its operations.[27] Little evidence of this proposition is provided by the results of this study, however.

While the results of this study indicate that firms relying upon internal growth exclusively have, on the average, better served stockholders' interests, I am obviously not implying that *all* mergers and merging firms have been unsuccessful. This subject will be discussed in more detail in Chapters 9 and 10. When one reflects upon the long line of studies concerning the relative success of mergers and the rather consistent pattern of lack of relative success, it is surprising to find so many ardent advocates of merger in business, government, and academia. Even if it was proved beyond a shadow of a doubt that mergers were the most profitable method of growth, serious public policy questions would remain.

Conclusions

In general, the major hypothesis tested in this study—that those firms which merge tend to be more oriented to managers' interests than to stockholders' interests—appears to have been true for large American industrial firms during the period examined. It further appears that the intensity of merger activity did make a difference in the growth patterns displayed by these firms. The differential effects of the various types of mergers will be examined in more detail in the next chapter.

These findings certainly suggest that the growing transfer of control from stockholders to managers may well be contributing to changing managerial behavior and performance, particularly regarding merging firms. In their quest to gain rapid control over capacity in their basic industry or in other industries, the managers of acquiring firms may well be unduly extravagant in their expenditures for the additional increments of capacity. While large merging firms in their entirety are subject to a "stock market test," the many hundreds of individual mergers and acquisitions consummated annually are not subject to as strong a market test. Since stockholders (in general) are more interested in profits than management groups (in general), it may well be that stockholders would make better investment decisions if given the opportunity. Assuming that decisions leading to a socially suboptimal allocation of resources are not in the best interests of stockholders, mergers which are unprofitable for stockholders will result in a net decrease in overall social welfare. The results of this study indicate that a number of firms have objective functions (or act as if they do) which result in a socially suboptimal allocation of capital by favoring the acquisition of existing productive capacity, rather than an expansion of the capital base through internal growth.[28]

The behavior of the professional managers of merging firms who have been active in increasing the size of the firms that employ them suggests that the theory of conspicuous investment (or expansion) is relevant in numerous cases. Further tests of this theory will be presented in the next chapter, where the *type* of merger program is included in the empirical tests.

NOTES

[1] The statistical tests reported in this chapter were part of a study conducted at Carnegie-Mellon University's Graduate School of Industrial Administration by John Bossons, Kalman J. Cohen, and me. Research funds were provided by Carnegie-Mellon University, the Ford Foundation, and the National Science Foundation. The computer programs used in the study were written by Ralph A. Sotak of Carnegie and James Burkhardt and Thomas Green of Notre Dame's computer center.

[2] The following statement, which admits that the profit motive has in fact been submerged in recent years, was made in an editorial advocating conglomerate mergers in a business periodical devoted to big business and their managers ("The Case for Conglomerates," *Fortune*, June 15, 1967, p. 164): "But haven't businessmen *always* been concerned with their profits? In a sense, the answer is no, they haven't always; at least, the concern in recent years has been far more sharply focused and systematic than it used to be." This is an interesting admission for this naturally biased big business magazine to make, and it tends to support the discussion here and in the previous chapter. The editorial referred to is curious since in the same issue it was reported that the median increase in earnings per share of the conglomerate firms was lower than the median for all the 500 largest firms and for single-product firms.

[3] If multiplied by 100, the relative change would become the percentage change. In the tests involving commercial banks reported in Chaps. 10 and 11, the percentage change was used since none of the banks had negative earnings during the period.

[4] Defined in this manner, Y^4 measures the percentage of capital gains (except that it is not multiplied by 100) received by stockholders during the time period. As an alternative, it would have been possible to measure the total yield received by stockholders during this period by adding to the capital gains the values of all cash dividends, rights, warrants, etc. This latter alternative was not chosen primarily because of the added costs of gathering and computing data that would have been incurred. Since the time period actually employed in the empirical study was a decade, it would have been necessary to know the precise dates of each distribution of cash dividends,

rights, warrants, etc., and then to use an internal-rate-of-return calculation in order to compute correctly the total yield to common stockholders. It is doubtful that the use of total yield instead of capital gains yield as one of the measures of stockholders' interests would significantly alter the conclusions derived in this paper.

[5] When one firm acquires another firm by merger, it is common for the first firm to issue new stock as compensation to the stockholders of the second firm. This will result in the dilution of the earnings received by the stockholders of the first firm if the ratio of the profits of the combined firm to the profits of the first firm is less than the ratio of the number of shares of stock outstanding in the combined firm to the number of shares of stock outstanding in the first firm. Thus in order to examine the effects of mergers on a firm's profits from the viewpoint of the premerger stockholders, it is necessary to adjust a firm's reported profits to determine the share attributable to the premerger stockholders. This is the rationale behind the numerators in Y^5 and Y^6.

A more precise definition of the numerators in Y^5 and Y^6 could be expressed algebraically in the following manner: $P_t^* - P_{t-1}^*$ is a measure of the increase in the share of profits between time $t-1$ and time t attributable to the stockholders at time $t-1$. It may, because of new issues of equity, differ from $P_t - P_{t-1}$, which is a measure of the total increase in profits between time $t-1$ and time t. Let N_t be the number of shares of common stock outstanding at time t, adjusted for stock splits and stock dividends. Then

$$P_t^* - P_{t-1}^* = P_t \frac{N_{t-1}}{N_t} - P_{t-1}$$

Utilizing the fact that EPS_t, the earnings per share (adjusted for stock splits and stock dividends) at time t, is

$$EPS_t = \frac{P_t}{N_t}$$

it is easy to show that

$$P_t^* - P_{t-1}^* = N_{t-1}(EPS_t - EPS_{t-1})$$

Thus, the numerators in Y^5 and Y^6 are equivalent to the number of shares outstanding at the beginning of the period multiplied by the increase in earnings per share (adjusted for stock splits and stock dividends) during the period.

[6] Because profits (whether measured by P or by P^*) are sometimes negative, it is not meaningful to define a relative change in profits variable in the same way that we have defined relative changes in sales, assets, number of employees, and market price. An absolute change in profits variable, however, would be dominated by scale effects, since the larger a firm is, the larger its increase in profits tends to be. Thus, two alternative procedures for scaling the increase in profits attributable to stockholders at the beginning of the period are adopted: In Y^5, the scaling is relative to beginning-of-period

assets, and in Y^6, the scaling is relative to beginning-of-period sales. There is no a priori reason for preferring one of these scalings to the other; both were included in order to test the sensitivity of the results to the choice of scaling variable. (As shown in the section headed "The Evidence," both scaling variables yield similar results.)

[7] William J. Fellner gives a vivid description of the distinction between managers' and stockholders' interests in his book *Competition among the Few,* New York: Alfred A. Knopf, Inc., 1949, p. 173: "Several other subtle relationships exist in regard to which the interests of managers and those of owners need not coincide. Mergers, for example, increase the prestige as well as the money earnings of certain managerial groups, namely, of the influential groups which survive the merger in leading positions. They frequently also bring considerable gains to financial groups carrying out the transactions resulting in the merger. Whether they enhance the earnings of the owners depends on specific circumstances and financial interests in these matters."

[8] The period 1951–1961 was used for this study because of the convenient availability of information about mergers. The number of mergers for each firm during this period was listed in a government document, Select Committee on Small Business, House of Representatives, *Mergers and Superconcentration: Acquisitions of 500 Largest Industrial and 50 Largest Merchandising Firms,* 87th Cong., 2d Sess., 1962, pp. 46–52. The number of mergers was tabulated from data supplied by the FTC; while the mergers reported were for the period 1951–1961, the firms considered were the 500 largest as of 1960.

In this study, the initial sample of firms consisted of the 500 largest industrials for 1961 (*not* 1960), as reported in the July, 1962, issue of *Fortune.* Data for variables other than merger activity were recorded for two points in time, 1951 and 1961. The market prices of common stock were the average of the highs and lows for each year, adjusted for stock splits and stock dividends. Of these 500 firms, only 478 could finally be used. Some firms had to be eliminated because of lack of data (e.g., Ford Motor Company's stock was not publicly traded in 1951) or because they did not exist in 1951 (e.g., Litton Industries).

In addition to *Mergers and Superconcentration* and *Fortune,* which were the major sources of information, some data for this study were obtained from *Moody's Industrial Manual,* Standard and Poor's reports, and direct questionnaires.

[9] More desirable methods of classification (for example, according to the ratio of assets, sales, etc., acquired by the merging firm to its existing assets, sales, etc.) were ruled out because the necessary data on many of the acquired firms have never been systematically collected, let alone reported, by either government agencies or private sources. Thus, researchers in this area are forced to use less than ideal data. While the use of the *number* of mergers reported for a firm as a surrogate variable for the *importance* of merger activity by the firm might conceivably introduce some bias into the results reported in this paper, it is important to recognize the direction of this possible bias. Unless it could be argued that there is a *negative* correlation between the number of mergers and the importance of merger activity (which is extremely implausible on a priori grounds), the analysis-of-variance tests that were employed would understate, rather than overstate, the

statistical significance of the relationship between the dependent variable and merger activity.

[10] Here and elsewhere where it is said that a dependent variable shows either a positive or a negative association with the intensity of merger activity, it is not necessarily implied that the relationship is strictly monotonic across all four merger groups. The implication, rather, is that if the mean values of the dependent variables for each merger group were plotted side by side, the line of best fit through these mean values would clearly slope upward when the association is called "positive," and downward when the association is called "negative."

[11] Here and elsewhere where analysis-of-variance test results are reported, it is implicitly assumed that the data possess the usual statistical properties (i.e., that the residuals are independent, normally distributed realizations of the same stochastic process). To the extent that some of these usual statistical assumptions might be violated, the analysis-of-variance results should, of course, be interpreted as descriptive statistics rather than as rigorous tests of hypotheses. Analysis of variance rather than regression analysis was adopted as the statistical test methodology in this study because the hypothesis being tested is that there is a tendency for the dependent variables to be merely monotonically related, rather than necessarily linearly related, to the intensity of merger activity.

[12] There are three additional potential explanatory variables that could usefully be included in further research: (1) the quality of management, (2) the ratio of "inside" directors to "outside" directors, and (3) the percentage of common stock controlled by a cohesive group of stockholders. While management quality is a difficult variable to quantify, it might be possible to use, as a proxy, the American Institute of Management's ratings of management. These ratings are based not only on profitability but also on a number of other considerations. The possible usefulness of an "inside directors–outside directors" ratio is suggested by Oliver E. Williamson's hypothesis, put forward in his article "Managerial Discretion and Business Behavior," *American Economic Review*, vol. 52, no. 5, p. 1044, December, 1963: "as the management representation on the board increases, there tends to be a subordination of stockholder for managerial interests." While the fraction of ownership represented by the "dominant" stockholder group would in principle be an interesting variable to explore, the relevant data are not easy to obtain in a consistent manner over a long period of time.

[13] Ten of the industries conform exactly to the two-digit SIC codes. Data for three of the industries (mining, textiles and apparel, and paper and printing) were obtained by grouping together closely related two-digit SIC codes. The "miscellaneous" industry is more heterogeneous than the others since it consists of all firms which do not fit into the other thirteen industries. It was not possible to use the more refined three- or four-digit SIC codes because this would have resulted in an insufficient number of observations in many of the cells of Table 8.3. A sample of several thousand firms would be required in order effectively to utilize a finer industrial classification. Moreover, the classification of diversified firms into industries would become progressively less accurate with increasing narrowness of the industrial classification.

[14] In this context, the observed differences between group means are called

"statistically significant" if the probability is less than 0.1 that these differences could be the result of chance. The choice of the cutoff level for stating that a test result is statistically significant depends upon the assessment made of the relative costs of type I and type II errors.

[15] It has been suggested that patents play a significant role in the electrical equipment industry and may well be among the more important assets obtained in a merger.

[16] *Fortune* (July 15, 1966, p. 214) has reported that only 14 of the current 500 largest firms have not engaged in mergers during the period 1955–1965.

[17] This problem is developed in more detail in my dissertation, *Corporate Mergers and Acquisitions Involving Firms in Missouri: Some Economic Results and Administrative Policies and Procedures,* Ann Arbor, Mich.: University Microfilms, 1962, pp. 209–215. See also Frank K. Reilly, "What Determines the Ratio of Exchange in Corporate Mergers?" *Financial Analysts Journal,* vol. 18, no. 6, pp. 47–50, November–December, 1962. Reilly found that the three foremost factors in determining the ratio of exchange in the twenty-five mergers he studied were common stock price (for most recent quarter *before* the merger proposal), common stock price (recent close), and earnings per share (last complete year). Reilly also found (p. 50) that "in nearly 88% of the mergers examined, based on the foremost factor, the surviving corporation paid a premium to the stockholders of the acquired corporation of about 7%. In the very few cases where there is a discount, there usually is an obvious reason and the discount is quite small." J. Fred Weston, in a paper in William W. Alberts and Joel E. Segall (eds.), *The Corporate Merger,* Chicago: The University of Chicago Press, 1966, states that at least a 20 percent premium over the existing market price must be paid by the acquiring firm, and he advocates paying premiums as high as 50 percent over the market value of a firm if synergy is present, since this would be its true worth. The following statement appears in "Tender Offer Success Needs Big Premiums," *Mergers and Acquisitions Monthly,* vol. 1, no. 5, p. 1: "The best play for making a successful tender offer these days is remarkably simple: Add plenty of money to the price levels of yesterday. At least 20 points above market would be a base minimum."

[18] See *The Wall Street Journal,* Feb. 5, 1965, p. 12. It should, of course, be emphasized that these "premiums" relate only to the market value of the firms before being integrated into the acquiring firm and so do not take into account any economies or diseconomies of integration. An article by Willard T. Grimm, "A Banker's Role in Corporate Merger Planning," *Banking,* vol. 59, no. 2, p. 45, August, 1966, reports the price–earnings paid ratio (based on 1965 earnings) in the industries with the most mergers during the first half of 1966. The ratio in the food industry (the most active industry) was 19.8, followed by electronics with 22.9. Two other top industries were finance-banking-insurance, with 22.8, and service, with 22.1.

[19] Henry G. Manne, "Mergers and the Market for Corporate Control," *Journal of Political Economy,* vol. 73, no. 2, p. 118, April, 1965.

[20] Discussion between Forrest D. Wallace, partner and managing director of the Chicago office, McKinsey and Company, and Robert A. Bicks, partner in the law firm of Breed, Abbot and Morgan, New York (and head of the Antitrust Division of the Department of Justice during part of the second Eisenhower term), in William W. Alberts and Joel E. Segall (eds.), *The Cor-*

porate Merger, Chicago: The University of Chicago Press, 1966, pp. 181–182.

[21] *The Wall Street Journal,* Feb. 14, 1967, p. 1, reported that "surplus executives dot the job market as a result of the merger binge." In line with my earlier observations concerning the attempt of merging firms to achieve financial and marketing economies rather than production economies, in the current wave, it is stated in this article: "A Philadelphia executive recruiter reports senior financial officers 'a drug on the market; hundreds available, no demand.' A San Francisco management consultant finds marketing executives among the first to go after a merger. Age is a key factor: 'Someone under 50 stays, someone over goes,' says another West Coast consultant." The displacement of a few executives should not be taken as an indication that economies of scale are actually achieved. I shall make a recommendation concerning the effective use of this surplus executive talent later in this book in the chapters on public policy considerations.

[22] A number of examples relative to these costs are available. *Forbes* reported in an article entitled "Diversification's Marriage Brokers," vol. 99, no. 4, pp. 38–39, Feb. 15, 1967: "For example, American Home Products recently paid investment banker Lehman Bros. a fee of $916,000 for services during the five years of study and negotiations that led to its merger with Ekco Products Co." With all this potentially lucrative demand for advice and assistance, accounting firms, management consultants, commercial banks, and brokerage houses are all looking for pieces of the action. One method of compensation is the "5-4-3-2-1 plan," which bases the payment upon 5 percent of an initial x dollars of assets, down to 1 percent of the remaining assets. Merger promotion can be a lucrative business, which prompts me to wonder occasionally why I devote so much time to writing on the subject instead of sharing in the action; at the same time, it becomes clearer why there are so many vested interests concerned with the acceleration of the movement.

[23] Richard B. Heflebower, "Corporate Mergers: Policy and Economic Analysis," *Quarterly Journal of Economics,* vol. 78, no. 4, p. 557, November, 1963.

[24] The timing of returns is important to shareholders since money has a "time value." Many firms prefer merger as a growth method because they believe that they can penetrate markets and acquire production facilities faster than they could build internally. The president of U.S. Industries, Incorporated (formerly the Pressed Steel Car Company), made the following statement in 1958 (John I. Snyder, Jr., "Strength through Growth," *Corporate Mergers and Acquisitions: Basic Financial, Legal, and Policy Aspects,* American Management Association, Management Report No. 4, New York, 1958, p. 127): "The company was faced in 1949 with the fact that it had to broaden its product base through diversification. The question facing management was: Should this be done through internal diversification or through acquisition? Our only recourse was diversification through acquisition. Product research and development or internal diversification is a time-consuming and expensive process. Pressed Steel Car Company could not afford this kind of money, nor could it wait too long to broaden its product base. We believe we took the right course." A national business weekly stated that from 1956 to 1964, per-share earnings for USI tumbled more than 60 percent, and for three years the company was in the red. A recent change in management has helped to increase the profitability of the firm by pruning product

lines and selling divisions that drained the firm financially and managerially. See "Taking USI out of the Limelight," *Business Week*, Jan. 21, 1967, pp. 51–54. The USI diversification program was started twenty years ago and is just beginning to show signs of positive progress. Perhaps the internal growth alternative should have received more attention initially.

[25] Productive assets employing the latest technological innovations are particularly important in the manufacturing sector. In other businesses, where physical assets (that is, machines and equipment) are not as important (such as retailing, banking, etc.), new locations in expansion may be most important. The same hypothesis was tested on a sample of 112 merchandising firms for the same time period, and the managers' interest variables were found to be significantly up in the direction of the merging firms, while the stockholder's interest variables were down, though not significant. The same pattern was found in a study of over sixty manufacturing and merchandising firms with headquarters in Missouri for the period 1950–1959.

[26] For a number of case studies, see *Corporate Growth through Merger and Acquisition,* American Management Association, Management Report No. 75, New York, 1963.

[27] While the merging firms have not performed as well as the internal growth firms for their stockholders (on the average), there is some evidence that the more active merging firms have performed a shade better than the other merging firms on market price and not quite as well on earnings per share. This may reflect the market's assessment of aggressive management and the hope that eventually something will work out or that experience gained in the merger process will eventually pay off in higher earnings. It also appears that the particular *type* of merger used by the active acquirers may contribute to this result, as will be discussed in the next chapter.

[28] Capacity utilization rates are deceptive and should be broken down into more meaningful subgroups for analysis. Groupings such as "profitable," "marginal," and "emergency" would be a starting point. Some industrial capacity is in the "antique" stage and would be used only in a national emergency, when cost would not be a prime consideration. Certainly some existing steel capacity would have to be classified in this latter category. In the final analysis, the economic strength of a firm as well as a nation depends upon the relative *productivity* of their assets. The ultimate fate of the American dollar and the British pound will be determined not only by administrative fiscal responsibility but by a *modern* productive industrial capacity capable of competing in world markets.

9

Conglomerates, Other Growth Strategies, and Performance

In addition to the great emphasis placed upon profit maximization as it relates in traditional economic theory to merger as an investment decision, the economies-of-scale assumption is constantly cited as a justification for utilization of this route to growth. Actually, the two factors are interrelated, and yet they are frequently discussed separately in the literature. Turner, for example, says that "growth by merger, like internal growth, will often yield substantial economies of scale—in production, research, distribution, cost of capital, and management."[1]

Even those economists who look upon mergers with disfavor appear to do so mainly because of traditional fears of market control, rather than because they question the economies of scale that allegedly result from combination. Those economists who favor merger as a growth form in a dynamic economy constantly cite the benefits which would accrue from realized economies of scale resulting from this type of economic event. Yet most of the literature suggests that not all types of mergers are expected to produce the same kinds of economies; that is, certain kinds of economies are associated more with particular types of mergers. Let us briefly examine this aspect of the merger question before discussing the results of tests designed to determine whether firms utilizing the various types of mergers demonstrated unique performance characteristics.

Merger Types and Economies of Scale

The various types of mergers were defined and discussed previously in Chapter 2; if you are not familiar with the distinguishing characteristics of the various types of mergers, you may wish to reexamine that chapter. Repetition will purposely be kept at a minimum, and the material will be brief and to the point as it relates to this particular topic.

Horizontal Mergers

When firms engaged in the same line of business combine, it is almost universally assumed that scale economies will result. This is particularly true if the firms are serving the same markets. Production economies are usually emphasized as well as the various other types of economies related to management services, promotional activities, capital costs, etc. The regulatory agencies base most of their decisions upon this assumption in approving the mergers of banks, railroads, etc. As stated previously, those which oppose mergers of this type generally do so for reasons other than possible expected economies of scale, such as the fear of increased market control or concentration.

Depending upon the definition used, there are few or no diversification aspects in this type of merger, except perhaps geographical extension of a firm's capacity and/or market.[2] The assumption concerning scale economies in the horizontal merger is that duplication can be eliminated to some degree and additional quantity discounts can be realized in purchasing, promotion, etc. The literature is replete with discussions of this type, concerning the possibilities of alleged economies of scale.

Vertical Mergers

Combination activity of this type is expected to yield economies in purchasing and/or distribution. When the thrust of the vertical integration is backward toward suppliers, it is generally assumed that it will cost less to make the product than to purchase it. The make-or-buy decision and value analysis are generally related to this type of merger. If the thrust is forward, it is generally supposed that distribution costs will be lowered and economies realized. There are also other aspects to this type of merger, such as the desire for uniform quality, continuity of supply, or a captive outlet. It is generally presumed that this type of merger will result in tangible economies of various kinds.

While a vertical merger will usually increase the assets of the acquiring firm (unless the transaction is accomplished solely through the use of cash), sales volume is less likely to increase than with the other types of mergers. The reason for this is that the sales figures of the acquired firm will not be additive unless some sales are made to firms other than the acquiring company. Thus, if economies are realized in this type of merger, profits could be increased without necessarily having an increase in sales volume added by the acquired firm.

Circular Mergers

This type of merger, which involves firms that make nonsimilar products but utilize the same distribution channels and perhaps the same research and development activities, etc., is definitely expected to result in scale economies. Depending upon the "degree of fit" between products, processes, management, etc., it is expected that mergers of this type will produce the synergistic effects discussed previously. Scale economies are expected mainly in the areas of marketing, management, research and development, and perhaps others as well. This type of merger has been utilized with increasing frequency during the current merger movement. In addition to scale economies, circular mergers are expected to produce synergistic results, which are multiplicative rather than simply additive. The arguments for circular mergers are persuasive, and while superficial, they appear to have a wide acceptance.

Conglomerate Mergers

Of the various types of mergers discussed up to this point, the conglomerate merger is the one that traditional economic theory would hold to have the least chance of achieving scale economies. For example, Turner, who has written the most extensive article to date on conglomerates, says:

> Economies of scale involve common supply or demand factors—products that can be produced with the same facilities, or sold to the same customers through the same distribution channels, or for which research and development in the two or more lines can be pooled. Since a "pure" conglomerate merger produces

> few economic interrelations between the products of the acquiring and the acquired firm, the possibility of significant economies is slight.[3]

The conglomerate merger route leads firms into areas which are removed from their basic operations; this is diversification to its extreme degree. Financial economies may be realized, but only if the "mutual fund" type of industrial firm can achieve and maintain satisfactory earnings.[4] If these "multiple oligopolists" can buy and sell divisions and/or subsidiaries in the marketplace, it is possible that this type of "industrial prostitution" or industrial mutual fund type of management (depending upon one's point of view) may be relatively more profitable than other types of mergers.

The economist adhering to traditional theory would have to rate the conglomerate as the form "least likely" to succeed in achieving scale economies in merging. Turner sums up this rather typical attitude in the following statement concerning conglomerates:

> It is not likely that economies in at least some of the management services will be of great significance. Also, advertising economies seem less likely to follow the "pure" conglomerate: different media and different appeals are commonly needed for products bought by different classes of customers, and the appeal of a strong trademark is more readily transferable to similar products, as from one household electrical appliance to another, than to widely different ones, as from furniture to toothpaste.[5]

Ansoff and Weston, reflecting on this anticipated relative lack of achievement of scale economies in conglomerate mergers, concluded the following about the relative performance of conglomerate mergers as compared with that of concentric mergers:

> Since conglomerate mergers achieve only additive results and concentric mergers attain multiplicative results, we would expect the latter to perform somewhat better as a group. Also, we would expect conglomerate mergers to present more diverse results than concentric mergers since the former are more dependent on the correctness of investment decisions in a highly dynamic environment.[6]

In summary, it has generally been held that mergers will result in the achievement of economies of scale. In addition, some types of mergers have been expected to yield greater economies than others. A likely ranking, based upon traditional economic theory, can be constructed. The highest degree of realization of economies of scale can be expected in the horizontal and circular types of mergers, followed by the vertical type. The least likely type of merger (according to traditional economic theory) would be the conglomerate. Although some might disagree with this ranking, I believe that it is reasonable, and I have not found anything in the literature indicating that either the vertical or, particularly, the conglomerate type of merger would be superior to the horizontal or circular type in the possible achievement of scale economies. Actually, the literature is almost universally in favor of the latter in this respect. The remainder of this chapter is devoted to presenting the results of empirical tests designed to determine whether the existing theories and assumptions are correct. According to traditional theory, mergers should result in size gains, scale economies, and the resulting benefits to stockholders and other interested groups.[7]

The Hypothesis

The results of the empirical tests reported in the previous chapter suggest that, in general, the use of merger by large firms has an effect upon their growth and profitability patterns, when considering intensity of merger activity. In this chapter, it is suggested that the utilization of various types of strategies may also contribute to differential effects upon the growth and profitability of large firms, as a result of variance in the amount and type of anticipated economies of scale. The specific hypothesis tested is stated as follows: The *form* of growth as well as the *type* of merger (if this method is utilized) will have differential effects upon the resulting growth of firms and particularly upon their profitability patterns. In traditional economic theory, it is assumed that merging firms—particularly the horizontal, vertical, and circular types—achieve economies of scale and thus should exhibit a relatively better performance on the profit-related variables.

The Variables

The three size-related dependent variables representing managers' interests used in the statistical tests are:

(1) $Y^1 = \frac{S_t - S_{t-1}}{S_{t-1}}$ = the relative change in sales from time $t-1$ (the beginning of the period) to time t (the end of the period)[8]

(2) $Y^2 = \frac{A_t - A_{t-1}}{A_{t-1}}$ = the relative change in assets from time $t-1$ to time t

(3) $Y^3 = \frac{E_t - E_{t-1}}{E_{t-1}}$ = the relative change in number of employees from time $t-1$ to time t

The three dependent variables representing profitability to stockholders used in the statistical tests of the hypothesis are the following:

(4) $Y^4 = \frac{MP_t - MP_{t-1}}{MP_{t-1}}$ = the relative change in market price per share (adjusted for stock splits and stock dividends) from time $t-1$ to time t

(5) $Y^5 = \frac{P_t^* - P_{t-1}^*}{A_{t-1}}$ = the increase in the share of profits from time $t-1$ to time t attributable to stockholders as of time $t-1$, relative to assets at time $t-1$[9]

(6) $Y^6 = \frac{P_t^* - P_{t-1}^*}{S_{t-1}}$ = the same as (5), except relative to sales at time $t-1$

The Evidence

The hypothesis was tested using the six variables $Y^1, \ldots, Y^6$, as defined, and the same sample of 478 large industrial firms that was used in the tests reported in the previous chapter. However, in the tests of the hypothesis as reported here, the firms were divided into the following five groups:

- Group 1 Pure internal growth firms—firms with no reported mergers, 1951–1961
- Group 2 Horizontal—firms engaged principally in this type of merger, 1951–1961
- Group 3 Vertical—firms engaged principally in this type of merger, 1951–1961
- Group 4 Circular—firms engaged principally in this type of merger, 1951–1961
- Group 5 Conglomerate—firms engaged principally in this type of merger, 1951–1961

Classifying the 430 merging firms into the five groups listed above was a difficult and time-consuming task. The merger pattern of each firm was examined and compared with objective criteria based upon the definitions of merger types used in this book.[10] Naturally, subjective judgments had to be made in some cases concerning the relationship of the firms. Initially, five major groups and five subgroups were defined, which included both pure and mixed patterns of activity:[11] pure horizontal, with a subgroup for geographical extension; mixed horizontal, with a subgroup for geographical extension; vertical, with pure and mixed subgroups; circular, with pure and mixed subgroups; and conglomerate, with pure and mixed subgroups. Tests were made to determine whether there was a significant difference in the performance of the subgroups within each classification. The results indicated that these subgroups were not necessary, so they were eliminated, and the five major groups (as defined) were used.[12]

Initial Tests

As a first step toward testing the hypothesis, the average (arithmetic mean) values of $Y^1, \ldots, Y^6$ were computed for all 478 firms in the sample, as well as for these same firms divided into the five groups. The results, which are shown in Table 9.1, provide (at least on the surface) striking confirmation of the first part of the hypothesis concerning the differential effects upon the growth and profitability variables when considering the form of growth and/or type of merger. There are considerable differences among the group means, which are statistically significant. The conglomerate merger type group dominates in all three of the size-related variables.

The picture revealed by the tests is quite different regarding the variables representing profitability to stockholders. All three dependent variables are statistically significant and strongly favor the pure internal growth firms rather than the merging firms, where scale economies should be expected.[13] A one-way analysis-of-variance test indicates that it is unlikely that these differences could have arisen as a result of chance. In order to examine this pattern of results in more detail, a number of other tests were conducted, as reported in the following sections of this chapter. One variable omitted in the first test was the industry membership of the various firms.

Further Tests Holding Industry Constant

Interindustry effects were held constant in another group of tests, much as was done in the tests reported in the previous chapter. Many economists and others believe that certain types of mergers will occur more frequently in some industries than in others because of environmental and other factors. The 478 firms in the sample were again divided into fourteen industry groupings (based on their principal lines of business and SIC codes). Table 9.2 shows the number of firms in each industry belonging to each of the five growth or merger type groups. One striking fact emerging from this table is that firms in each industry tend to utilize the various growth methods and types of merger. Pure internal growth and conglomerates are represented in thirteen and twelve industries, respectively. This appears to be an indication that managerial preference is stronger than any particular industry environmental factors and that this preference is influenced more by the total economic environment than by a narrowly defined industry environment. Conglomerate firms were assigned to the industry where the highest percentage of their business was conducted.

In order to hold interindustry effects constant, the type of analysis reported above in the section headed "Initial Tests" and in Table 9.1 was repeated fourteen additional times, each time using only those firms belonging to the same industry. The results for the three size-related variables are presented in Tables 9.3 to 9.5, while the results for the three profit-related variables are shown in Tables 9.6 to 9.8.

With the interindustry effects held constant, the statistical tests still tend to confirm the hypothesis that the type of growth and/or merger affects growth, although not as strongly as appeared to be the case on the basis of the evidence presented in Table 9.1. The basic difference is that when the effects of growth (including merger type) are analyzed within specific industries, the growth and/or merger type does not always have a significant effect. Thus, of the six dependent variables related to size and profitability, $Y^1, \ldots, Y^6$, the observed differences between group means are statistically significant in, respectively, three, four, two, five, five, and six.

Few of the size-related variables were statistically significant, which is not too surprising since intensity of merger activity was not included in these tests. In the industries where the observed differences were statistically significant, out of the nine combinations of size-related variables and industry for which growth and/or merger type mattered, the conglomerate type had the highest mean growth rate in six cases, the internal growth type had the highest mean in two cases, and the circular type had the highest mean in one case.

In the more important area of profitability, of the sixteen combinations of profit-related variables and industry for which growth and/or merger type mattered, eleven favored the internal growth firms, and five favored the conglomerates. This is an interesting development since the merger types which are rather commonly believed to yield economies-of-scale benefits are completely out of the picture.

TABLE 9.1 Means of the Variables for Pure Internal Growth Firms (No Merger) and Merger Type Groups

Variable	*Pure Internal Growth*	*Horizontal*	*Vertical*	*Circular*	*Conglomerate*	*F-ratio**
Size-related:						
Y_1	1.5967	1.3546	1.0541	1.6303	5.1113	$\mathit{11.33}^{(0.005)}$
Y_2	1.6395	1.6616	1.6933	1.8007	5.0439	$\mathit{8.17}^{(0.005)}$
Y_3	0.4275	0.7188	0.3268	0.9649	2.6456	$\mathit{6.59}^{(0.005)}$
Profit-related:						
Y_4	6.8035	2.2638	1.4284	2.3643	4.3424	$\mathit{4.35}^{(0.005)}$
Y_5	0.1212	0.0305	0.0130	0.0210	0.0421	$\mathit{3.96}^{(0.005)}$
Y_6	0.1089	0.0199	0.0105	0.0150	0.0343	$\mathit{4.35}^{(0.005)}$
Number of firms	48	195	22	167	46	

* The *F*-ratios shown for each variable are based on one-way analysis-of-variance tests of the significance of the observed differences in group means for that variable. The italicized *F*-ratios are those for which the probability is less than 0.10 that the observed differences in group means could be the result of chance; in these cases, the significance levels are shown in parentheses as superscripts to the *F*-ratios. This note applies also to Tables 9.3 to 9.8.

TABLE 9.2 Number of Firms in Each Industry and in Each Growth Group

Industry	*All Firms*	*Pure Internal Growth*	*Merger Type*			
			Horizontal	*Vertical*	*Circular*	*Conglomerate*
Mining	8	2	3	1	—	2
Food	66	6	32	1	25	2
Textiles and apparel	21	—	11	3	5	2
Paper and printing	34	4	21	3	4	2
Chemicals	58	5	21	—	28	4
Petroleum	32	4	20	4	3	1
Stone, glass, and clay	15	1	9	—	5	—
Primary metals	47	6	22	2	13	4
Fabricated metals	20	1	5	—	12	2
Machinery	52	6	18	—	25	3
Electrical equipment	45	3	15	1	20	6
Transportation equipment	46	5	7	4	15	15
Instruments	8	1	2	1	4	—
Miscellaneous	26	4	9	2	8	3

TABLE 9.3 Means of Y^1 (Growth in Sales) in Each Industry for All Firms and by Merger Type Group

Industry	*All Firms*	*No Mergers*	*Horizontal*	*Vertical*	*Circular*	*Conglomerate*	*F-ratio*
Mining	1.085	0.869	0.593	−0.199	—	2.679	0.70
Food	1.102	0.334	1.096	0.502	1.378	0.343	0.54
Textiles and apparel	0.856	—	0.422	1.587	1.435	0.701	1.29
Paper and printing	1.714	0.678	1.274	1.452	5.215	1.796	*2.56*(0.10)
Chemicals	1.814	1.377	1.785	—	2.046	0.881	0.46
Petroleum	2.027	0.637	2.551	0.634	0.852	2.636	0.31
Stone, glass, and clay	0.954	0.983	0.973	—	0.915	—	0.01
Primary metals	0.547	0.415	0.564	0.654	0.373	1.094	0.79
Fabricated metals	2.690	1.495	1.445	—	1.223	15.206	*6.43*(0.005)
Machinery	1.519	4.360	0.979	—	1.169	1.998	2.17
Electrical equipment	3.161	0.307	2.084	2.646	3.161	7.366	1.62
Transportation equipment	3.350	3.505	1.442	1.203	1.469	6.642	1.40
Instruments	3.243	9.914	3.747	0.824	1.929	—	2.75
Miscellaneous	1.867	0.318	1.389	0.682	0.419	10.014	*10.33*(0.005)

TABLE 9.4 Means of Y^2 (Growth in Assets) in Each Industry for All Firms and by Merger Type Groups

Industry	*All Firms*	*No Mergers*	*Horizontal*	*Vertical*	*Circular*	*Conglomerate*	*F-ratio*
Mining	2.065	1.615	1.383	0.333	—	4.405	0.70
Food	1.069	0.580	1.085	0.850	1.214	0.589	0.29
Textiles and apparel	0.935	—	0.769	1.320	1.146	0.749	0.36
Paper and printing	2.304	0.802	1.882	1.868	6.396	2.213	2.02
Chemicals	1.781	1.680	2.197	—	1.572	1.178	0.78
Petroleum	1.845	1.149	2.067	1.477	1.092	2.034	0.31
Stone, glass, and clay	1.415	1.260	1.364	—	1.538	—	0.10
Primary metals	1.286	1.334	0.986	4.592	1.050	1.088	*3.22*(0.025)
Fabricated metals	1.740	2.297	1.379	—	1.687	2.688	0.29
Machinery	2.121	1.821	1.307	—	1.554	12.325	*8.69*(0.005)
Electrical equipment	3.689	0.521	3.179	1.123	3.866	6.383	0.53
Transportation equipment	2.959	1.900	1.359	1.114	1.348	6.162	1.06
Instruments	4.410	18.000	4.458	1.230	1.783	—	*7.74*(0.05)
Miscellaneous	2.353	1.057	2.131	0.730	0.748	10.110	*10.33*(0.005)

TABLE 9.5 Means of Y^3 (Growth in Number of Employees) in Each Industry for All Firms and by Merger Type Group

Industry	*All Firms*	*No Mergers*	*Horizontal*	*Vertical*	*Circular*	*Conglomerate*	*F-ratio*
Mining	0.361	0.174	−0.335	−0.489	—	2.017	0.99
Food	0.393	−0.035	0.453	−0.049	0.451	0.217	0.32
Textiles and apparel	0.413	—	0.291	0.690	0.628	0.125	0.48
Paper and printing	1.628	0.160	1.385	1.036	5.084	1.101	1.70
Chemicals	0.854	0.508	0.806	—	1.048	0.190	0.90
Petroleum	1.351	0.125	1.774	0.343	0.223	1.888	0.20
Stone, glass, and clay	0.236	0.189	0.174	—	0.358	—	0.21
Primary metals	0.131	0.411	0.102	0.124	0.031	0.171	0.75
Fabricated metals	1.476	0.786	0.652	—	0.816	7.848	$9.24^{(0.005)}$
Machinery	0.834	0.670	0.486	—	0.666	4.601	$6.55^{(0.005)}$
Electrical equipment	1.768	0.217	0.890	0.585	1.758	4.966	1.37
Transportation equipment	1.023	0.902	0.287	−0.149	0.213	2.528	1.52
Instruments	1.427	3.975	1.956	0.074	0.864	—	1.24
Miscellaneous	1.710	−0.019	0.768	0.469	3.304	3.418	0.59

TABLE 9.6 Means of Y^4 (Growth in Market Price) in Each Industry for All Firms and by Merger Type Group

Industry	*All Firms*	*No Mergers*	*Horizontal*	*Vertical*	*Circular*	*Conglomerate*	*F-ratio*
Mining	0.935	1.163	1.119	2.231	—	−0.214	1.57
Food	1.741	0.986	1.923	0.000	1.853	0.481	0.16
Textiles and apparel	0.668	—	0.839	1.004	0.414	−0.137	0.25
Paper and printing	2.880	4.171	2.546	1.656	3.059	5.280	0.57
Chemicals	4.144	20.031	2.744	—	2.718	1.616	$3.59^{(0.025)}$
Petroleum	0.973	0.184	1.207	0.536	1.333	0.927	0.94
Stone, glass, and clay	2.255	6.083	2.337	—	1.342	—	$9.23^{(0.005)}$
Primary metals	1.328	2.937	0.932	1.522	1.100	1.635	1.76
Fabricated metals	2.061	15.200	0.912	—	1.697	0.546	$18.09^{(0.005)}$
Machinery	3.007	5.144	1.987	—	2.735	7.196	2.07
Electrical equipment	3.920	2.159	4.073	4.889	3.814	4.610	0.11
Transportation equipment	2.466	2.416	1.426	1.699	2.627	3.011	0.26
Instruments	20.403	102.500	20.439	3.261	4.147	—	$14.85^{(0.025)}$
Miscellaneous	5.436	2.481	4.234	−0.021	1.606	26.833	$5.16^{(0.005)}$

TABLE 9.7 Means of Y^5 (Growth in Profits for Original Stockholders Scaled by Assets) in Each Industry for All Firms and by Merger Type Group

Industry	*All Firms*	*No Mergers*	*Horizontal*	*Vertical*	*Circular*	*Conglomerate*	F-*ratio*
Mining	−0.001	0.105	−0.054	−0.014	—	−0.022	3.74
Food	0.033	0.054	0.029	0.000	0.037	−0.002	0.14
Textiles and apparel	0.016	—	−0.000	0.077	0.004	0.041	1.61
Paper and printing	0.023	−0.008	0.007	0.037	0.028	0.219	*2.18*$^{(0.10)}$
Chemicals	0.085	0.267	0.105	—	0.048	0.010	*2.87*$^{(0.05)}$
Petroleum	0.003	−0.021	0.020	−0.027	−0.014	−0.028	0.81
Stone, glass, and clay	0.048	0.186	0.049	—	0.020	—	2.40
Primary metals	−0.025	0.027	−0.032	0.014	−0.009	−0.025	1.73
Fabricated metals	0.008	0.104	0.015	—	0.021	−0.134	1.15
Machinery	0.024	0.142	0.018	—	0.007	−0.033	*3.32*$^{(0.05)}$
Electrical equipment	0.072	0.058	0.111	0.027	0.017	0.172	1.07
Transportation equipment	0.019	0.096	−0.004	0.011	0.018	0.007	0.19
Instruments	0.367	1.890	0.368	0.138	0.043	—	*11.26*$^{(0.025)}$
Miscellaneous	0.028	0.055	−0.007	−0.125	0.004	0.268	*5.72*$^{(0.005)}$

TABLE 9.8 Means of Y^6 (Growth in Profits for Original Stockholders Scaled by Sales) in Each Industry for All Firms and by Merger Type Group

Industry	*All Firms*	*No Mergers*	*Horizontal*	*Vertical*	*Circular*	*Conglomerate*	F-*ratio*
Mining	0.017	0.149	−0.044	−0.013	—	−0.010	*10.09*$^{(0.025)}$
Food	0.019	0.027	0.015	0.000	0.024	0.003	0.23
Textiles and apparel	0.014	—	0.001	0.059	0.008	0.031	1.45
Paper and printing	0.014	−0.011	0.002	0.022	0.016	0.182	*2.98*$^{(0.05)}$
Chemicals	0.066	0.156	0.083	—	0.044	0.012	2.02
Petroleum	0.014	−0.019	0.035	−0.014	−0.008	−0.041	0.67
Stone, glass, and clay	0.043	0.136	0.051	—	0.011	—	1.55
Primary metals	−0.017	0.017	−0.031	0.005	−0.008	−0.029	1.83
Fabricated metals	−0.027	0.056	0.007	—	0.010	−0.372	*3.31*$^{(0.05)}$
Machinery	0.050	0.392	0.013	—	0.002	−0.008	*3.24*$^{(0.05)}$
Electrical equipment	0.040	0.052	0.049	0.048	0.009	0.113	1.38
Transportation equipment	0.021	0.056	−0.003	0.015	0.011	0.031	0.24
Instruments	0.178	0.874	0.154	0.117	0.032	—	*9.13*$^{(0.05)}$
Miscellaneous	0.035	0.039	−0.005	−0.104	0.003	0.322	*4.62*$^{(0.01)}$

On balance, then, when interindustry effects are held constant, the type of growth and/or merger type does not appear to exert as strong an influence on the growth variables as when industry is not held constant. The evidence is more consistent with regard to the profit-related variables, where the patterns display a more significant effect. The pure internal growth firms did tend to display a better profit-related performance, being challenged only by the conglomerates.

It is interesting to note at this point that the conglomerates, which have the least chance according to traditional economic theory of achieving scale economies, performed relatively better than the horizontal, vertical, and concentric groups. Needless to say, these results suggest that both the assumptions and the theories regarding scale economies and the mergers of large firms should be subjected to considerably more empirical testing before they are accepted. The efficiencies resulting from pure investment in new plant and equipment appear to produce more economies than investments in mergers.

Tests Holding Merger Types Constant

In the previous chapter, it was demonstrated that merger intensity is an important variable, having an impact upon the growth and profitability patterns of large firms. In order to determine whether merger intensity was important within the merger type groups, additional tests were conducted holding merger types constant. Two different groups representing merger intensity were used in the tests. One was the two-way classification of low (one to five) and high (six-plus) merger intensity groups; the other was the three-way intensity classification as used in the previous chapter. The results were essentially the same and are presented for the two-way classification in Table 9.9.

It appears that intensifying merger activity within merger types contributes significantly to size in the horizontal, vertical, and concentric types. While the size-related dependent variables increase with merger intensity in the conglomerate group, this has no statistical significance. It is interesting to note that none of the profit-related variables are statistically significant and that the pattern of results is mixed, indicating an independent rather than a complementary alignment of managers' and stockholders' interests, as assumed in traditional economic theory and discussed in the two previous chapters.

Tests Holding Merger Intensity Constant

Further one-way analysis-of-variance tests were conducted to determine the relative effect of merger types when intensity of merger activity is held constant. The results of these tests are presented in

TABLE 9.9 Means of the Variables by Merger Intensity Group within Merger Types

Variable	Horizontal			Vertical			Circular			Conglomerate		
	Low (1–5)	*High (6-plus)*	F-*ratio**	*Low (1–5)*	*High (6-plus)*	F-*ratio**	*Low (1–5)*	*High (6-plus)*	F-*ratio**	*Low (1–5)*	*High (6-plus)*	F-*ratio**
Size-related:												
Y_1	1.1008	1.7521	*4.23*$^{(0.05)}$	0.6095	1.4986	*4.17*$^{(0.10)}$	1.2356	1.9444	*3.81*$^{(0.10)}$	2.7447	5.8551	1.06
Y_2	1.3994	2.0722	*4.47*$^{(0.05)}$	0.7917	2.5948	*3.33*$^{(0.10)}$	1.2686	2.2240	*4.96*$^{(0.05)}$	1.8753	6.0397	1.64
Y_3	0.4650	1.1163	*5.50*$^{(0.025)}$	0.0038	.6497	*5.96*$^{(0.025)}$	0.7677	1.1218	0.78	0.5730	3.2970	2.62
Profit-related:												
Y_4	2.3896	2.0670	0.26	1.3340	1.5227	0.07	2.4595	2.2886	0.12	1.5291	5.2266	1.26
Y_5	0.0372	0.0201	0.90	−0.0028	.0289	0.71	0.0243	0.0184	0.25	0.0601	0.0364	0.06
Y_6	0.0254	0.0112	1.37	0.0069	.0140	0.06	0.0197	0.0112	1.09	0.0626	0.0253	0.23
Number of firms	118	77		11	11		74	93		11	35	

* The *F*-ratios shown for each variable are based on one-way analysis-of-variance tests of the significance of the observed differences in group means for that variable. The italicized *F*-ratios are those which are significant, and the levels of significance are shown in parentheses as superscripts to the *F*-ratios.

TABLE 9.10 Means of the Variables by Merger Type Group within Merger Intensity Groups

Variable	*Occasional (1–5)*					*Moderate (6–10)*					*Active (11-plus)*				
	Horizontal	*Vertical*	*Circular*	*Conglomerate*	*F-ratio**	*Horizontal*	*Vertical*	*Circular*	*Conglomerate*	*F-ratio**	*Horizontal*	*Vertical*	*Circular*	*Conglomerate*	*F-ratio**
Size-related:															
Y_1	1.110	0.610	1.236	2.745	*3.10*$^{(0.05)}$	1.643	1.386	1.875	4.624	1.96	2.079	1.696	2.098	6.583	*3.59*$^{(0.025)}$
Y_2	1.394	0.792	1.269	1.875	1.12	1.609	2.819	2.113	5.190	*2.14*$^{(0.10)}$	3.462	2.202	2.469	6.542	2.00
Y_3	0.466	0.004	0.768	0.573	0.79	1.005	0.606	0.972	2.683	1.51	1.449	0.727	1.453	3.660	1.79
Profit-related:															
Y_4	2.370	1.334	2.460	1.529	0.49	2.181	1.789	2.607	3.007	0.20	1.726	1.056	1.587	6.538	*2.46*$^{(0.10)}$
Y_5	0.038	−0.003	0.024	0.060	0.77	0.012	0.038	0.026	0.047	0.47	0.044	0.013	0.001	0.030	0.17
Y_6	0.026	0.007	0.020	0.063	1.12	0.008	0.023	0.015	0.024	0.31	0.021	−0.002	0.002	0.026	0.10
Number of firms	118	11	74	11		58	7	64	13		19	4	29	22	

* The *F*-ratios shown for each variable are based on one-way analysis-of-variance tests of the significance of the observed differences in group means for that variable. The italicized *F*-ratios are those which are significant, and the levels of significance are shown in parentheses as superscripts to the *F*-ratios.

TABLE 9.11 Number of Firms in Each Merger Type Group and Merger Intensity Group

	Merger Intensity			
Merger Type	*Occasional (1–5)*	*Moderate (6–10)*	*Active (11-plus)*	*Total*
Horizontal	118	58	19	195
Vertical	11	7	4	22
Circular	74	64	29	167
Conglomerate	11	13	22	46
Total	214	142	74	430

Table 9.10, and the number of firms in each classification is presented in Table 9.11. The only dependent variables which were statistically significant between the merger type groups with "occasional" and "moderate" intensity held constant were sales in the occasional group and assets in the moderate group. The conglomerate firms had the largest increase in these size-related variables. The conglomerates also had a significant impact among the merger types in the "active" merging group. The size-related variable sales was statistically significant, and the highest mean was recorded by the conglomerate firms. In addition, these firms also improved their market price significantly better than the active acquiring firms using the other merger types. It is becoming apparent that the conglomerate type of merger is a special case and is worthy of more analysis. This type of merger appears to exert the strongest influence among the merger types in the various tests; the section headed "The Conglomerate Merger: A Special Case" will be devoted to an analysis of the conglomerate merger as a special case among merger types.

Tests Relating Growth and Merger Types

Since the results of these tests indicate that the economies-of-scale assumptions regarding the various types of mergers are questionable, more tests were conducted in an attempt to clarify the differences between the merger type groups. The results presented in Table 9.1 suggest that the conglomerate merger type group clearly leads in size maximization and is second to the internal growth firms in profitability to stockholder gains. There did not appear to be much difference in the performance of the horizontal and concentric groups, while the vertical

TABLE 9.12 Means of the Variables for Three Merger Type Groups

Variable	*Merger Type Groups*			F-ratio*
	Horizontal	*Vertical*	*Circular*	
Size-related:				
Y_1	1.355	1.054	1.630	1.09
Y_2	1.662	1.693	1.801	0.14
Y_3	0.719	0.327	0.965	1.13
Profit-related:				
Y_4	2.264	1.428	2.364	0.61
Y_5	0.031	0.013	0.021	0.55
Y_6	0.020	0.011	0.015	0.33
Number of firms	195	22	167	

* None of the *F*-ratios are statistically significant.

group displayed the poorest performance of all. In order to determine whether there was a significant difference between these latter three groups, another one-way analysis-of-variance test was conducted, and the results are presented in Table 9.12. None of the dependent variables were statistically significant in this test. Thus, the remaining two groups, the pure internal growth firms and the conglomerate group, appear to exert the strongest influence.

The pure internal growth firms were compared with the horizontal, vertical, and concentric groups, and in a separate test the internal growth firms were compared with the conglomerates. The results are presented in Table 9.13 and reveal a striking and important finding regarding merger and internal growth. When the pure internal growth group is compared with the three merger type groups which are usually expected to produce economies-of-scale advantages, there is no statistically significant difference in the size-related variables; yet all three profit-related variables are statistically significant and strongly favor the internal growth group.

A completely different pattern emerges when the pure internal growth group is matched with the conglomerate group. The three size-related dependent variables are all increasing considerably more in the conglomerate group, and each is statistically significant. By contrast, the three profit-related variables are not statistically significant, and yet they favor the internal growth group. It appears that the conglomerates are size maximizers par excellence. The results of these tests (added to

TABLE 9.13 Means of the Variables for the Pure Internal Growth Group and Three Merger Type Groups and for the Pure Internal Growth Group and the Conglomerate Group

Variable	Internal Growth	Horizontal	Vertical	Circular	F-ratio*	Internal Growth	Conglomerate	F-ratio*
Size-related:								
Y^1	1.597	1.355	1.054	1.630	0.67	1.597	5.111	*6.66*$^{(0.025)}$
Y^2	1.640	1.662	1.693	1.801	0.11	1.640	5.044	*5.75*$^{(0.025)}$
Y^3	0.428	0.719	0.327	0.965	1.30	0.428	2.646	*9.39*$^{(0.005)}$
Profit-related:								
Y^4	6.804	2.264	1.428	2.364	*5.55*$^{(0.005)}$	6.804	4.342	0.60
Y^5	0.121	0.031	0.013	0.021	*6.65*$^{(0.005)}$	0.121	0.042	1.69
Y^6	0.109	0.011	0.015	0.033	*7.15*$^{(0.005)}$	0.109	0.034	1.58
Number of firms	48	195	22	167		48	46	

* The *F*-ratios shown for each variable are based on one-way analysis-of-variance tests of the significance of the observed differences in group means for that variable. The italicized *F*-ratios are those which are significant, and the levels of significance are shown in parentheses as superscripts to the *F*-ratios.

those of all the other tests) certainly suggest that the managers of merging firms are, on the average, not primarily profit maximizers and, further, that the economies-of-scale assumption is highly questionable with regard to mergers.

Perhaps these findings should not be considered too surprising since the merging firms in the sample are already large and, in addition, are publicly owned, with the resulting separation between owners and professional managers, as discussed previously. However, the emergence of the conglomerates and the unique performance characteristics of this type of merger deserve additional discussion and analysis.

The Conglomerate Merger: A Special Case

In Chapter 5, discussion centered upon the growing importance of this type of merger during the current merger wave. This fact, coupled with its unique performance characteristics revealed by the empirical tests reported in this chapter, justifies additional discussion of this merger type at both a micro- and a macroeconomic level.

The Conglomerate: A Micro View

The conglomerate merger brings together two or more firms with unrelated product lines and distribution methods. It should not be necessary to emphasize that conglomerate diversification can be accomplished through internal growth; that is, the merger route is not the *only* method of accomplishing a diversification objective. Yet it is a fact of economic life that during the relatively prosperous 1950s and, particularly, in the 1960s, the merger route became the superhighway to conglomeration.

A closer investigation of the firms in the conglomerate merger group suggests that there are at least two different subgroups in the population. One subgroup can be labeled the "defensive conglomerates"—firms which have moved from their basic industry into other, unrelated industries because of either real or imagined declining opportunities or a relatively poor current position, as well as a desire for continuity of the firm. In some cases, past management mistakes and inadequate forecasting were among the contributing factors at the time of the decision. Impatience with existing growth rates, which hinders the realization of size maximization objectives, was also a major aspect of the desire to move into "greener pastures" where risk would be minimized. These defensive conglomerates have accelerated their growth rates; however, their profitability performance has been disappointing.[14] These firms generally attempt to integrate the acquired firm into their organizations, in contrast to the other subgroup of conglomerates. This practice tends to complicate an already difficult management situation. Admittedly, sustained prosperity has helped these firms; however, they will most likely be as affected by any prolonged economic decline as their less diversified brethren, or perhaps even more.[15]

The other subgroup can be termed the "offensive conglomerates."[16] These are the flamboyant, wheeling-and-dealing firms which have been called the "firms of the future" and the "free-form" or "multimarket" firms. This group has promoter-type managers, who are quietly reminiscent of the more colorful merger promoters of the past. They use the promoter's lingo and have a knack for verbally dressing up their divisions with such titles as "energy resource base," "recreation and leisure-time division," "education technology group," and so on.

A potentially dangerous weapon in the promoter's kit that has been used in recent years has to do with the method of reporting financial data and the creation of new types of securities to be used in the process of active acquisition. Many of the activities of these firms remind one of abuses in similar speculative periods in the past. The really difficult task is to separate the innovative and imaginative moves of these firms from "shoddy" promotional and operational practices.

Two related problems deserve brief but special mention because of their potential impact upon investors. One area of concern is the method of accounting utilized by some of these firms concerning their acquisitions.[17] An example was cited in the financial press as follows:

> Two of the basic principles of accounting are uniformity and consistency, yet Teledyne, Kidde and most of the other conglomerates blithely have used pooling of interest for acquisitions effected above book value, and purchase of assets for companies bought below book. In fact, Gulf & Western somehow managed to use both methods in booking the acquisition of New Jersey Zinc. The accounting technique used is the one that best served their interest in maximizing reported earnings. Obviously this is neither uniform nor sound accounting practice. Neither does it create a consistent balance sheet or income statement.[18]

The other problem arises from increased use of convertible securities by conglomerates in the consummation of acquisitions. Most of these firms continue to report earnings on common stock currently outstanding, disregarding the potential dilution effects of conversion. This fact was recognized in the financial press as follows:

> All of the conglomerates are subject to substantial dilution from myriad convertible issues, and all publish lavish annual reports with glossy photographs and much purple prose about their technological and research capabilities. But none shows (as McGraw-Hill does, for example) their earnings per share assuming full conversion.[19]

The promotional flair is also revealed in the annual reports of offensive conglomerates; as observed in *Barron's:*

> Incidentally, conglomerates always show their past records in the most favorable light in their annual reports. Thus Teledyne, in its latest report, shows growth from 1961 to 1966 (a period of rising prosperity and profits for almost everybody), but makes no adjustment for subsequent poolings of interests of acquisitions. A footnote in small print details what the far less impressive figures would have been on the basis of including the operations of pooled companies prior to the years of acquisition—which is the practice the SEC generally makes companies follow in prospectuses. In other words, the annual report of a conglomerate is a promotional document in regard to accounting as well as imagery.[20]

Abuses of this type are serious enough to command the attention of the accounting profession and the Securities and Exchange Commission, the agency created to deal with similar types of promotional abuses which occurred during the merger wave of the 1920s.

On the brighter side, some special features of the offensive conglomerates are worthy of note. Naturally they are not uniform in their operational or organization structures; however, the few successful firms among them do have imaginative administrative arrangements. These firms tend to delegate a considerable amount of operational authority, with the result that each division and/or subsidiary function somewhat like a smaller, independent firm. The top administrative group contains specialists in the various functional areas who are removed from the problems of the individual units (although they are familiar with them). This top layer plays the role of an "inside management consulting group," dividing time among the various units. Actually, this system is not unique to conglomerates, but their very nature almost demands an arrangement of this sort, and the few successful ones have implemented it.

Maintaining a multitude of autonomous divisions and/or subsidiaries in a "portfolio of firms" is one method of staving off diseconomies of scale.[21] In addition, this practice minimizes the postmerger integration problems which plague many merging firms. In essence, these firms are similar to investment trusts or mutual funds since they also have a "portfolio," except that the conglomerate firm gains *control* in the investment process.[22] Control is an asset which permits power to be exercised if needed and is an integral part of the conglomerate pattern. In allocating resources among various unrelated products, divisions, etc., the conglomerate substitutes a simulated and synthetic market for the actual capital market. The divisions and/or subsidiaries vie with one another for the available capital and other resources. This development is, indeed, a novel fabrication of capitalism. Manager-investors are spending stockholders' funds and paying "premiums" to acquire control in the process. Stockholders could diversify their own portfolios at market price.

A few of the conglomerates possess the unique feature of being a sort of "minimarket," with the top administrators functioning as quasi-entrepreneurs. That is, the conglomerate firm is owned by the public, and the top management of this publicly held firm then buys a number of other firms and behaves like an owner of these firms and in addition has managerial *control*. This latter feature distinguishes the true conglomerate from a regular mutual fund. Yet there is an important basic similarity between the conglomerate and the mutual fund: the importance of management in making diverse investment decisions. In the final analysis, the owner-investor is interested in the profitability performance at the micro level of the firm (or fund) in which he invests.[23] The conglomerate (like a mutual fund) will have to stand and fall on its record in prosperous times as well as over the long pull. The real test for the conglomerates is yet to come, unless the business cycle has been rendered obsolete through government planning and improved monetary and fiscal policy (and antitrust policy remains unchanged).

With the exception of a handful of offensive conglomerates, the record to date, during a prolonged period of prosperity, has not been exceptional. *Fortune* attempted to determine the relationship between diversification and growth in earnings per share between 1956 and 1966 and found that "there isn't any relationship to speak of between diversification and earnings growth."[24] The median growth rate for firms in the conglomerate category was 5.86 percent a year, while the median for the single-category firms was 6.27 percent.[25] Conglomeration was determined by the major categories in which a firm was doing business, and merger was not directly considered in this study; thus one of the leading conglomerates in the *Fortune* study was IBM, which has been a leader among the internal growth firms.

Many investors have been wisely cautious in their approach to conglomerates, basically because of the many uncertainties associated with them, compounded by their methods of reporting performance on a consolidated basis. This fact has caused the promoter-managers of conglomerates to seek a new "yardstick" for performance, other than traditional methods; as noted in a national business weekly "the conglomerates are aiming for a reappraisal from Wall Street, and they have their own ideas on just how that should be done. They are sensitive about the fact that the market does not value them on a par with other corporations, as witness their price-earnings ratios. Most of them are below the current 14.9 of the Dow-Jones industrial average."[26]

The conglomerate has been singled out for special attention because of its relative newness as a merger form and because of its unusual performance characteristics, compared with those of the other traditional merger type groups. It is these latter groups that are expected to yield superior economies-of-scale performance, according to traditional theories concerning merger, and yet the empirical tests reported suggest that this has not been the case during this time period.

The Conglomerate: A Macro View

In discussing the effect of the antitrust laws in curbing waves of merger activity in Chapter 8, it was pointed out that while these laws have not stopped waves of mergers they have influenced the form and shape of the movements. The growth in the use of conglomerate mergers is no doubt a response to the tightening of the Clayton Act in 1950 by the

Celler-Kefauver amendment, which changed the *legal* environment. Perhaps a more basic factor has been the *economic* environment of prolonged prosperity.[27] Nevertheless, the increased use of the conglomerate merger poses special problems in the public policy area which are still unresolved.

Traditional market control arguments used in horizontal mergers are not necessarily applicable. Any case against conglomerate mergers must be based upon a broader economic and social approach. As Turner stated: "Thus, a quick survey of the three broad categories of mergers would suggest the following relative hierarchy of rules: hardest on horizontal merger, easier on vertical, and least severe on conglomerates."[28]

Some of the economic complaints which have been lodged against the conglomerate relate to the following: (1) predatory pricing, that is, picking areas or products where smaller firms could be eliminated or disciplined by pricing policies; (2) adverse effects upon entry since giant firms enter numerous industries and their size and related power are viewed as unhealthy threats; and (3) reciprocity effects, that is, the fact that firms may have to purchase products from one division of a conglomerate in order to sell products to other divisions of the same company. These are real problems and should not be discounted or dismissed lightly.

On the other side of the coin is the fact that conglomerates may enter various industries and, depending upon the degree of competition in the industry entered and the previous performance of the firm acquired, add a competitive dimension to the industry. This is the usual defense of the conglomerate put forward by its proponents. It is a legitimate and logical argument and is a stronger defense than those usually offered by the proponents of other merger types. The really critical question, however, is not whether conglomeration is desirable, but whether the merger route should be permitted and encouraged when the internal growth alternative can be utilized to accomplish the same diversification objective. Actually, the same basic alternative is present when considering growth by any merger type and should receive more consideration.

The very feasible internal growth alternative should be explored in more detail since it has both short- and long-run ramifications for business behavior and industrial structure. Entry into an industry by merger has a substitution effect, with the actual benefits being contingent upon the quality of the management of the acquiring firm. Entry via the internal growth route provides a new, *additional* competitor armed with new, modern productive capacity. The obvious advantages of this type of growth were discussed in some detail in the previous chapter. These advantages should not be underestimated or dismissed lightly, even by the proponents of mergers. Individuals and agencies which favor increased use of the internal growth alternative should earnestly require more explicit proof from special interest groups concerning the alleged advantages to be gained from merger activity and the growth of economic power centers.

It is interesting to note that a member of the board of editors of *Fortune* magazine (which appears to be a chief proponent of the conglomerate firm), Gilbert Burck, told me (during a telephone conversation in November, 1966) that he had found only three firms among the conglomerate group that were relatively successful.[29] Perhaps he was a bit conservative, and yet the number is so small that it should cause thoughtful people (those interested in the structure of our economy) to wonder whether all the "economic pollution" problems caused by numerous mergers are worth the extremely dubious benefits which are alleged to exist.

In an editorial devoted to making a case for conglomerates, *Fortune* praised the conglomerate and referred to the single-product firm as "stuck in cement." Perhaps it is better to be stuck in cement than in cement, glue, tar, gum, girdles, revolving doors, elevators, mousetraps, molasses, and cells of various types (even the detention variety). It is ironic that the same issue of *Fortune* reported that the performance of the single-product firms in terms of earnings-per-share growth was superior to that of the conglomerates during this relatively prosperous period. Current, unpublished research by Donald F. Eslick confirms this finding by *Fortune* as well as some of the findings reported here. Eslick studied the effects of product diversification upon the profitability of the 500 largest industrials for the 1955–1965 time period. According to Eslick:

> My overall results indicate that there is a relatively significant negative relationship between firms' rates of change in profit and the number of products [they produce]. In addition, when one looks at the composition of products produced by these firms, we observe that the number of products which a firm produces within its broadly defined primary industry has no significant influence on profitability, but the number of products outside the primary industry has a significant negative influence on profitability.[30]

Performance Tests among Conglomerate Subgroups and Aggressive Pure Internal Growth Firms

In order to determine whether there are different performance characteristics among the conglomerate subgroups (as defined), additional tests were conducted. The offensive conglomerates were dis-

TABLE 9.14 Means of the Variables for Three Conglomerate Subgroups and Aggressive Pure Internal Growth Firms Compared with Offensive and Defensive Conglomerates

Variable	*Conglomerates*				*Aggressive Pure Internal Growth*	*Defensive Conglomerate*	*F-ratio**	*Aggressive Pure Internal Growth*	*Offensive Conglomerate*	*F-ratio**
	Unique	*Defensive*	*Offensive*	*F-ratio**						
Size-related:										
Y_1	1.704	2.682	9.659	$4.21^{(0.25)}$	3.284	2.682	0.07	3.284	9.659	$6.41^{(0.025)}$
Y_2	1.495	3.006	9.143	$2.81^{(0.10)}$	3.257	3.006	0.01	3.257	9.143	$5.87^{(0.025)}$
Y_3	1.421	1.178	5.049	$3.54^{(0.05)}$	0.835	1.178	0.12	0.835	5.049	$9.02^{(0.005)}$
Profit-related:										
Y_4	1.243	2.257	8.317	$2.51^{(0.10)}$	15.892	2.257	$4.45^{(0.05)}$	15.892	8.317	0.90
Y_5	0.010	0.033	0.067	0.13	0.305	0.033	$7.00^{(0.025)}$	0.305	0.067	$2.56^{(0.10)}$
Y_6	0.015	0.023	0.058	0.14	0.277	0.023	$5.30^{(0.05)}$	0.277	0.058	2.11
Number of firms	7	22	17		18	22		18	17	

* The *F*-ratios shown for each variable are based on one-way analysis-of-variance tests of the observed differences in group means for that variable. The significance levels are shown in parentheses as superscripts to the *F*-ratios.

tinguished by both their relative growth of assets and the intensity of their merger activity. Firms following the conglomerate strategy that had a growth of 125 percent or more of assets and ten or more mergers were included in this subgroup. Firms with one or two relatively small conglomerate mergers were isolated and included in the "unique" category, and the remainder of the firms were included in the "defensive" subgroup.

The results of the tests are presented in Table 9.14 and reveal that among the conglomerates, the offensive subgroup had the largest gains in all the variables. Each of the size-related variables was statistically significant, and the market price of common stock variable was also significant, suggesting a superior performance for the offensive subgroup of conglomerates.

The same criterion of a growth in assets of 125 percent during the period was applied to the pure internal growth group, and these firms constituted a special subgroup termed "aggressive" pure internal growth firms. Internal growth is usually considered a slow method of growth, and yet the firms in this subgroup have demonstrated that it is possible to grow internally at a rate which is higher than that of the total economy.[31] Separate tests comparing the performance of the aggressive pure internal growth firms with that of the offensive and defensive conglomerates were conducted, and the results of these tests are presented in Table 9.14. All the profit-related variables were statistically significant and favored the aggressive pure internal growth firms over the defensive conglomerates. The comparison of the aggressive pure internal growth firms and the offensive conglomerates was also revealing. The offensive conglomerates led by a wide margin in all the size-related variables, and each was statistically significant. The opposite pattern emerged with the profit-related variables, which favored the aggressive pure internal growth group, with the P^*-assets variable being statistically significant.

One important fact continually stands out in the analysis of the growth patterns of the conglomerates, and this is the consistently larger gain in sales and assets than in the market price of common stock during this time period.[32] This pattern of results suggests that the theory of conspicuous investment (or expansion) is again substantiated in this group, which is usually active in the merger process.[33]

The growing importance of the conglomerate "portfolio" type of merger, which substitutes the judgment of manager-investors for stockholder-investors in diversification activities, is a matter of genuine concern in modern capitalism.[34] Since it appears that if such a thing as synergy does exist, the synergistic benefits are serendipitous, then stockholders, whose objectives are more economic and rational, should be better able to allocate resources.

NOTES

[1] Donald F. Turner, "Conglomerate Mergers and Section 7 of the Clayton Act," *Harvard Law Review*, vol. 78, no. 7, p. 1317, May, 1965.

[2] My personal preference is to classify mergers involving firms making the same products as "horizontal," with a subclass for those with geographical extension features. Others, such as the FTC and Turner, classify mergers between firms with similar products but in different geographical markets as "mixed conglomerates." The difficulty with this latter treatment is that semantic problems arise in discussions of conglomerates in general.

[3] Turner, *op. cit.*, p. 1330. Turner's article is interesting despite its length (82 pp.) and the fact that it is all theory, with no empirical evidence presented.

[4] Since the "true" conglomerate must continually and actively make acquisitions, it generally will use stock in most of the transactions. The higher the relative price of the stock, the better chance it will have in arriving at an acceptable exchange ratio. Naturally, the market price of the stock is influenced by the amount and quality of earnings of these firms.

[5] Turner, *op. cit.*, pp. 1330–1331.

[6] H. Igor Ansoff and J. Fred Weston, "Merger Objectives and Organization Structure," *The Quarterly Review of Economics and Business*, vol. 2, no. 3, p. 53, August, 1962.

[7] If scale economies are being realized, this should be reflected in the relative profitability of the firms involved.

[8] If multiplied by 100, the relative change would become the percentage change.

[9] A more complete description concerning variables (5) and (6) is presented in the previous chapter.

[10] The merger pattern of each firm was conveniently available in a government document: Select Committee on Small Business, House of Representatives, *Mergers and Superconcentration: Acquisitions of 500 Largest Industrial and 50 Largest Merchandising Firms*, 87th Cong., 2d Sess., 1962, pp. 54–213. Additional data were obtained from *Moody's Industrial Manual* for the firms in the sample which were not listed.

[11] The "pure" category included firms concentrating upon one type of merger (horizontal, vertical, concentric, or conglomerate), while the "mixed" category included firms making various types of mergers. The major group for a mixed firm was determined by the principal type of merger in the mixed pattern.

[12] The only statistically significant variables in the subgrouping test were employees in the vertical group, which favored the mixed category, and sales in the concentric group, which favored the pure subgroup.

[13] The geographical extension or diversification subgroup performed much like the pure horizontal subgroup; thus it seems that there is no particular advantage to be gained from either kind of merger of this type. The performance characteristics were quite different from those for the pure conglomerate group.

[14] For example, see Thomas O'Hanlon, "The Odd News about Conglomerates," *Fortune*, June 15, 1967, p. 177.

[15] Ansoff and Weston (*loc. cit.*) conducted a test comparing the results of five firms following the concentric strategy and seven conglomerate firms during the recession of 1957–1958. They found that "the recession drop in both sales and profits was substantially smaller for the firms following

the concentric strategy." Since the sample was so small, the results can be considered only suggestive; however, it is the only evidence available, and to date there have not been any prolonged recessions in the 1960s.

[16] In addition to the two groups of conglomerates identified in this discussion, there are other scattered firms which do not fit either main category. These are firms which have made one or perhaps two conglomerate acquisitions during the period and should be considered "unique" cases. Two examples are the Ford Motor Company, which purchased Philco appliances, and distributes them through different retail outlets from the ones used for its automotive products, and Anheuser-Busch, Inc., which acquired the St. Louis Cardinals baseball team. In the initial years of this latter acquisition, the brewery attempted to run the baseball team and eventually discovered that it was better to delegate this job to baseball men. The results in recent years have been apparent. In contrast to firms in this subgroup, the "offensive conglomerates" are merging actively.

[17] Admittedly, improper accounting procedures could be used by nonmerging firms also; however, mergers can become complicated events and provide more opportunities for those inclined to "massage" the figures.

[18] Barton M. Biggs, "Day of Reckoning?" *Barron's*, vol. 47, no. 14, p. 3, Apr. 3, 1967.

[19] *Ibid.*

[20] *Ibid.*, p. 12.

[21] For an interesting discussion of the optimum size of a firm, see Joel Dean and Winfield Smith, "The Relationships between Profitability and Size," in William W. Alberts and Joel E. Segall (eds.), *The Corporate Merger*, Chicago: The University of Chicago Press, 1966, pp. 3–22.

[22] There is evidence of a growing concern over the increasing economic power of mutual funds and other institutional investors and the influence they could have upon the market prices of issues in which they trade. While it is prudent to be concerned with power centers of any kind, this development may well represent a new type of "countervailing power" in the world of big business. These groups generally do not seek control of the firms in which they invest funds, and yet they can exercise a more powerful voice than smaller investors concerning the affairs of the firm. It is possible that these professional investors may act as a lever in the process of alignment of interests among the various groups in the large publicly held firms.

[23] One of the leaders in the conglomeration movement, Charles B. Thornton, is quoted as having made the following comment concerning the role of profits in the growth process: "Profits is only one of the motives. A stronger motive is a deep, pioneering spirit." See "Corporations: Where the Game Is Growth," *Business Week*, September 30, 1967, p. 99.

[24] O'Hanlon, *op. cit.*, p. 176.

[25] *Ibid.*

[26] "Looking for a New Yardstick," *Business Week*, Aug. 20, 1966, pp. 119–120.

[27] A decline in business conditions accompanied by a drop in common stock prices would tend to limit the amount of merger activity of these firms. The existing legal environment is permissive; thus, relative prosperity is the key factor in this "go or no-go" situation.

[28] Turner, *op. cit.*, p. 1322.

[29] An editorial that appeared in the June 15, 1967, issue of *Fortune*, entitled "A

Case for Conglomerates," pp. 163–164, seems a bit paradoxical since the same issue reported on a *Fortune* study of conglomerates that found the median growth rate in earnings per share to be lower than that of the single-category firms and the 500 largest firms as a group. For an interesting article discussing some of the management problems of conglomerates see Gilbert Burck, "The Perils of the Multi-Market Corporation," *Fortune,* February, 1967, pp. 130f.

[30] These remarks were contained in an unpublished address given by Professor Donald F. Eslick at a conference sponsored by Loyola University's School of Business Administration in cooperation with the Chicago Association of Commerce and Industry, Chicago, Jan. 19, 1968.

[31] Use of the criterion of 125 percent increase in assets during the period produced the following percentages of qualified firms in each merger type group: pure internal growth, 37.5 percent; horizontal, 40.5 percent; vertical, 31.8 percent; circular, 43.1 percent; and conglomerate, 56.5 percent. The fact that such a high percentage of pure internal growth firms have grown rapidly and profitably is an interesting and significant one, worthy of attention.

[32] The same pattern of results is apparent when the median growth rates of the various groups are compared.

[33] While the administrative staff of a mutual fund is generally small, the conglomerate can develop an expensive administrative superstructure since it possesses *control* of the firms in its "portfolio." A business weekly reported on the developments in a conglomerate (which has had an attrition of management personnel) when it stated: "Litton lost some executives prematurely because the company fell down in the area of recognition. . . . A survey showed that too few Litton officers had any public identity. 'We had lots of presidents of divisions, but not many corporate vice-presidents compared to others,' Ash adds. 'We found General Electric had 49 vice-presidents, IBM 42, and Lockheed 25, while we had 13.' " This situation did not last for long as the article further states: " 'In the past four weeks,' says Ash, 'Litton has promoted two officers to executive vice-president, several more to the title of senior vice-president, and it has created a dozen new vice-presidents.' " See "Litton: B-school for conglomerates," *Business Week*, Dec. 2, 1967, pp. 89–90.

[34] One objective of diversification is to minimize various risks, yet it appears as if new developments will actually increase some important risks related to the conglomerates. One of these developments is a new method of negotiating labor contracts called "coordinated collective bargaining" which is advocated by Jack T. Conway in his article "Coordinated Bargaining . . . 'Historical Necessity,' " *IUD Agenda,* January–February, 1967, pp. 22–27.

10

Some Empirical Tests: Large Commercial Banks[1]

The pros and cons of bank mergers and multiple-office banking are in the forefront of bank policy considerations today.[2] Commercial banks have joined the industrial and merchandising firms, as well as the transportation companies, to swell a rising tide of mergers. The Comptroller of the Currency has reported that nearly two thousand banks with resources of over $40 billion were acquired by other banks between 1950 and 1962.[3] This increase in merger activity has been accompanied by renewed research efforts into the economic effects of mergers upon banking structure and performance.[4] This special concern related to banking mergers is in contrast to the scant attention which the industrial, transportation, and insurance mergers have received.[5]

Commercial bank mergers are of particular interest since banking is regulated considerably more than most other types of business activity. This regulation is carried out both at the national and the state levels. The basic forms of public control (as exercised by the various regulatory agencies) are related to entry, branching controls, and merger activity. Horvitz has stated that "probably the most important decisions of regulatory authorities which affect competition in banking are those with respect to bank mergers."[6]

In the unregulated industries, firms are considerably freer to use mergers as a means of growth, provided they do not violate the antitrust laws in the process. A number of mergers are consummated by the interested management groups without a vote or the consent of the stockholders. In commercial banking, the situation is quite different. A commercial bank may not expand through the acquisition or consolidation of another bank without the prior approval of the agencies that are responsible for its regulation. Since approval must be obtained from the regulators, there is an implication that they are to represent the various "publics" which may be affected by the action.[7] The results of the study presented in this chapter give some indication of the relative benefits that have accrued to the various interested groups affected by these approved mergers.

Mergers for Whom? The Interested Groups

For the individual large publicly held bank, it appears reasonable to expect that where management is separated from ownership, there may be different goals for the two groups as discussed previously. The studies of Berle and Means, Burnham, Gordon, Maurer, and others[8] have shown in various degrees that many large firms are not controlled by the owners because ownership is so widely diffused. Rather, control often rests in salaried professional managers, who frequently have little or no equity in the corporations they operate.[9] In the study of large publicly held commercial banks reported in this chapter, three special interest groups are examined separately: bank management, bank stockholders, and, since banking is a regulated industry, the "public."

Management Interests

While there is no separate behavioral theory of the banking firm, it appears reasonable to assume that many large banking institutions do not behave very differently from other large firms in oligopolistic industries, that is, that the profit maximization principle (which economists assume in perfectly competitive markets) is replaced by a "satisficing" or "utility maximization" concept. The literature is replete with discussions on this subject, and it should not be necessary to examine it in much detail here. An example or two will suffice.[10]

In discussing managerial behavior in the large organization, Maurer observed:

> Such an enterprise is too big for any one owner or group of owners to control. It is run, therefore, not primarily for the stockholders, who generally become used to a socially approved return on their investment, but for the enterprise itself. The aim of the enterprise is not immediate or even future maximum profits, once thought to be the goal of all enterprise, but healthy, future existence, to which the size of profits is an important but secondary consideration.[11]

This discussion is not meant to imply that bank managers are not interested in profits but that they assign to profits the role of serving as a constraint in the decision-making process. The introduction of noneconomic goals influences the value judgments and decisions of managers of large enterprises.[12] The Alhadeffs have commented on the role of noneconomic factors in the growth decisions of banks: "Consideration of prestige, or the desire for sheer size of bank are no doubt important in stimulating individual bank expansion—and an excellent way to become a banking giant is to expand the number of branches."[13]

In discussing some of the factors concerning bank mergers, a government publication stated: "Factors such as prestige and the desire or need for higher lending limits are still important."[14]

The variables typically referred to in discussions of the growth of commercial banks are such size-related variables as assets, deposits, number of employees, and perhaps the amount of loans outstanding. Banks are usually ranked by size according to assets or deposits.[15] In their study of the growth of large banks, the Alhadeffs stated that they "measured a bank's success in meeting the challenge of its environment by the growth of its assets."[16] The number of employees in a bank is listed in the various financial manuals, as well as in Dun and Bradstreet's *Directory of Million Dollar Corporations.*

Note that all four of these growth variables—assets, deposits, number of employees, and loans—represent an economic or a human resource at the control of bank managers. Control over these types of resources clearly conveys a great deal of economic power to bank managers and, secondarily, a great deal of social and/or political power.

In this regard, it is perhaps worth elaborating on the reasons for including loans in this category. When a banker agrees to lend a customer money, this not only lets that banker play a direct role in the allocation of economic resources, but also puts him in the position of "doing a favor" for the customer. Within broad limits, bankers like to lend money; the more money they lend, the more favorably they are regarded by the customers. In addition, of course, there are important feedback relationships between a bank's lending policies and the size of future deposits. As Chandler has stated: "A banker knows that his total lending power is not independent of his lending policies to customers. If he acquires a reputation of meeting all reasonable loan demands of customers, he will be able to attract and retain more deposits, and thus to lend more."[17]

In summary, bank managers' main interests may be identified as a desire for growth in assets, deposits, loans, and number of employees. In the statistical tests of the underlying hypothesis reported in this chapter, the following variables are used to represent the primary interests of bank managers:

(1) $Y^1 = 100\left(\frac{A_t - A_{t-1}}{A_{t-1}}\right)$ = the percentage change in total assets from time $t-1$ to time t

(2) $Y^2 = 100\left(\frac{D_t - D_{t-1}}{D_{t-1}}\right)$ = the percentage change in total deposits from time $t-1$ to time t

(3) $Y^3 = 100\left(\frac{L_t - L_{t-1}}{L_{t-1}}\right)$ = the percentage change in loans and discounts from time $t-1$ to time t

(4) $Y^4 = 100\left(\frac{E_t - E_{t-1}}{E_{t-1}}\right)$ = the percentage change in number of employees from time $t-1$ to time t

Stockholder Interests

The holders of bank stock are interested in the growth of the market value of their holdings and hence, *ceteris paribus,* in the growth of earnings per share. Many things affect the price of a stock, but the principal factor on which all the returns that accrue to the common stockholders are ultimately based is earnings per share. The price is affected by both the amount and the quality of earnings.[18] The academic and professional literature is replete with material on this subject, and again there is no point in recapitulating the discussion here. The current market price reflects investors' expectations about a stream of discounted future earnings.

If managers of large banks are making profitable growth decisions, including the use of mergers that are approved by the regulatory agencies, this should be reflected in the market value of the stock of these banks. Certainly stockholders may also be interested in the growth of the banking institution, but only if this is accomplished without a dilution in earnings per share. Bigness, as such, has little intrinsic value to stockholders if earnings per share or return on investment is not increased.[19]

The following two variables are used to represent the bank stockholders' interests in the statistical tests:

(5) $Y^5 = 100\left(\frac{EPS_t - EPS_{t-1}}{EPS_{t-1}}\right)$ = the percentage change in net operating earnings per share (adjusted for stock splits and stock dividends) from time $t-1$ to time t (this variable was used since none of the banks had negative earnings)

(6) $Y^6 = 100\left(\frac{MP_t - MP_{t-1}}{MP_{t-1}}\right)$ = the percentage change in market price per share of common stock (adjusted for stock splits and stock dividends) from time $t-1$ to time t[20]

Public Interests

The public that has an interest in the outcome of approved bank mergers can be divided into two basic groups, depositors and borrowers. Depositors can be further subdivided into various classes, such as business firms (of varying sizes), government units, and households (both families and individuals).

In discussing the interests of the depositor, Crosse said:

> The depositor is interested in the safety of his particular deposit; he is interested in compensation for the use of his money either in the form of interest or services. He is interested in the efficiency of his bank as reflected in the accuracy of the posting of entries to his account. And finally, he is interested in an intangible quality which I shall call "recognition." He resents having a bank teller ask him whether he has an account in the bank. He wants to be known to *his* bank.[21]

While conceivably it is possible to measure these interests as identified by Crosse, it is beyond the scope of this study. It can be assumed, however, that banks that are satisfying depositors will retain present depositors as well as attract other depositors from institutions that are not fulfilling their needs. Banks in the former category should then exhibit a more rapid deposit growth than those in the latter.[22]

The borrower must also be considered; in this regard, Crosse stated: "The borrower from a bank (who, of course, may also be a depositor) wants availability of credit first, understanding of his business or credit needs second, and a competitive rate, somewhere down the line. He is less interested in the absolute rate than in knowing that his bank is not charging him more than another bank would."[23]

Hall and Phillips have attempted to determine how much importance the regulatory authorities attach to bank customers (both depositors and borrowers).[24] They have concluded that "the Federal banking authorities share a common approach to their duties under the Bank Merger Act of 1960. . . . Great stress is placed on the advantages to customers from the creation of larger banking organizations."[25] Thus, if mergers are approved, the regulators must believe that the public interests are best served by a combination of banking units, provided that managements of these banks are willing to combine and have made formal application to do so.[26]

The benefits to the public of increased competition in banking have not been mentioned. There are conflicting viewpoints on this subject, despite the fact that it has been included in the list of factors to be considered by the regulatory agencies. Hodgman believes that ". . . the public interest will be better served if competition within the banking industry becomes more vigorous than it presently is."[27] There is the problem of striking the delicate balance between vigorous competition and safety.[28] Crosse has stated that ". . . the public is vitally concerned with competition: it wants enough to insure generally good service at reasonable prices to the broad aggregate of individual borrowers and depositors—but not so much as to threaten bank failure."[29]

Despite the recognition of the value of competition to the public, the bank regulators have not given the factor much weight. The only government agency that has been active in this area of the public interest is the Antitrust Division of the Justice Department.[30] Hall and Phillips came to the general conclusion that competition (as defined by the economist) is not the most important consideration in the decision making of the regulatory agencies; they stated: "Increases in concentration as a result of a merger are regarded as a necessary price to pay to increase the availability of local banking services."[31] No attempt was made in this study to measure the direct effect of approved bank mergers upon competition. Instead, the variables are related more closely to bank regulators' view of the public interest.

In summary, the public interest variables included in this study are constructed to measure the aggregate rate of expansion for those banks brought together through merger. The purpose of the study is to determine whether these variables have grown significantly more for merging banks than for pure internal growth banks. Presumably, these variables will be positively associated with banks that are better serving their customers. The variables are:

(7) $Y^7 = 100\left(\frac{A_t - A^*_{t-1}}{A^*_{t-1}}\right)$ = the percentage change in total assets from time $t-1$ to time t for the entire network of banks which by time t have been combined into a single bank

(8) $Y^8 = 100\left(\frac{D_t - D^*_{t-1}}{D^*_{t-1}}\right)$ = the percentage change in total deposits from time $t-1$ to time t for the entire network of banks which by time t have been combined into a single bank

(9) $Y^9 = 100\left(\frac{L_t - L^*_{t-1}}{L^*_{t-1}}\right)$ = the percentage change in total loans from time $t-1$ to time t for the entire network of banks which by time t have been combined into a single bank[32]

The Formal Hypothesis

In addition to the variables $Y^1, \ldots, Y^9$ defined in the previous sections, for purely statistical reasons a set of related variables will also be defined:

(10) $Z^i = ln(Y^i + 1) \qquad i = 1, \ldots, 9$

On a priori grounds, it is clear that the relative change form of dependent variable (the Y^i) is truncated since it cannot assume a value less than zero. The logarithmic form of dependent variable (the Z^i), is not truncated. Hence, the residuals in the analysis-of-variance tests when the relative change form of dependent variable is used are less likely to be approximately normally distributed than when the logarithmic form of dependent variable is used, since the latter can in principle assume any values, negative or positive.

The analysis-of-variance tests reported in the section headed "The Evidence" have been performed on both the Y form and the Z form of the dependent variables. In general, similar results have been obtained. Since each Z variable is a monotonic transformation of the corresponding Y variable, the formal hypotheses to be stated apply equally well to the Z and to the Y variables. For semantic simplicity, the hypotheses will now be stated in terms of only the Y variables; it should be understood that they apply equally well, *mutatis mutandis,* to the Z variables

In terms of the Y variables, the direct hypothesis to be tested can be stated as follows: Since the managers of commercial banks must always obtain approval of mergers prior to their consummation from the relevant regulatory authorities, and sometimes from their stockholders as well, it is natural to presume that these merger proposals receive considerable attention from bank managers, the various regulatory authorities, and possibly also stockholders. Thus, the variables representing the interests of each of these groups should be positively associated with both the existence and the intensity of merger activity. Less formally stated, the hypothesis to be tested is that among large commercial banks, those which have engaged in approved mergers will display higher relative increases in all the growth variables than those which have not used mergers as a method of growth. If the potential conflicts of interest between managers and stockholders that have been discussed above do in fact exist in commercial banks, there would be an exception in terms of the stockholders' interest variables Y^5 and Y^6. In this case, these variables would be negatively associated with mergers. If the interests of managers and stockholders prove to be independent, rather than complementary or conflicting, there would be no significant association between Y^5 and Y^6, on the one hand, and merger activity, on the other.

The Evidence

Data for the decade 1952–1962 for a sample of 165 large domestic commercial banks were obtained.[33] The commercial banks included in this study acquired over 418 banks between 1952 and 1961, participating in approximately one-third of the mergers during this period.

Two different measures of merger activity were used in this study. A first measure was a simple dichotomy considering only whether a bank had or had not engaged in any merger during the decade. Thus, "not merging" and "merging" were the two classifications in this simpler breakdown. A second breakdown[34] of merger activity, which is more appropriate as a measure of the intensity of merger activity, divided the 165 banks in the study into three classes: those which did not merge at all during this decade, those which had engaged in only one or two mergers during this decade, and those which had engaged in three or more mergers during this decade.

Initial Tests

As an initial test of the underlying hypotheses, the average (i.e., arithmetic mean) values of $Y^1, \ldots, Y^9$ for the two merger groups as well as for the three merger groups were computed for all 165 commercial banks in the sample. As far as they go, the results, which are shown in Table 10.1, provide a striking confirmation of the direct hypothesis with respect to the four variables (Y^1, Y^2, Y^3, and Y^4) representing management interests. Each of these variables shows a significant positive association with merger activity, and one-way analysis-of-variance tests indicate that it is extremely unlikely that this association could have arisen as a result of chance.[35]

The results for the two variables representing stockholder interests (Y^5 and Y^6) are negatively associated with merger activity, indicating that the hypothesized conflict of interests between managers and stockholders seems to be real. The degree of significance attributed to the negative association between stockholder interest variables and merger activity is somewhat less, however, than the degree of positive association between management interest variables and merger activity; in fact, although market price (Y^6) is negatively associated with merger activity in both the twofold and the threefold merger group classifications, the statistical significance for this variable is lacking in the threefold merger group classification.

In no case is there any statistically significant association between the public interest variables and merger activities. Since a prima facie case for bank mergers serving the public interest could be made only if there were a positive association between the public interest variables and merger activity, the lack of any significant association seems to belie the contention that mergers involving large banks typically are in the public interest because they result in better services to bank customers.

The results of these initial tests suggest that mergers *do* matter

TABLE 10.1 Means of the Variables by Merger Group

	Two Merger Groups (Case IA)			*Three Merger Groups (Case IIA)*			
Variable	*Not Merging*	*Merging*	*F-ratio**	*Not Merging*	*1 or 2 Mergers*	*3 or More Mergers*	*F-ratio**
Management interest:							
Y_1	44.5	103.1	*17.48*$^{(0.01)}$	44.5	79.0	128.1	*14.77*$^{(0.01)}$
Y_2	40.4	103.6	*16.42*$^{(0.01)}$	40.4	79.7	128.4	*12.89*$^{(0.01)}$
Y_3	105.0	205.7	*14.61*$^{(0.01)}$	105.0	176.7	235.8	*9.61*$^{(0.01)}$
Y_4	43.4	113.6	*16.87*$^{(0.01)}$	43.4	93.4	134.5	*11.14*$^{(0.01)}$
Stockholder interest:							
Y_5	99.0	64.3	*8.05*$^{(0.01)}$	99.0	65.7	62.8	*4.03*$^{(0.05)}$
Y_6	200.5	165.1	*2.85*$^{(0.10)}$	200.5	171.1	158.8	1.56
Public interest							
Y_7	44.5	48.2	0.28	44.5	48.7	47.6	0.15
Y_8	40.4	44.4	0.35	40.4	45.1	43.7	0.19
Y_9	105.0	119.3	1.04	105.0	130.2	108.0	1.58
Number of banks	49	116		49	59	57	

* The *F*-ratios shown for each variable are based on one-way analysis-of-variance tests of the significance of the observed differences in group means for that variable. In the fourth column, the *F*-ratios are based on a classification of banks into two merger groups; in the rightmost column, the *F*-ratios are based on a classification of banks into three merger groups. The italicized *F*-ratios are those for which the probability is less than 0.10 that the observed differences in group means could be the result of chance; in these cases, the significance levels are shown in parentheses as superscripts to the *F*-ratios.

Source: Kalman J. Cohen and Samuel Richardson Reid, "The Benefits and Costs of Bank Mergers," *Journal of Quantitative and Financial Analysis,* vol. 1, no. 4, p. 30, December, 1966.

in the growth patterns displayed by large commercial banks. The more actively a bank merges, the more it tends to further the self-interests of managers rather than the interests of stockholders, and there is no significant evidence that the public interest is being served by bank mergers.[36]

Tests Holding State Branching Regulation Constant

The results of these initial tests, taken by themselves, are not entirely conclusive. It is implicitly assumed when one-way analysis-of-variance tests are used that except for the independent variable (merger activity, in the above tests), there are no other omitted variables which exert *systematic* effects upon the dependent variables (i.e., upon Y^1, . . . , Y^9). It could be argued that this assumption is not likely to be satisfied for the sample of large commercial banks that have been analyzed. For example, it is conceivable that the apparent systematic association between merger activity and the variables representing the interests of managers and stockholders, as well as the conclusion to be drawn from the lack of definite association between merger activity and variables representing the public interest, is spurious. The results reported in Table 10.1 might well be due to some other variable(s) systematically related to both merger activity, on the one hand, and to the variables representing management, stockholder, and public interests, on the other. It is unsafe to conclude that the apparent effects of mergers are the real effects without employing further analyses which hold constant the effects of such possible missing variables.

One obvious variable omitted from the initial tests is state regulation concerning branching by commercial banks. In the United States, some states (so-called unit banking states) do not permit commercial banks to establish any branches whatsoever. Other states permit commercial banks to establish branches throughout the entire state (the so-called statewide branching states). In between, some states permit branching which is less than statewide (the so-called limited branching states). It may well be that mergers occur more frequently in those states which permit branching than in unit banking states and that the observed growth patterns in such variables as assets, deposits, loans, number of employees, earning per share, and market price may differ markedly from state to state, depending on branching regulations. In order to determine whether the apparent effects of mergers revealed in Table 10.1 could be entirely due to interstate differences in branching regulations that are systematically related to merger activity, further statistical tests were conducted.

These further tests consisted of dividing the 165 commercial banks in the sample into groups on the basis of similarity in state branching regulations. In some of the tests, two branching divisions were used (unit banking states and branching states); in other tests, states were divided into three branching groups (unit banking states, limited branching states, and statewide branching states). Within each branching classification, the type of analysis reported in the section headed "Initial Tests" and in Table 10.1 was repeated in order to hold branching regulation effects constant. Each time, only those banks which were in the same branching regulation category were used. Regardless of whether two or three branching regulation groups are used, the results are similar. Further, it does not really matter whether two or three merger groups are used or whether the relative change or logarithmic definitions of the dependent variables are employed. A typical set of results, which display the pattern that develops, is shown in Table 10.2. The logarithmic form, rather than the relative change form, of the dependent variables has been employed in Table 10.2.

When state branching regulation effects are held constant, the statistical results, although slightly weaker, are similar to those reported in Table 10.1 (which did not hold state branching regulation effects constant). The basic difference is that when the effects of mergers are analyzed within specific state branching regulation classes, mergers do not always matter as much as they appear to in a gross sense.

In examining whether each dependent variable has the hypothesized direction of relationship with merger activity, it is most meaningful to consider only those state branching regulation classes for which the effects of mergers on that variable are statistically significant. Table 10.2 reveals that for each state branching regulation class in which the observed differences in merger group means are statistically significant, there is a positive association between the dependent variable representing management interests and merger activity and a negative association between the dependent variable representing stockholder interests and merger activity. In no case, when state branching regulation effects are held constant, do any significant associations, either positive or negative, appear between public interest variables and merger activity.

It appears, then, that when state branching regulation effects are held constant, the evidence is consistent with the hypothesis of a conflict of interests between managers and stockholders. To the extent that mergers have significant effects on the growth patterns displayed by commercial banks within state branching regulation classes, the more actively a bank merges, the more it tends to further management inter-

TABLE 10.2 Means of the Variables by Merger Group within State Branching Regulation Classes (Case IIIC)

Variable	Unit Branching			Limited Branching			Statewide Branching		
	Not Merging	Merging	F-ratio*	Not Merging	Merging	F-ratio*	Not Merging	Merging	F-ratio*
Management interest:									
Z^1	14.3	25.0	*11.55*$^{(0.01)}$	14.5	26.5	*14.47*$^{(0.01)}$	25.6	31.5	0.45
Z^2	12.6	23.9	*11.50*$^{(0.01)}$	13.4	26.4	*13.19*$^{(0.01)}$	24.5	30.2	0.42
Z^3	27.7	39.1	*6.61*$^{(0.05)}$	28.2	44.0	*12.27*$^{(0.01)}$	35.9	44.5	0.59
Z^4	12.0	25.8	*17.30*$^{(0.01)}$	14.8	25.6	*8.56*$^{(0.01)}$	23.7	37.3	1.53
Stockholder interest:									
Z^5	29.3	23.2	0.87	25.0	18.0	*3.25*$^{(0.10)}$	31.2	16.5	*3.10*$^{(0.10)}$
Z^6	44.5	44.8	0.00	40.3	37.4	0.72	63.1	41.1	*4.38*$^{(0.05)}$
Public interest:									
Z^7	14.3	12.0	0.64	14.5	15.2	0.13	25.6	18.4	1.17
Z^8	12.6	10.8	0.38	13.4	14.1	0.14	24.5	17.2	1.22
Z^9	27.7	27.0	0.03	28.2	32.5	1.51	35.9	31.1	0.32
Number of banks	20	13		25	73		4	30	

* The *F*-ratios shown for each variable are based on one-way analysis-of-variance tests (within each state branching regulation class) of the significance of the observed differences in group means for that variable. The italicized *F*-ratios are those for which the probability is less than 0.10 that the observed differences in group means could be the result of chance; in these cases, the significance levels are shown in parentheses as superscripts to the *F*-ratios.

Source: Kalman J. Cohen and Samuel Richardson Reid, "The Benefits and Costs of Bank Mergers," *Journal of Financial and Quantitative Analysis,* vol. 1, no. 4, p. 35, December, 1966.

ests at the expense of stockholder interests, and it does not appear in any significant way to further the interests of the public.[37]

Tests Holding Region Constant

Another variable that may have been omitted from the tests reported in Tables 10.1 and 10.2, thus affecting the results, is the geographical region in which a commercial bank is located. Because not all regions of the United States grow at the same rate, it may well be that the growth patterns of commercial banks are systematically affected by the general economic growth of the region in which they are situated. If there are also marked geographical differences in the merger activity of banks, the patterns of association and lack of association of the different growth variables with merger activity displayed in Tables 10.1 and 10.2 may be spurious, being due instead to the systematic influence of geographical region on both the dependent variables and the merger activities of commercial banks. Thus, further tests are necessary to determine whether the apparent effects of mergers revealed in Tables 10.1 and 10.2 could be due entirely to geographical differences that are systematically related to the merger activity groups.

For this purpose, the 165 commercial banks in the sample were divided into four groups on the basis of the geographical regions in which they were located: East, Central, South, and West. Table 10.3 shows the results of the one-way analysis-of-variance tests that were performed on each of the dependent growth variables (in their logarithmic forms) within each geographical region separately.

The data in Table 10.3 indicate that when geographical effects are held constant, the results of the analysis-of-variance tests still repeat the basic pattern previously observed. In every case, within each geographical region there is a positive association between growth in each management-related variable and merger activity; this positive association is statistically significant in fifteen of the sixteen cases shown in Table 10.3. There are only two cases in Table 10.3 where a stockholder interest variable is significantly associated with merger activity. In each of these cases, the significant association is negative, indicating a conflict of interest between managers and stockholders. In contrast to the results shown in Tables 10.1 and 10.2, Table 10.3 shows two cases (in the South) where the association between a public interest variable and merger activity is significant. In both cases, this association is negative, implying that the public interest has been harmed by merger activity among commercial banks in the South during this decade.

In summary, the picture revealed in Table 10.3, in conjunction with

TABLE 10.3 Means of the Variables by Merger Group within Geographical Regions (Case IIID)

Variable	East			South			Central			West		
	Not Merging	*Merging*	F-ratio*	*Not Merging*	*Merging*	F-ratio*	*Not Merging*	*Merging*	F-ratio*	*Not Merging*	*Merging*	F-ratio*
Management interest:												
Z^1	16.2	30.9	*5.97*$^{(0.01)}$	18.2	25.9	*3.36*$^{(0.05)}$	11.5	21.1	*11.29*$^{(0.01)}$	16.8	31.4	*6.75*$^{(0.01)}$
Z^2	15.2	31.5	*5.30*$^{(0.01)}$	16.6	24.4	*3.33*$^{(0.05)}$	10.2	20.5	*13.16*$^{(0.01)}$	15.6	30.2	*6.66*$^{(0.01)}$
Z^3	28.2	46.0	*5.06*$^{(0.01)}$	33.5	42.3	2.59	23.2	38.6	*7.32*$^{(0.01)}$	31.1	46.7	*5.26*$^{(0.05)}$
Z^4	15.5	30.3	*5.76*$^{(0.01)}$	14.7	28.4	*4.30*$^{(0.05)}$	11.5	23.9	*11.81*$^{(0.01)}$	18.4	31.5	*4.17*$^{(0.05)}$
Stockholder interest:												
Z^5	31.9	16.9	*4.29*$^{(0.05)}$	25.2	18.4	1.86	27.4	21.7	1.39	26.3	16.1	1.97
Z^6	44.5	37.1	1.80	40.0	41.3	0.06	44.4	36.6	*2.89*$^{(0.10)}$	49.0	44.0	0.34
Public interest:												
Z^7	16.2	16.0	0.00	18.2	13.9	*4.84*$^{(0.05)}$	11.5	12.5	0.26	16.8	22.0	0.87
Z^8	15.2	14.7	0.01	16.6	12.6	*3.72*$^{(0.05)}$	10.2	11.9	0.74	15.6	20.8	0.85
Z^9	28.2	31.2	0.24	33.5	29.9	1.07	23.2	30.0	1.81	31.1	36.8	0.85
Number of banks	8	42		15	30		17	25		9	19	

* The *F*-ratios shown for each variable are based on one-way analysis-of-variance tests (within each geographical region) of the significance of the observed differences in group means for that variable. The italicized *F*-ratios are those for which the probability is less than 0.10 that the observed differences in group means could be the result of chance; in these cases, the significance levels are shown in parentheses as superscripts to the *F*-ratios.

Source: Kalman J. Cohen and Samuel Richardson Reid, "The Benefits and Costs of Bank Mergers," *Journal of Quantitative and Financial Analysis,* vol. 1, no. 4, p. 38, December, 1966.

the pictures portrayed in Tables 10.1 and 10.2, again indicates that to the extent that mergers have significant effects on the growth patterns of commercial banks, the more actively a bank merges, the more it tends to further the interests of management. Mergers by banks do not appear to promote the interests of stockholders; sometimes, in fact, they are significantly deleterious to stockholders' interests. Finally, commercial bank mergers have only a negative effect on the public interest variables.[38]

Tests Holding Both State Branching Regulation and Geographical Region Constant

In order to hold constant both the direct effects of, and the possible interactions between, state branching regulation and geographical region, the one-way analysis-of-variance tests of each dependent growth variable were repeated as shown in Table 10.4. The results in Table 10.4 are representative of those obtained when other forms of state branching regulation and geographical region cross-classification tests were run using either two or three merger groups and either the relative change or the logarithmic form of the dependent variables (see Table 10.5). Again, these results more or less confirm the pattern already noted.

When both state branching regulation and geographical region effects are held constant, there is a pronounced tendency for the management interest variables to be positively and significantly associated with intensity of merger activity among commercial banks. What previous tests indicated was a potential *conflict* of interests between managers and stockholders now appears, in Table 10.4, to be perhaps an independence of interests. It is clear that stockholder interest variables are *not* significantly and positively associated with intensity of merger activity; on the other hand, there is no striking evidence in Table 10.4 that they are significantly and negatively associated with merger activity. Finally, Table 10.4 reveals no consistent strong association between public interest variables and intensity of merger activity.

Summary of Statistical Results

The results obtained in the analysis-of-variance tests reported in detail in Tables 10.1 to 10.4 are repeated in summary form in Table 10.5, along with a summary of the results from a great many other forms of analysis-of-variance tests that were run on the sample of 165 large commercial banks. It definitely appears, on the basis of all the evidence presented in Tables 10.1 to 10.5 and discussed above, that mergers exert

TABLE 10.4 Means of the Variables by Merger Group within State Branching Regulation and Geographical Region Cross-classifications (Case IVE)

Variable	*Branching—East*				*Unit—South*				*Branching—South*			
	No. of Mergers				*No. of Mergers*				*No. of Mergers*			
	0	*1–2*	*3*	F-*ratio**	*0*	*1–2*	*3*	F-*ratio**	*0*	*1–2*	*3*	F-*ratio**
Management interest:												
Z^1	16.2	24.8	34.0	*4.83*(0.05)	19.8	34.0	—	*9.79*(0.01)	16.8	18.8	36.1	*5.93*(0.01)
Z^2	15.2	23.6	35.4	*4.92*(0.05)	17.7	33.6	—	*9.01*(0.05)	15.7	17.2	34.0	*5.35*(0.05)
Z^3	28.2	42.2	47.9	*2.87*(0.10)	31.0	43.5	—	2.86	35.7	36.7	53.3	*2.75*(0.10)
Z^4	15.5	29.5	30.8	*2.85*(0.10)	11.4	30.6	—	*15.14*(0.01)	17.6	17.4	50.5	*8.25*(0.01)
Stockholder interest:												
Z^5	31.9	17.8	16.4	2.13	24.1	22.6	—	0.02	26.2	17.7	17.2	1.03
Z^6	44.5	34.7	38.3	1.18	39.4	52.8	—	1.45	40.5	38.9	39.4	0.02
Public interest:												
Z^7	16.2	14.8	16.6	0.13	19.8	19.0	—	0.03	16.8	13.3	12.0	1.81
Z^8	15.2	13.7	15.3	0.11	17.7	18.3	—	0.02	15.7	12.0	10.1	2.26
Z^9	28.2	31.0	31.3	0.12	31.0	31.8	—	0.01	35.7	31.1	26.1	1.91
Number of banks	8	14	28		7	5	0		8	17	8	

TABLE 10.4 **Means of the Variables by Merger Group within State Branching Regulation and Geographical Region Cross-classifications (Case IVE) (Continued)**

	Unit—Central				*Branching—Central*			
	No. of Mergers				*No. of Mergers*			
Variable	*0*	*1–2*	*3*	F-*ratio**	*0*	*1–2*	*3*	F-*ratio**
Management interest:								
Z^1	11.2	18.9	—	2.72	11.7	18.8	24.0	*4.24*$^{(0.05)}$
Z^2	9.8	17.9	—	*3.10*$^{(0.10)}$	10.5	17.7	23.9	*5.28*$^{(0.05)}$
Z^3	24.1	26.8	—	0.15	22.5	40.8	40.9	*2.80*$^{(0.10)}$
Z^4	10.9	19.5	—	*4.20*$^{(0.05)}$	11.9	20.0	29.0	*4.97*$^{(0.05)}$
Stockholder interest:								
Z^5	40.0	21.5	—	2.25	18.6	18.7	24.6	0.95
Z^6	51.5	36.9	—	1.55	39.4	34.9	38.0	0.31
Public interest:								
Z^7	11.2	6.8	—	1.89	11.7	13.8	13.4	0.30
Z^8	9.8	5.8	—	1.53	10.5	13.0	13.1	0.57
Z^9	24.1	16.1	—	1.82	22.5	35.8	29.8	1.45
Number of banks	7	4	0		10	10	11	

TABLE 10.4 Means of the Variables by Merger Group within State Branching Regulation and Geographical Region Cross-classifications (Case IVE) (Continued)

Variable	Unit—West				Branching—West			
	No. of Mergers				No. of Mergers			
	0	1–2	3	F-ratio*	0	1–2	3	F-ratio*
Management interest:								
Z^1	11.3	19.8	—	*4.13*$^{(0.10)}$	27.8	40.8	31.4	0.97
Z^2	10.0	17.7	—	3.25	26.8	39.8	30.3	1.00
Z^3	27.9	45.7	—	*5.73*$^{(0.05)}$	37.5	58.9	41.0	1.93
Z^4	14.0	25.9	—	2.18	27.1	43.0	27.9	1.58
Stockholder interest:								
Z^5	22.8	25.5	—	0.09	33.4	13.0	13.8	1.20
Z^6	42.2	42.6	—	0.00	62.5	46.6	43.2	0.68
Public interest:								
Z^7	11.3	8.3	—	0.42	27.8	36.0	20.4	*2.93*$^{(0.10)}$
Z^8	10.0	6.3	—	0.59	26.8	35.1	19.4	*2.98*$^{(0.10)}$
Z^9	27.9	31.7	—	0.28	37.5	53.0	30.8	*3.86*$^{(0.05)}$
Number of banks	6	4	—		3	5	10	

* The *F*-ratios shown for each variable are based on one-way analysis-of-variance tests (within each state branching regulation and geographical cross-classification) of the significance of the observed differences in group means for that variable. The italicized *F*-ratios are those for which the probability is less than 0.10 that the observed differences in group means could be the result of chance; in these cases, the significance levels are shown in parentheses as superscripts to the *F*-ratios.

Source: Kalman J. Cohen and Samuel Richardson Reid, "The Benefits and Costs of Bank Mergers," *Journal of Quantitative and Financial Analysis,* vol. 1, no. 4, pp. 40–41, December, 1966.

TABLE 10.5 Summary of Analysis-of-variance Results

	Design of Analysis							*Results of Analysis**																							
								Management Interest																							
	Form of Dependent Variable		*No. of Merger Classes*		*No. of State Branching Regulation Classes*			*Assets*						*Deposits*						*Loans*						*Employees*					
								Up		*Down*		*Mixed*		*Up*		*Down*		*Mixed*		*Up*		*Down*		*Mixed*		*Up*		*Down*		*Mixed*	
Case	*Logarithmic*	*Relative Change*	*2*	*3*	*2*	*3*	*Geographical Region*	*Sig.*	*Not*	*Sig.*	*Not*	*Sig.*	*Not*	*Sig.*	*Not*	*Sig.*	*Not*	*Sig.*	*Not*	*Sig.*	*Not*	*Sig.*	*Not*	*Sig.*	*Not*	*Sig.*	*Not*	*Sig.*	*Not*	*Sig.*	*Not*
IA		x	x					1						1						1						1					
IB		x	x		x			2						2						2						2					
IC		x	x			x		2	1					2	1					2	1					2	1				
ID		x	x				x	4						4						3	1					4					
IE		x	x		x		x	4	3					3	4					3	4					4	3				
IIIA	x		x					1						1						1						1					
IIIB	x		x		x			2						2						2						2					
IIIC	x		x			x		2	1					2	1					2	1					2	1				
IIID	x		x				x	4						4						3	1					4					
IIIE	x		x		x		x	4	3					3	4					3	4					3	4				
IIA		x		x				1						1						1						1					
IIB		x		x	x			2						2						2						2					
IIC		x		x		x		2	1					2	1					2					1	2	1				
IID		x		x			x	3				1		2	1			1		2	1			1		2					2
IIE		x		x	x		x	5	1				1	4	2				1	2	4			1		4	1				2
IVA	x			x				1						1						1						1					
IVB	x			x	x			2						2						2						2					
IVC	x			x		x		2	1					2	1					2					1	2					1
IVD	x			x			x	3				1		4						3				1		3				1	
IVE	x			x	x		x	4	2				1	6					1	4	2				1	4	1			1	1
Total								51	13	0	0	2	2	50	15	0	0	1	2	43	19	0	0	3	3	48	12	0	0	2	6

TABLE 10.5 Summary of Analysis-of-variance Results (Continued)

Case	Results of Analysis*																													
	Stockholder Interest																		Public Interest											
	Earnings per Share						Market Price						Assets—Star						Deposits—Star						Loans—Star					
	Up		Down		Mixed		Up		Down		Mixed		Up		Down		Mixed		Up		Down		Mixed		Up		Down		Mixed	
	Sig.	Not	Sig.	Not	Sig.	Not	Sig.	Not	Sig.	Not	Sig.	Not	Sig.	Not	Sig.	Not	Sig.	Not	Sig.	Not	Sig.	Not	Sig.	Not	Sig.	Not	Sig.	Not	Sig.	Not
IA			1						1					1						1						1				
IB			1	1						2				1		1				1		1				1		1		
IC			1	2					1	2				1		2				1		2				1		2		
ID			1	3				1	1	2				3	1					2	1	1				3		1		
IE		3	1	3				1		6				3	1	3				3	1	3				4		3		
IIIA			1							1				1						1						1				
IIIB			1	1				1		1				1		1				1		1				1		1		
IIIC			2	1				1	1	1				1		2				1		2				1		2		
IIID			1	3				1	1	2				1	1	2				2	1	1				3		1		
IIIE		2	1	4				2		5				1	1	5				2	1	4				5		2		
IIA			1							1								1						1						1
IIB			2							2						1		1				1		1				1		1
IIC				3					1	1		1				1		1		1		1		1				1		2
IID				2		2				1		3			1			2		1	1			2				1	1	2
IIE		2		3		2		1		3		3				3	1	3		2		3	1	1		2		3	1	1
IVA			1							1										1										1
IVB				1	1			1				1				1		1				1		1				1		1
IVC				2		1		1		1		1		1		2				1		2						1		2
IVD				3		1				1		3		1	1			2		1	1			2				1		3
IVE		1		4		2		2		2		3		1		3	1	2				4	1	2		3		2	1	1
Total	0	8	15	36	1	8	0	12	6	35	0	15	0	20	6	27	2	13	0	22	6	27	2	11	0	26	0	24	3	15

*The "Results of Analysis" section of this table gives the number of classes for a given analysis-of-variance design for which the merger group means have an increasing (i.e., up), decreasing (i.e., down), or nonmonotonic (i.e., mixed) association with merger activity. An association is called "significant" (i.e., sig.) if the probability is less than 0.10 that the observed differences in group means could be the result of chance; otherwise, the association is called "not significant" (i.e., not).

Source: Kalman J. Cohen and Samuel Richardson Reid, "The Costs and Benefits of Bank Mergers," *Journal of Quantitative and Financial Analysis*, vol. 1, no. 4, pp. 44–45, December, 1966.

a strong effect on the growth patterns displayed by large commercial banks. Although there are situations in which mergers do not appear to matter, whenever they do matter in a significant way they clearly are positively associated with the management interest variables. Thus, it appears safe to conclude that in trying to promote mergers involving commercial banks, managers are at least in part tending to increase their own status, prestige, and control over economic resources.

The picture with respect to the effects of merger activity on the stockholder and the public interest variables is not so strong. Nevertheless, some interesting patterns do emerge. To the extent that merger activity is significantly associated with any of the stockholder interest variables, this association is negative. In addition, although tests conducted one at a time should normally consider only those analysis-of-variance results which are statistically significant, the preponderance of negative associations, in contrast to the positive or mixed associations, does suggest that the hypothesized conflict of interests between managers and stockholders may actually exist in large commercial banks. Finally, the lack of statistically significant positive associations between the public interest variables and the intensity of merger activity, combined with the fact that to the extent that the association appears to be statistically significant it is negative rather than positive, does serve to cast strong doubts upon the viewpoint that the larger banks which result from merger activity are in fact better able to serve their customers.

Further Explanations of the Differences among Merger Groups

The large banks that have not merged during the period—that is, the pure internal growth banks—have had relatively higher net operating earnings per share than the merging banks. A brief discussion of some of the factors which may account for these differences follows.

Pure Internal Growth Banks

The managers of nonmerging banks may well be more interested in profitability than in increasing the size of their banks. Certainly the growth of these banks has been less rapid than the growth of the merging banks. In the nonmerging banks, however, this growth has probably been more orderly and accomplished with less strain on the organization. As a result, the costs of expansion, in both the short and the long run, may well be lower for these banks.

It will be noted that the largest number (in absolute terms) of pure internal growth banks are located in states permitting branching.[39] If these banks are branching, and many of them are, they must be using the *de novo* method of expansion. While this method does not eliminate a competitor or potential competitor, it does offer some definite advantages. As stated previously, costs may well be lower for newer and more modern facilities since the internal growth bank is not paying a premium for a bundle of assets and liabilities. The quality content of a bundle assembled by the acquired bank's management may have a wide variance. Certainly the loans and investments may be of a different mix from those of the acquiring bank. In addition, the deposit mix may also be quite different from what the acquiring bank desires.[40] The non-merging banks that are branching *de novo* also have the advantage of being able to choose the location of the new branch. The bank establishing branches by acquiring existing banks is generally restricted to the location of that established bank. The importance of location has been emphasized by a Chicago banker, who wrote: "A new bank has the opportunity to select a site which is most convenient to its potential clientele and to construct facilities geared to modern banking services and public taste. But most banks, already have quarters in varying stages of obsolescence, perhaps on sites of lessened convenience due to shifts of residential and business areas."[41]

Thus, while the expansion of the large pure internal growth banks has not been as rapid as that of the merging banks, this growth has perhaps been more orderly, and it has certainly, on the average, been more profitable.

External Growth Banks

It is obvious from the data presented in this chapter that those banks using merger as a growth method have enlarged themselves considerably more than banks depending upon pure internal growth. Many consider this increase in the size of the banking firm a benefit. One must also remember that this type of growth incurs a number of "costs."

The most obvious cost is the price paid for the acquired bank. There is reason to believe that many acquiring banks have paid premiums to the owners of the acquired banks.[42] Phillips has equated the payment of a premium with increased efficiency, stating: ". . . the fairly rapid development of branch operations in the wake of legislative changes in states such as Virginia and New York, and the premiums paid for the acquisition of small banks, especially when *de novo* entry is barred, are evidence that, at least in some types of operations, branch banking is more efficient than is unit banking."[43]

If the managers of acquiring banks are paying a premium for the banks they acquire, they can most likely rationalize this on the grounds that they are eliminating a competitor or potential competitor. The rationale is that the increased market share gained should lead eventually to increased profits. Time may also be a factor, since acquiring an existing bank will speed the process of entry into the target marketing area. Thus, premiums may be paid both to eliminate a competitor and to "buy" time. In relation to the former point, Jacobs states:

> The existence of entry restrictions tends to bias the buy-or-branch "de novo" decision toward the buy side. The expected value of the probability distribution around expected earnings is higher for the purchase of an existing bank than it would be with free entry. The additional value of the purchase due to restricted entry is the value attached to the probability that an additional charter will not be granted when sought. If the bank branched "de novo" an additional competitor would be on the scene for certain.[44]

A number of other costs are assumed by the acquiring bank in addition to the "search" and "closing" costs which accompany any merger transaction. Crosse has enumerated some of the more obvious ones:

> The first thing is a complete refurbishing of building and equipment at considerable expense. Then the employees of the small bank are brought into the salary program and pension plan of the larger bank which appreciably raises salary costs. Under most merger agreements, former management is retained, at least for a while, but the need for succession is met by bringing in an additional officer or two at the large bank's salary scale. The acquiring bank also usually pays the competitive rate on time and savings deposits which in many cases is more than the absorbed bank was paying. Thus, the new branch starts off immediately with higher costs than the former unit bank.[45]

Some of the other less obvious costs are related to the management group itself. The planning and execution of growth in a firm can be time-consuming, whether it is internal or external growth. Baumol pointed this out when he said: ". . . growth is what strains the firm's entrepreneurial resources and adds to the company's risks, and it may be expected that after some point the resulting increases in costs will catch up with the marginal revenues derived from more rapid expansion."[46]

External growth by merger can be particularly costly in this regard since the increment of growth is generally larger than it would be in a pure internal growth bank. In addition, a problem that is often overlooked is the integration of the acquired bank into the organization of the acquiring bank. Bringing together two or more formerly independent economic and behavioral systems (regardless of size differences) can be a difficult and expensive process.[47]

Thus, merging involves a number of costs, some of which are obvious, and others not so obvious. It appears that the managements of a number of banks using merger as a means of growth have not considered all the costs, have underestimated the costs, or have overestimated the benefits which might accrue to the other interested parties in the merger.

The evidence suggests that large banking firms using merger as a means of growth in a regulated oligopolistic industry may well be "deposit maximizers" subject, of course, to a profit constraint. It is even possible that beyond some point in growth, the desire for deposits competes with the desire for profits. That is, the higher costs incurred by acquisition, plus increased marketing outlays—such as for advertising, impressive banking offices, etc.—and perhaps higher interest rates paid, may eventually lead to reduced net operating earnings.

Bank Mergers and the Public

The results of this study suggest that the public interest as defined in the section headed "Public Interests" has not been well served by bank mergers. There are, of course, a number of other ways of examining the public interest.

The regulatory agencies appear to favor the availability of local banking services. This has tended to confuse the situation, since in many localities there exist alternatives to, or substitutes for, most banking services. Actually, there is only one major service which banks provide that is relatively unique—demand deposits (checking accounts). Since the public has no satisfactory substitute for checking account services, it is logical to assume that the general public would wish to have them provided at the lowest possible cost.[48] Some recent studies indicate that the cost of these services generally increases after a merger.

Horvitz and Shull studied the changes in policy of banks after a merger.[49] They reported that "in 12 of these cases the changes resulted in a net reduction in the monthly service charges, while in 26 there were net increases."[50] They further stated that "in only two out of 16 was there a net decrease in the cost of maintaining a special checking account at the office of the acquired bank."[51] The New York study also found that ". . . increases greatly exceeded reductions."[52] The New York study, in discussing mergers, stated: "The major detrimental effects would be higher service charges in special and regular checking accounts of individuals and small businesses."[53] In his study of Iowa banks, Kaufman found that service charges were higher in markets where concentration was highest.[54]

To date, there have not been any studies demonstrating that the public has benefited from lower checking account service charges after banks have merged. One Federal Reserve official, who appears to favor higher charges for the public, made the following remarks in discussing the policies of merging banks: "The large bank also tends to impose higher (and I think more realistic) service charges on deposit accounts."[55] He further states that as a compensation for higher check-writing costs, the depositor gains "better facilities and better management which, as I have pointed out above, the large bank immediately sets out to supply."[56]

It is difficult to see how the public has gained from these bank mergers, which are approved by the regulatory agencies that are supposed to be promoting the public interest. Concentration has increased in banking markets which are already highly concentrated, and there is no evidence of "efficiencies," since the stockholder has not benefited particularly, nor has the public been offered banking services at lower prices. The structural changes in this quasi-regulated industry do not appear to benefit the public.

NOTES

[1] This chapter is based on an article Kalman J. Cohen of Carnegie-Mellon University and I coauthored, entitled "The Benefits and Costs of Bank Mergers," *Journal of Financial and Quantitative Analysis,* vol. 1, no. 4, pp. 15–57, December, 1966. This study was supported by funds provided by Carnegie's Graduate School of Industrial Administration, the National Science Foundation, and the Ford Foundation.

[2] See Howard D. Crosse, *Management Policies for Commercial Banks,* Englewood Cliffs, N.J.: Prentice-Hall, Inc., 1962, p. 19.

[3] See *100th Annual Report of the Comptroller of the Currency,* 1962, p. 11.

[4] For a summary of these studies, see "Research into Banking Structure and Competition," *Federal Reserve Bulletin,* November, 1964, pp. 1383–1399.

[5] It is unfortunate that despite the recent flurry of research activity, as noted previously, economists have provided very little theory regarding mergers to aid in the decision-making processes of the courts and the regulatory agencies. In his article entitled "Corporate Mergers: Policy and Economic Analysis," *Quarterly Journal of Economics,* November, 1963, p. 553, R. B. Heflebower made the following comment: "The literature on mergers is abundant but the theoretical analysis of growth by merger is almost non-

existent. Recent statistical studies of factors related to growth of firms do not introduce method of growth as a variable."

[6] Paul M. Horvitz, "Stimulating Bank Competition through Regulatory Action," *Journal of Finance,* vol. 20, no. 1, p. 5, March, 1965.

[7] In his article entitled "Banking Structure and Competition," *Journal of Finance,* May, 1965, p. 350, Howard D. Crosse, a former vice-president of the Federal Reserve Bank of New York, made the following remark concerning public policy as it relates to bank structure: "The big question is 'the best for whom?' If it were only the bank stockholder, we could leave banking structure to market forces and the Department of Justice. But we are talking about money in which everybody has a vital interest."

[8] For additional discussion of this subject, see A. A. Berle, Jr., and Gardiner C. Means, *The Modern Corporation and Private Property,* New York: Commerce Clearing House, Inc., 1932; A. A. Berle, Jr., *The Twentieth Century Capitalist Revolution,* New York: Harcourt, Brace & World, Inc., 1954; A. A. Berle, Jr., *Power without Property,* New York: Harcourt, Brace & World, Inc., 1959; Richard Eells, *The Meaning of Modern Business,* New York: Columbia University Press, 1960; R. A. Gordon, *Business Leadership in the Large Corporation,* Washington, D.C.: The Brookings Institution, 1945; J. Burnham, *The Managerial Revolution,* New York: The John Day Company, Inc., 1941; E. S. Mason (ed.), *The Corporation in Modern Society,* Cambridge, Mass.: Harvard University Press, 1959; H. Maurer, *Great Enterprise: Growth and Behavior of the Big Corporation,* New York: The Macmillan Company, 1955; and a series of pamphlets on the corporation published by the Fund for the Republic.

[9] Gerald L. Nordquist, "The Breakup of the Maximization Principle," *Quarterly Review of Economics and Business,* vol. 5, no. 3, p. 37, Fall, 1965.

[10] See Richard M. Cyert and James G. March, *A Behavioral Theory of the Firm,* Englewood Cliffs, N.J.: Prentice-Hall, Inc., 1963; and Oliver E. Williamson, *The Economics of Discretionary Behavior: Managerial Objectives in a Theory of the Firm,* Englewood Cliffs, N.J.: Prentice-Hall, Inc., 1964.

[11] There is some evidence that in the large banks, a separation of ownership and control exists. In a study undertaken by G. R. Whitaker, Jr., for the House Committee on Banking and Currency, *The Market for Bank Stock,* 1964, p. 8, it is noted: "In 1962, there are no banks in the largest size class where officers and directors own over 50 percent of the outstanding stock. . . ."

[12] Armen A. Alchion and Reuben A. Kessel have indicated that nonpecuniary factors play an important role in the reward structures perceived by the managers of firms possessing some degree of monopoly power. In their article entitled "Competition, Monopoly, and the Pursuit of Money," in *Aspects of Labor Economics,* Princeton, N.J.: Princeton University Press, 1962, p. 164, they state: "If wealth cannot be taken out of an organization in salaries or in other forms of personal pecuniary property, the terms of trade between pecuniary wealth and nonpecuniary business-associated forms of satisfaction turn against the former. More of the organization's funds will now be reinvested (which need not result in increased wealth) in ways that enhance the manager's prestige or status in the community." Because of the entry restrictions imposed by the various regulatory authorities, it is likely that this analysis is pertinent to the behavior of commercial bankers.

[13] Charlotte P. Alhadeff and David A. Alhadeff, "Recent Bank Mergers," *Quarterly Journal of Economics,* vol. 69, no. 4, pp. 516–517, November, 1955.

When expanding by branching, a bank has a choice between *de novo* branching and merging with an existing bank; the latter method is frequently utilized since it provides relatively quick entry into an area and also eliminates a potential competitor in the process.

[14] Select Committee on Small Business, Senate, *Special Staff Report of the Board of Governors of the Federal Reserve System: Recent Developments in the Structure of Banking*, 1962, p. 7.

[15] For example, in the list of the fifty largest commercial banks that *Fortune* magazine publishes each summer, banks are ranked primarily in decreasing order of their assets and secondarily in decreasing order of their deposits.

[16] David Alhadeff and Charlotte Alhadeff, "Growth of Large Banks: 1930–1960," *Review of Economics and Statistics*, vol. 46, no. 4, p. 356, November, 1964.

[17] Lester V. Chandler, *The Economics of Money and Banking*, 4th ed., New York: Harper & Row, Publishers, Incorporated, 1964, p. 127.

[18] For a more complete discussion, see Franco Modigliani and Merton H. Miller, "The Cost of Capital, Corporation Finance, and the Theory of Investment," *American Economic Review*, vol. 48, no. 3, pp. 261–297, June, 1958; and Merton H. Miller and Franco Modigliani, "Dividend Policy, Growth, and the Valuation of Shares," *Journal of Business*, vol. 34, no. 4, pp. 411–433, October, 1961.

[19] See Myles L. Mace and George G. Montgomery, Jr., *Management Problems of Corporate Acquisitions*, Cambridge, Mass.: Harvard University Press, 1962, especially, p. 11. Another view has been expressed by M. A. Shapiro, leading bank stock specialist, who is quoted in an article by Hubert Bratter, "The Comptroller's Proposal for Strengthening Dual Banking," *Banking*, December, 1964, p. 41, as saying: "Primary interest of stockholders is soundness and growth of their bank. Legal and administrative obstacles and complex laws and regulations block expansion through branches, mergers, and holding companies. Overlapping jurisdiction confuses stockholders."

[20] In principle, it would also be desirable to measure the total yield received by bank stockholders during this period by adding the values of all cash dividends, rights, warrants, etc., issued between time $t-1$ and time t to the capital gains. This alternative way of measuring stockholders' interests was not used because of the large additional data gathering and computational costs that would have been incurred. The length of time actually employed in the empirical study for the interval between time $t-1$ and time t was a decade; hence it would have been necessary to ascertain the precise dates of each distribution of cash dividends, rights, warrants, etc., and then to use an internal-rate-of-return calculation in order correctly to compute the total yield to common stockholders. It is doubtful that the conclusions arrived at in this chapter would have been significantly altered if total yield instead of capital gains yield had been used as a measure of stockholders' interests.

[21] Crosse, "Banking Structure and Competition," p. 351.

[22] Other things being equal, such as population growth, area income, etc.,

[23] Crosse, "Banking Structure and Competition." Most economists, businessmen, and borrowers would most likely place a higher value on the rate than Crosse does.

[24] George R. Hall and Charles F. Phillips, Jr., *Bank Mergers and the Regulation Agencies*, Washington, D.C.: Board of Governors of the Federal Reserve System, 1964, p. 156.

[25] *Ibid.* While their study was based on published merger decisions since the passage of the Bank Merger Act of 1960, the factors considered probably had not changed much since the passage of the act. Most merger applications submitted have been approved by the agencies, even after considering the "competition" factor included in the act. Tynan Smith stated the following in an unpublished paper presented in St. Louis on Oct. 20, 1965, to the Committee on Financial Analysis: "In his recent statement on the proposed bank merger legislation, Governor Mitchell relied upon a survey of bank merger cases decided by the Board during the past three and one-half years to point out the relative unimportance of competitive factors in most of the Board's decisions. This analysis was in effect an updating of the analysis of merger decisions during the years 1960 through 1962 which was prepared a year ago by George Hall and Charles Phillips."

[26] In his article "Banking Structure and Competition," p. 351, Crosse says the following: "There can be little question but there are great pressures in the economy for a more concentrated banking structure. Without regulatory controls there would be a great many more mergers and a great many more new branches established. This trend represents the judgment of bank management representing the long-range interests of the stockholders. These are the views of management both in the acquiring bank and those that are acquired. It takes two to tango! It is clear that bankers believe sincerely that there are efficiencies of scale, if not economies. And I think they are right."

[27] Donald R. Hodgman, "Competition in Banking and Its Regulation," *The Bankers Magazine,* vol. 147, no. 1, p. 54, Winter, 1964.

[28] For a discussion of this problem, see Franklin R. Edwards, "The Banking Competition Controversy," *National Banking Review,* vol. 3, no. 1, pp. 1–34, September, 1965.

[29] Crosse, "Banking Structure and Competition," p. 351.

[30] Governor George Mitchell has stated that "during the past 3½ years the Board of Governors has considered 107 merger cases. It has approved 97 applications and denied 10." Governor Mitchell's complete statement, made before the House Committee on Banking and Currency on Aug. 26, 1965, is reprinted in *Federal Reserve Bulletin,* September, 1965, pp. 1248–1253. During this same period the Justice Department has disapproved of a majority of the mergers while considering the "competitive factor."

[31] Hall and Phillips, *op. cit.,* p. 158.

[32] Note that the variables A^*_{t-1}, D^*_{t-1}, and L^*_{t-1} are operationally defined in terms of the variables A_{t-1}, D_{t-1}, and L_{t-1}, respectively. For example, A^*_{t-1} is the sum of A_{t-1} for those banks which by time t have been combined into one single bank.

An example can be provided to clarify the distinction between the public interest variables Y^7 to Y^9 and the related management interest variables Y^1 to Y^3. Suppose that between time $t-1$ and time t, bank U had absorbed, through mergers, bank V and bank W to form bank UVW. Bank U, as the dominant bank of the three, is regarded as the surviving bank from the mergers. Assume that the total assets (in billions of dollars) of the three banks at time $t-1$ were 4.0 for bank U, 0.8 for bank V, and 0.2 for bank W and that at time t, the total assets of bank UVW were 6.0. For bank UVW, $A_t = 6.0$, $A_{t-1} = 4.0$, and $A^*_{t-1} = 5.0$. Hence, for bank UVW, $Y^1 = 50$, and $Y^7 = 20$.

[33] The period 1952–1961 was used for this study because of the convenient

availability of information about bank mergers. The merger activity of large banks (those with over $100 million of assets) was listed in Select Committee on Small Business, Senate, *op. cit.* The mergers listed were consummated between July 1, 1952, and June 30, 1961. We then eliminated any mergers occurring prior to Dec. 31, 1952, and added mergers completed between July 1, 1961, and Dec. 31, 1961. The banks listed were then checked with the 300 largest commercial banks as of Dec. 31, 1952. Those large banks with the desired balance sheet, income statements, and market price information available in *Moody's Bank and Finance Manual* constituted the sample. Data on the deposits, assets, and loans at time $t-1$ of banks acquired during the period were obtained from the *Rand McNally International Bankers Directory* and *Polk's Bank Directory.*

[34] The two classes of banks that merged during the decade were divided in such a way that they formed two groups containing approximately equal numbers of banks. Thus, during this decade 49 of the 165 banks did not merge at all, and of the 116 banks that did merge, 59 had one or two mergers, and 57 had three or more mergers.

[35] It should be realized, of course, that an F-ratio large enough to be statistically significant indicates that the between-group variability is considerably greater than the within-group variability.

[36] As shown by the rows for cases IIIA and IVA in Table 10.5, when the one-way analysis-of-variance tests are run on the logarithmic (that is, Z) form of the dependent variables, the results are essentially similar to those reported in Table 10.1.

[37] As shown by the results displayed in Table 10.5, other forms of the analysis-of-variance tests holding constant the effects of state branching regulation classes tend to confirm the evidence presented in Table 10.2.

[38] The other analysis-of-variance results summarized in Table 10.5 conform to the apparent effects of mergers holding geographical region constant that are reported in Table 10.3.

[39] This is true mainly because a majority of the states permit some type of branching. Bank mergers have occurred principally in states permitting statewide or limited branch banking. See "Changes in Banking Structure: 1953–62," *Federal Reserve Bulletin,* September, 1963, pp. 1192–1193.

[40] There have been cases of postmerger deposit shrinkage caused by depositors who, for one reason or another, withdrew their funds and transferred them to other banking institutions.

[41] Robert Lindquist, *The Bank and Its Public: Philosophy and Technique of Bank Public Relations,* New York: Harper & Row, Publishers, Incorporated, 1956, p. 62.

[42] It may well be that the principle gains from bank mergers accrue to the shareholders or owners of the acquired banks. W. Ralph Lamb reports in his book *Group Banking,* New Brunswick, N.J.: Rutgers University Press, p. 65, that a "particularly strong factor causing bank mergers has been the attractive prices and terms which have been offered to shareholders." The following statement appeared in *The Ninety-ninth Annual Report of the Comptroller of the Currency,* 1961, pp. 14–15: "Shareholders of the banks which consolidated or merged with 59 national banks received cash and stock representing a premium of . . . $34,370,761 or an average of 2.24% of the aggregate deposits acquired by the continuing banks. . . . The

shareholders of six national banks and seven state banks, which were purchased by 13 national banks, received $7,193,000, in cash or stocks, or $1,452,414 in excess of the selling banks' aggregate capital structures. This amounted, on the average, to 2.72% of the selling banks' deposits. . . ."

[43] Almarin Phillips, "Competition, Confusion, and Commercial Banking," *Journal of Finance,* vol. 19, no. 1, p. 36, March, 1964.

[44] Donald R. Jacobs, "The Interaction Effects of Restrictions on Branching and Other Bank Regulations," *Journal of Finance,* vol. 20, no. 2, p. 347, May, 1965.

[45] Crosse, "Banking Structure and Competition," p. 351.

[46] William J. Baumol, "On the Theory of the Expansion of the Firm," *American Economic Review,* vol. 52, no. 5, p. 1078, December, 1962.

[47] See Timothy Costello, Joseph F. Kubis, and Charles L. Shaffer, "An Analysis of Attitudes toward A Planned Merger," *Administrative Science Quarterly,* vol. 8, no. 2, pp. 235–249, September, 1963. These authors analyzed questionnaire data from eighty-seven middle management personnel in a bank planning a merger with a larger bank. Among their findings were: "Attitudes toward the merger tended to be unfavorable, although they ranged from very favorable to very unfavorable. Favorable attitudes were related to older age, lack of previous success in the organization, high morale, and high *F*-scale scores (authoritarianism). Unfavorable attitudes toward the merger seemed to be principally associated with: younger age, a pattern of success in the organization, low current morale, and low authoritarianism."

[48] This area of bank pricing was pretty much swept under the rug until recently. The regulatory agencies (with the possible exception of the Comptroller of the Currency) have not provided proper safeguards for the public. Horvitz (*op. cit.,* p. 9) has stated: "Another area in which price competition could be stimulated is in the area of service charges on checking accounts. Until recently, many local clearing houses had apparently set service charges on checking accounts to be charged by their members. Recent action by the Justice Department and the banking regulatory agencies, culminating in the conviction on price fixing charges of several banks in Minnesota, has greatly reduced this overt setting of prices. It is still not clear, however, whether collusion in the setting of service charges has been completely eliminated or simply driven underground." The Comptroller of the Currency has instructed the National Bank Examiner to examine service charge practices to determine whether they are established independently.

[49] Paul M. Horvitz and Bernard Shull, "The Impact of Branch Banking on Bank Performance," *National Banking Review,* vol. 2, no. 2, pp. 143–188, December, 1964.

[50] *Ibid.,* p. 160.

[51] *Ibid.*

[52] *Branch Banking, Bank Mergers, and the Public Interest: A Summary Report,* New York State Banking Department, January, 1964, p. 34.

[53] *Ibid.*

[54] George G. Kaufman, "Bank Market Structure and Performance: The Evidence from Iowa," *Southern Economic Journal,* vol. 32, no. 4, pp. 429–439, April, 1966.

[55] Crosse, "Banking Structure and Competition," p. 353.

[56] *Ibid.,* p. 354.

11

Some Empirical Tests: Regulation, Bank Mergers, and Branching Activity[1]

The structure and performance of the commercial banking industry depend to a considerable degree upon the type of legal and regulatory environment in existence at both the national and the state levels. State laws regarding branching have a particularly important influence on the magnitude of merger activity, as well as on the amount of new entry into the banking industry.

The dramatic changes that took place in the structure of banking between 1953 and 1962 are presented in Table 11.1.[2] It is obvious that the vast majority of mergers (92.5 percent) were consummated in states which permit branching. The absorption of banks through merger in unit states was more than offset by the 687 new entrants during this decade. It is also interesting to note that in both absolute and relative terms, there was less entry of new banks in the thirty-two states permitting branching than in the eighteen unit banking states during this period.[3]

For those who believe in the preservation and promotion of bank-

TABLE 11.1 Changes in Commercial Banking Structure, 1953–1962

	Total	*States with Branching*	*Unit Banking States*
No. of Banks, 1953	*14,073*	*7,010*	*7,036*
New banks organized	1,113	426	687
Mergers and absorptions	1,669	1,544	125
Voluntary liquidations and suspensions	91	38	53
Number of banks, 1962	13,426	5,854	7,572
Net change	—647	—1,156	509
Number of states		32	18

Source: Kalman J. Cohen and Samuel Richardson Reid, "Effects of Regulation, Branching, and Mergers on Banking Structure and Performance," *Southern Economic Journal,* vol 34, no. 2, p. 232, October, 1967.

ing alternatives, the future is indeed bleak unless there is legislative and regulatory agency recognition of the problem.[4] In the absence of this recognition, it appears that banking alternatives will decline at an accelerating rate in the years ahead. This pessimistic outlook stems from the following factors: First, the majority of bank mergers occur in states which permit branch banking; and second, it is highly probable that branching laws will be liberalized in many states in the future as a result of redistricting, which will eventually cause a shift in the balance of power away from the rural areas and toward the metropolitan areas.

With the increased power of the metropolitan areas in the various state legislatures, it is reasonable to expect the influence of the larger city bankers to grow. These bankers generally favor liberalized branching since they would like to follow the flight of some of their depositors and customers to the outlying areas. The increased power of the larger city bankers increases the probability that they will have a more direct influence on state banking laws. Any changes which occur, however, will not come easily. In fact, it is likely that many battles will result.[5]

Aversion to competition (which could result from increased banking alternatives) is not necessarily a function of bank size. The small country banker in a one-bank town is certainly more of a monopolist than his banking brother in the larger city, where banking alternatives exist. These smaller rural bankers will rely upon the rural legislators to protect and preserve their isolated position. The resulting conflict between bankers as well as state legislators will undoubtedly be resolved in a variety of ways. It is highly doubtful that the public will have an opportunity directly to influence the resultant banking structure in a particular state, since these matters will likely be settled in places other than the ballot box.[6] Big city bankers recognize the large information dissemination costs involved when the branching issue is put to a direct vote of the electorate. It seems reasonable to predict that the pressure for liberalized branching in the future will be exerted upon the legislators in the form of more persuasive lobbying activities at all levels of government, rather than through direct appeals to the public.[7]

One final pessimistic note will be sounded before we examine some examples of recent changes in state laws regarding branching and mergers. The commercial banking industry, perhaps more than any other industry, has been subjected to a considerable amount of analysis in recent years by commissions, committees, regulatory agencies, judicial bodies, and the academic community.[8] A consensus of these groups and individuals is that there is a need for increased competition in the banking field. Despite this consensus and the many proposals that have emanated from various sources aimed at promoting competition, Congress has failed to pass any significant legislation designed to facilitate accomplishment of this objective.[9] It is curious that a pro-merger attitude is so widespread among legislators and regulatory agencies, in spite of a lack of any clear-cut, demonstrable evidence to support this position. The assumed benefits of bank mergers seem to be almost universally accepted as a fact of economic life.[10] Perhaps the main reason for this attitude (as well as the lack of legislative initiative and regulatory change) is the considerable power possessed by the banking industry in general and by some groups of bankers in particular.[11]

It is a recognized fact that bankers' associations can and do exert powerful influence on legislative matters pertaining to banking at both the national and the state levels. It is no secret that legislators at both levels have been subject to pressure from the lobbying activities of these groups.[12] It would be naïve to expect bankers' associations—which are composed of groups and individuals who, given an alternative, would prefer a "quiet life"—to be in favor of changes that would promote competition.[13] No doubt many individual bankers and their trade associations adhere to the belief that there is too much competition in the industry at the present. Indeed, in some banking markets, intense forms of nonprice competitive battles have been waged, involving advertising expenditures, fancy offices, credit card plans, and the like.[14]

In summary, it appears reasonable to conclude that despite the relatively large input in the form of studies of the commercial banking industry and the resulting proposals for change that would stimulate competition, the output, in the form of new legislation, has been disproportionately low.[15] The future holds little promise for improvement since legislative redistricting will result in increased power for the larger city bankers and hence pressure for liberalized branching and an accompanying increase in merger activity. Two interesting examples of recent changes in state laws are presented in the next section.

Some Recent Changes in State Branching Laws

Even prior to the Supreme Court decision pertaining to apportionment, liberalization of branching laws (or more liberal interpretations of them) had taken place in some states.[16] One recent, unsuccessful attempt to liberalize the branching laws was made in Illinois, a unit state, where a proposal was defeated during the 1965 legislative session. Even here, however, it is expected that renewed attempts to obtain such legislation will be made in the future.[17]

New York and Virginia have made important changes in their banking laws in recent years. I shall briefly outline the major changes in the banking laws of these states and then present the results of some statistical tests designed to measure the impact of these changes upon the performance of some of the banks located in these states.

New York Laws

In 1934, New York passed a law which divided the state into nine banking districts, a division which is still in effect. During the next quarter century, very few laws concerning banking institutions were passed by the State Legislature, and those which did pass were relatively insignificant. In 1960, however, the State Legislature passed the Omnibus Banking Act. This was the culmination of almost a decade of discussion and debate.

The main provisions of the 1960 Omnibus Banking Act, as it relates to commercial banks, are:

(1) *Branching Powers.* The law permits New York City commercial banks to have branches in counties surrounding the city which have a population of at least 700,000 people. At the present time, this includes Nassau and Westchester Counties. Likewise, Nassau and Westchester County commercial banks may open branches in New York City. A commercial bank in an incorporated village of 30,000 or more population is now allowed to open branches.

Previously this was not allowed unless the location was classified as a city.
(2) *Mergers.* The law provides for merger or purchase of assets of banking institutions involving New York City and Westchester or Nassau County banks. According to the new law, the size of the new bank must be taken into consideration in evaluating prospective mergers; if it is deemed that the bank is so big that it would hinder competition or could cause unsound banking, or if the merger is not in the public interest, then it should not be approved.
(3) *Holding Companies.* Until the passage of the Bank Holding Company Act of 1956, there was no legislation dealing with such companies in New York State. In 1957, a "freeze" was placed on all bank holding companies regarding both their expansion and their formation. With the passage of the Omnibus Banking Act of 1960, however, this freeze was lifted. The law provides for bank holding companies, but whenever a holding company has subsidiaries in two or more banking districts, it must have the approval of the State Banking Board.

In summary, it appears safe to conclude that the passage of the Omnibus Banking Act in New York State has provided a number of banks with new alternatives regarding their choice of methods of growth.

Virginia Laws

Prior to 1948, Virginia permitted branching of both types, that is, *de novo* branching and merger with, or acquisition of, another bank to be operated as a branch. A bank having a paid up and unimpaired capital and surplus of $50,000 or more could establish branches within the confines of the city, town, or village in which it was located. Banks could also open branches in cities with a population of 50,000 or more. Regarding merger and acquisition, banks could merge with or acquire other banks in the same or contiguous counties or banks located not more than twenty-five miles away. The merged or acquired banks could be operated as branches without regard to capitalization or population. Either type of branching was subject to the approval of the state regulatory authorities.

Only one bank took full advantage of these provisions, and yet this was enough to cause resistance; as Haymes and Phillips observed:

> Only one bank, the Bank of Virginia, took full advantage of the opportunity to expand into other cities. It opened branches not only in Richmond and the nearby city of Petersburg, but also in Norfolk, Newport News, Portsmouth, and Roanoke. Many smaller banks, concerned about the expansion of the Bank of Virginia, began to bring pressure to bear in the late 1940's for a revision of the law. The larger banks, other than the Bank of Virginia, appeared to be somewhat apathetic. The Bank of Virginia posed no threat to their existence. Nor were they taking advantage of the

opportunity to expand into other cities. Nevertheless, the pressure continued until in 1948 the law was amended to prohibit branching outside of the immediate area in which a bank was located.[18]

Thus, pressure from a particular subset of bankers led to the passage of the 1948 amendment (further amended in 1952), which prohibited a bank from branching outside its environs. The pressure for change continued, however, and those favoring the development of large banks through merger and branching pointed out the disadvantage of Virginia banks in competing for large loans. Haymes and Phillips stated their position as follows:

> The law effectively prevented all Virginia banks from competing for large loans with banks in the District of Columbia, Maryland, and North Carolina. Virginia had no cities of sufficient size to foster the development of banks as large as some of those in Washington and Baltimore, and the law prohibited the development of branch banking organizations as large as some of those in North Carolina.[19]

Arguments of this nature, coupled with the implication that large banks can stimulate economic development, led to changes in the banking laws which permitted the establishment of branches outside the immediate area of the bank. Branching in Virginia is now permitted anywhere in the state, but *only* by merger. This is an interesting development since it appears that the legislation was designed to gain the support (or at least diminish the resistance) of the smaller and rural bankers. The value of a bank charter (issued by the state in the public interest) has automatically increased since the only way an established bank can gain entry into a new area is to absorb an existing bank. This is a striking illustration of the type of legislative trade-offs which will result when powerful lobbyists and legislators team up to obtain specialized legislation.

The main provisions of the 1962 amendment as it applies to commercial banks are:

> (1) *Branching Powers.* A bank having paid-up and unimpaired capital and surplus of $50,000 or over may continue to establish *de novo* branches within the limits of the city, town, or county in which it is located. Branches may be established elsewhere by merger with banks located in any other county, city, or town.[20] Thus, *de novo* branches continue to be restricted to the immediate area of the existing bank; however, statewide branching is permitted, but *only* through merger.
>
> (2) *Mergers.* The 1962 amendment encourages mergers, since the only method of developing a statewide network of branches is through the merger route. As previously noted, a law of this type obviously places a premium upon the property of the existing bank charter holder.

> (3) *Holding Companies.* There have not been any restrictions upon bank holding companies operating in Virginia. Even prior to the 1962 amendment, it was possible to engage in statewide banking operations through the holding company device. As of September 15, 1963, there were four bank holding companies operating within the state, with a combined total of 144 banking offices and approximately $946 billion in deposits.

In the short span of time since its enactment, the 1962 amendment has generated a considerable amount of discussion. For example, regarding the problems of interpretation, Horvitz has commented: "Another example of a state law subject to diverse interpretation is that of Virginia. Virginia allows branching statewide if and only if the branch is acquired by merger. The question has been raised as to whether such procedural restrictions bind the Comptroller in his decisions or whether he is bound only by the geographical limitations of state law."[21]

Impact of Mergers on Bank Performance in New York and Virginia

It has been recognized that the changes discussed above in the state banking laws of New York and Virginia have had an impact upon banking structure and competition in these states. Governor Mitchell, in discussing Virginia, stated: "For example, in Virginia, a State where there has been a great deal of merger activity in the past three years (47), the preponderance of cases have involved the extension of service areas for banking institutions that are, under a recent State statute, becoming statewide in their operations."[22]

In an attempt to analyze the impact of the 1960 change in New York State laws in one area, Motter and Carson made a detailed case study of Nassau County.[23] Entry by New York City banks led to an increase in the total number of commercial banks operating in the county and to a reduction in the concentration of banking offices. The structure of commercial banking was changed significantly in the brief, three-year period following the change in branching laws; Motter and Carson stated:

> The number of commercial banks represented increased in 14 of the 16 submarkets and remained constant in the other two during 1961–63. . . . In six of the submarkets, there was an increase of three or more in the number of banks represented. The number of commercial banking offices increased in every submarket with the increase ranging from one to seven offices. . . . If variety in the size and scope of operations of banks represented leads to a "balanced" banking structure, Nassau County had such a structure by the beginning of 1964.[24]

It is clear that the recent changes in New York and Virginia laws were designed to have a major impact upon the branching and merging activities of the commercial banks in these states. The resulting changes in banking structure clearly have an impact upon banking performance. In observing the changes taking place in these states, Phillips expresses a common belief that the merging banks have become more efficient: ". . . the fairly rapid development of branch operations in the wake of legislative changes in states such as Virginia and New York, and the premiums paid for the acquisition of small banks, especially where *de novo* entry is barred, are evidence that, at least in some types of operations, branch banking is more efficient than is unit banking."[25]

Bank performance, however, is not a simple, unidimensional concept that can be defined and measured in operational terms, since there are a number of different groups interested in various aspects of banking activity. Furthermore, banking is a regulated industry, so that some of the conventional marketplace tests of business firms are not directly applicable. The purpose in this section and the section headed "Pros and Cons of Branching by Merger and *de Novo* Branching" is to attempt to measure the impact of bank merger and branching activity upon the various groups that have an interest in commercial bank expansion. In this section, the emphasis is on the impact of bank mergers upon the performance of two statewide samples of commercial banks.

Interested Groups

In the previous chapter, three groups were identified as primarily affected by commercial bank behavior: bank management, bank stockholders, and the public. Bankers, like their executive counterparts in other industries, clearly have a vital interest in the survival and growth of their firms. The holders of bank stocks, just like the holders of any corporate equities, will benefit if the increments in growth prove to be profitable. The public represents primarily the customers for the various types of banking services. At one extreme, lack of survival by banks can result in considerable financial losses or (at a minimum) serious inconvenience to some bank customers, especially the depositors. The public should also be interested in the growth of banks when this leads to improved services at lower costs. Thus, the interests of each group are not homogeneous and should be examined in more detail.

Management Interests For operational purposes, it is reasonable to identify some of the major interests of bank managers with the desire for growth of assets, deposits, loans, and number of employees.[26] Each of these dimensions of management-related growth represents an economic or a human resource over which bank managers have some degree of control. This control directly conveys a large amount of economic power to bankers, and it also indirectly results in their having a considerable amount of political and/or social power. Since the prestige and status of bankers generally increase with the relative size of the banks with which they are associated, such variables as assets and deposits, which generally are used to rank banks by size, are clearly important to managers.

The following variables are used to represent the primary interests of bank managers in the statistical results reported in this chapter:

(1) $Y^1 = 100\left(\frac{A_t - A_{t-1}}{A_{t-1}}\right)$ = the percentage change in total assets from time $t-1$ to time t

(2) $Y^2 = 100\left(\frac{D_t - D_{t-1}}{D_{t-1}}\right)$ = the percentage change in total deposits from time $t-1$ to time t

(3) $Y^3 = 100\left(\frac{L_t - L_{t-1}}{L_{t-1}}\right)$ = the percentage change in loans and discounts from time $t-1$ to time t

(4) $Y^4 = 100\left(\frac{E_t - E_{t-1}}{E_{t-1}}\right)$ = the percentage change in number of employees from time $t-1$ to time t

Stockholder Interests It seems reasonable to believe that most investors who buy bank stocks are interested in them primarily as a vehicle for financial returns rather than as a means of control. Thus, bank stockholders are interested mainly in the growth of the market value of their holdings. The growth in net operating earnings per share is also of direct interest, because earnings are both the source of dividends and the ultimate foundation of capital gains. Size of bank per se is not likely to be of direct relevance to the rational stockholder, since growth may or may not be accomplished in a profitable manner.

The variables used to represent the primary interests of bank stockholders in the statistical results reported here are:

(5) $Y^5 = 100\left(\frac{EPS_t - EPS_{t-1}}{EPS_{t-1}}\right)$ = the percentage change in net

operating earnings per share (adjusted for stock splits and stock dividends) from time $t-1$ to time t (this variable was included since none of the banks had negative earnings)

(6) $Y^6 = 100\left(\frac{MP_t - MP_{t-1}}{MP_{t-1}}\right)$ = the percentage change in market price per share of common stock (adjusted for stock splits and stock dividends) from time $t-1$ to time t

Public Interests Despite the fact that banking is a regulated industry, in most areas it is not regulated to the extent that local or regional banking monopolies have been created (as is usually the case with public utilities).[27] Thus, most bank customers have at least some degree of choice concerning which of several alternative banking institutions they will do business with. Therefore, a type of market success test can be used to measure, at least partially, the extent to which banks are able to serve the interests of the public. Banks that are doing a good job of satisfying the needs of their customers at reasonable prices will retain their present customers and also attract new customers from other institutions that are not doing as good a job in this respect. Thus, banks in the former category should exhibit more rapid growth in assets, deposits, and loans than banks in the latter category, *ceteris paribus.*

While this type of growth is somewhat analogous to some of the variables previously indicated as representing the interests of bank managers, there is an important distinction. To the extent that banks grow by means of mergers and acquisitions, the growth variables in assets, deposits, and loans, which serve best to reflect the extent to which these banks are serving the interests of the public, should relate to the whole set of banks which by the end of some period have been consolidated into a single bank, rather than to the single surviving bank. Thus, the public interest variables used in this research have been developed to measure the aggregate rate of expansion of those banks which have been brought together through merger. These variables, which presumably are positively associated with banking systems that are better able to serve customers' needs, are:

(7) $Y^7 = 100\left(\frac{A_t - A^*_{t-1}}{A^*_{t-1}}\right)$ = the percentage change in total assets

from time $t-1$ to time t for the entire network of banks which by time t have been combined into a single bank

(8) $Y^8 = 100\left(\frac{D_t - D^*_{t-1}}{D^*_{t-1}}\right)$ = the percentage change in total deposits from time $t-1$ to time t for the entire network of banks which by time t have been combined into a single bank

(9) $Y^9 = 100\left(\frac{L_t - L^*_{t-1}}{L^*_{t-1}}\right)$ = the percentage change in total loans from time $t-1$ to time t for the entire network of banks which by time t have been combined into a single bank

The Hypothesis Tested

In the study discussed in the previous chapter concerning the effects of bank mergers on the growth patterns displayed by large banks over a ten-year period, the following hypothesis was tested:

> Since the managers of commercial banks must always obtain approval of mergers prior to their consummation from the relevant regulatory authorities, and sometimes also from their stockholders as well, it is natural to presume that these merger proposals receive considerable attention by bank managers, by the various regulatory authorities, and, possibly also, by stockholders. Thus, the variables representing the interests of each of these groups should be positively associated both with the existence and the intensity of merger activity. Less formally stated, the hypothesis to be tested is that among large commercial banks, those which have engaged in approved mergers will display higher relative increases in all of the growth variables than those banks that have not used mergers as a method of growth.[28]

It was recognized, however, that there could be some potential conflicts of interest between managers and stockholders. If bank managers were motivated primarily by the desire for growth in assets, deposits, loans, and number of employees, they might sometimes employ means of achieving these objectives that lead to decreases in earnings per share and market price of common stock, i.e., that are against the best interests of bank stockholders. If this were commonplace, the variables representing the interests of stockholders (Y^5 and Y^6) would be negatively associated with mergers. To the extent that the interests of bank managers and stockholders are independent, rather than being conflicting or complementary, there would be no significant association between the stockholder interest variables and merger activity.

One of the reasons for undertaking the statistical tests reported in this chapter was to determine whether the conclusions previously reached about the effects of bank mergers on the performance and growth patterns of a nationwide sample of 165 large commercial banks would remain valid when considerably more homogeneous groups of banks were examined for relatively brief periods of time. The recent legislative changes in New York and Virginia served to unleash a flurry of bank merger activity in these states. Thus, it was possible to obtain a substantial sample of banks in these two states which merged in a relatively short time, as well as another sample of banks which did not merge during the same period.

In addition to providing additional evidence on the hypotheses presented in the previous chapter, analyzing the effects of bank mergers in New York and Virginia is one means of assessing some of the impact of these legislative changes. To the extent that different interest groups have benefited to greater or lesser degrees from this legislation, it may be possible to derive some judgments about the overall effects of these laws upon general economic well-being. In particular, since the effects of bank mergers and bank branching are in part separable and in part intermingled, the evidence presented here is one important part of the total evidence needed for these overall judgments. Furthermore, some guides to future possible legislative changes in other states may be derived from a careful statistical examination of the New York and Virginia experiences.

The Evidence

Data for a three-year period determined by the date of passage of the recent changes in banking legislation were obtained for samples of commercial banks in New York and Virginia. In particular, the triennium 1959–1961 was used for New York banks, and the triennium 1961–1963 was employed for Virginia banks. The samples consisted of all commercial banks in the respective states for which it was possible to obtain information concerning all the relevant variables.[29] In order to test the hypotheses, the average (i.e., arithmetic mean) values for all the growth variables were computed separately for those banks in each of the two which did engage in mergers during the study period and those banks which did not. These results are presented in Table 11.2.

TABLE 11.2 Effects of Merging on Growth of Banks in New York and Virginia

Variable	New York Banks			Virginia Banks		
	Not Merging	*Merging*	*F-ratio**	*Not Merging*	*Merging*	*F-ratio**
Management interest:						
Y^1—assets	19.5	40.0	*19.20*$^{(0.01)}$	5.6	42.7	*6.69*$^{(0.05)}$
Y^2—deposits	20.2	38.9	*14.63*$^{(0.01)}$	4.2	41.9	*6.60*$^{(0.05)}$
Y^3—loans	18.3	50.6	*23.84*$^{(0.01)}$	20.4	65.8	*5.74*$^{(0.05)}$
Y^4—no. of employees	6.9	25.1	*15.61*$^{(0.01)}$	13.2	52.1	*3.31*$^{(0.10)}$
Stockholder interest:						
Y^5—earnings per share	14.2	1.5	1.26	19.5	2.3	*4.03*$^{(0.10)}$
Y^6—market price	39.3	45.6	0.47	39.3	39.0	0.00
Public interest:						
Y^7—assets*	19.5	18.3	0.16	5.6	12.2	1.92
Y^8—deposits*	20.2	17.5	0.62	4.2	11.6	1.70
Y^9—loans*	18.3	25.9	2.47	20.4	31.2	1.85
Number of banks	35	11		4	7	

*The *F*-ratios shown for each variable are based on one-way analysis-of-variance tests of the significance of the observed differences in group means for that variable. The italicized *F*-ratios are those for which the probability is less than 0.10 that the observed differences in group means could be the result of chance; in these cases, the significance levels are shown in parentheses as superscripts to the *F*-ratios.

Source: Kalman J. Cohen and Samuel Richardson Reid, "Effects of Regulation, Branching, and Mergers on Banking Structure and Performance," *Southern Economic Journal,* vol. 34, no. 2, p. 241, October, 1967.

It appears that management interests have been well served by bank merger activity in both states. All four of the variables representing management interests are positively and significantly associated with merger activity in both New York and Virginia. That this association could have resulted from chance factors is unlikely, as the one-way analysis-of-variance tests indicate.

Stockholder interests do not appear to have been furthered by the bank mergers in New York and Virginia. In fact, earnings per share in Virginia are significantly and negatively associated with merger activity, perhaps indicating that there may well be a conflict of interest between managers and stockholders, at least in the short run. The minor differences between bank merger groups with respect to market price are not statistically significant.

The public interest variables fail to show any significant association with merger activity. Since mergers per se lead to a reduction in the number of banking alternatives available to customers, one could not make even a prima-facie case for bank mergers being in the public interest unless there were a significant positive association between the public interest variables (as we have defined them) and merger activity. Thus the statistical findings in New York and Virginia indicate that most bank customers, at least in the short run, have not benefited from bank expansion via the merger route.

The one-way analysis-of-variance tests that were employed implicitly assume that except for merger activity, there are no other omitted variables exerting *systematic* effects upon the dependent growth variables. With this in mind, a variety of additional tests were run holding constant such variables as population, counties or banking districts, asset size groups, etc. Furthermore, variants of all these tests were also run employing a logarithmic rate of growth rather than a percentage rate of growth as the dependent variable. Since the results in all cases are basically consistent with the results presented in Table 11.2 and already discussed, they are not reported here in any detail. The results of the above tests suggest that mergers do matter and that they may affect not only the structure of banking in a state but also the interests (as defined) of the various groups.[30]

Pros and Cons of Branching by Merger and *de Novo* Branching

Since more liberalization of branching restrictions is anticipated in the future, concern is naturally centered upon the method of branching to be employed. In the absence of restrictive bank merger legislation, it is likely that the merger alternative will receive considerable attention from bank managers. In most branching states (except, as noted above, in Virginia), the alternative to branching by merger is *de novo* branching. Banks that are making branching decisions with the objective of maximizing profits rather than maximizing deposits need an effective cost-benefit analysis to aid managerial decision making.[31] Some of the uncertainties that tend to complicate the branching decision are discussed below.

Types of Branching

The *de novo* method of branching provides an opportunity to construct modern facilities in a location which may be more convenient than that of the existing bank. The various costs (construction, personnel, etc.) are relatively easy to compute, and many banks have established branches in this way, particularly in areas where previously there was no banking facility. The decision becomes more complicated when a prospective branch is desired in an area where there is an existing banking operation. The acquisition of a going banking concern will not only speed entry into the area but also eliminate a competitor or potential competitor in the process. If the probabilities are high that a new banking charter will not be granted in the area by the regulatory authorities, the payment of a premium to the existing bank is rationalized on these grounds. The benefit to the acquiring bank's management of avoiding competition is deemed to justify the extra cost. The stockholders will not benefit from the premium paid, however, unless the elimination of a competitor results in sufficient additional earnings to compensate for the dilution effects of the premium. The effect upon the public is not so clear, depending upon the pricing and other policies of the branch bank substituted for the existing bank. There is some evidence (as discussed in the previous chapter) that in the majority of cases, the costs of important services, such as checking accounts, actually rise.[32] The loss of a possible banking alternative represents another cost to the public, the severity of which depends to a large degree on the existing level of bank concentration in the area.

The effects of mergers per se need not necessarily be the same as the effects of branching per se, since the *de novo* method of branching may also be utilized. Since both types of activities frequently occur at the same time, it is difficult separately to identify and measure their differential effects. Since this is an important aspect of the branching problem, however, an attempt was made to determine the relative impact of each alternative.

Results of Tests

As was pointed out above, in many discussions of the pros and cons of bank mergers, conclusions are frequently reached which are then purported to imply something about the desirability or undesirability of bank branching. One of the contentions in this study is that since these are two distinct types of activities that banks may undertake, it is important to try to discuss the benefits and costs of each separately. For this reason, the results of some statistical tests which were made on both a nationwide sample of commerical banks covering a ten-year period and a sample of banks in New York covering a three-year period will be reported and discussed.

In general, these tests show that when one attempts to distinguish carefully between the effects of mergers and the effects of branching on various bank growth variables, mergers are found to exert a much stronger impact upon bank performance than branching.

Nationwide Large Bank Sample In the study of the effects of mergers on a nationwide sample of large banks, reported in the previous chapter, one variable that was statistically held constant was state branching laws. The general nature of the conclusions reached has already been indicated in the section headed "Impact of Mergers on Bank Performance in New York and Virginia." A somewhat more refined version of the previous tests is presented in Table 11.3. Rather than consider only whether or not state laws permit banks to establish branches, the new test considers the actual rate of branching activity among banks as a possible explanatory variable for the observed differences in growth patterns. Clearly all those banks in the sample which are located in states that do not permit branching are in the "no change in branches" category. There are, however, also some banks in the "no change in branches" category located in states that do permit branching. Furthermore, those banks which increased their number of branches during the decade 1952–1962 have been divided into two groups: a "small change in branches" group, consisting of banks that added between one and nine branches during this period, and a "large change in branches" group, which includes those banks which added ten or more branches during this decade.

The dependent variables employed in the tests summarized in Table 11.3 are defined in logarithmic rather than relative change form.[33] The banks in the sample are also divided into three merger groups: those which did not merge at all, those which had one or two mergers, and those which had three or more mergers during this decade.

The results of the analysis-of-variance tests reported in Table 11.3 tend to confirm the conclusions already reached in the previous study of the effects of mergers on this nationwide sample of large banks. When intensity of branching activity is held constant, merger activity has a significant and positive association with each of the management interest variables.[34] When branching activity is held constant, the effects of mergers on the variables representing the interests of stockholders and the public are much less clear-cut. As was concluded in the previous study of the sample of large banks, it appears that managers promote bank mergers at least in part in the pursuit of their own self-interests, without this necessarily implying corresponding gains for bank stockholders or for the public.

In Table 11.4, the roles of branching activity and bank mergers have been reversed. Tables 11.3 and 11.4 both pertain to the same nationwide sample of large banks for the decade 1952–1962, but the one-way analysis-of-variance tests reported there are interpreted differently. Table 11.3 emphasizes the effects on bank growth of merger activity, holding branching activity constant. In contrast, Table 11.4 emphasizes the effects on bank growth of branching activity, holding merger activity constant.

The most striking property of Table 11.4 is that in contrast to the results of the analysis-of-variance tests reported earlier, no significant association at all is shown between the variables representing management interests and the alleged explanatory variable on which the test is focused. That is, when merger activity is held constant, there is no significant association evident between any of the management interest variables and intensity of branching activity. The general lack of significant association between the variables representing the interests of stockholders and the public and the alleged explanatory variable on which the test focuses is more consistent with the type of results previously obtained. Although in two cases the *F*-ratio between market price and branching activity is statistically significant, there does not appear to be a strong and consistent relationship here that can safely be inferred only from the data contained in Table 11.4.

When the results presented in Tables 11.3 and 11.4 are compared it appears that merger activity, rather than branching activity, is the more important explanation of the differences in the bank growth variables. There may well be strong interaction effects between mergers and branching that are not apparent from the tests reported here. Nonetheless, to the extent that one or the other of these forces appears to have a strong impact upon bank growth and performance, it would be mergers, and not branching.

The Sample of Banks in New York State Tests similar to those reported for the nationwide sample have also been performed on the sample of banks from New York State for the triennium 1959–1961.[35] The results shown in Table 11.5 tend to confirm (although primarily only for those banks experiencing a large increase in number of branches) the conclusions already reached about the effects of merger activity. In particular, bank mergers, whenever they have a strong impact, appear to promote management interests rather than the interests of either stockholders or the public.

While there are several significant *F*-ratios in Table 11.6, the effects of branching on bank growth appear to be less strong than the effects of

TABLE 11.3 Large Banks: Effects of Merging on Growth, Holding Branching Activity Constant

Variable	*No Increase in Branches*			*Small Increase in Branches (1–9)*				*Large Increase in Branches (10-plus)*			
	No Mergers	*1–2 Mergers*	F-*ratio**	*No Mergers*	*1–2 Mergers*	*3-plus Mergers*	F-*ratio**	*No Mergers*	*1–2 Mergers*	*3-plus Mergers*	F-*ratio**
Management interest:											
Z^1	15.1	25.0	*10.60*$^{(0.01)}$	14.1	21.7	26.7	*5.38*$^{(0.01)}$	19.8	26.3	33.9	*2.72*$^{(0.10)}$
Z^2	13.5	23.9	*10.33*$^{(0.01)}$	12.9	21.8	24.6	*3.97*$^{(0.05)}$	19.0	25.3	33.7	*2.82*$^{(0.10)}$
Z^3	28.7	39.1	*6.07*$^{(0.05)}$	31.0	41.7	41.3	*3.16*$^{(0.05)}$	21.0	43.5	47.0	*3.15*$^{(0.05)}$
Z^4	13.3	25.8	*14.57*$^{(0.01)}$	14.5	23.8	29.0	*2.45*$^{(0.10)}$	18.7	28.2	33.5	2.14
Stockholder interest:											
Z^5	30.4	23.2	1.40	21.8	20.3	19.0	0.14	30.4	14.8	16.5	1.81
Z^6	44.9	44.8	0.00	36.9	40.6	30.8	1.54	60.4	34.9	40.9	*5.76*$^{(0.01)}$
Public interest:											
Z^7	15.1	12.0	1.21	14.1	16.2	13.6	0.38	19.8	14.9	17.9	0.80
Z^8	13.5	10.8	0.88	12.9	15.1	13.0	0.30	19.0	14.1	16.1	0.70
Z^9	28.7	27.0	0.18	31.0	35.5	28.5	1.22	21.0	30.8	31.1	0.99

* The *F*-ratios shown for each variable are based on one-way analysis-of-variance tests of the significance of the observed differences in group means for that variable. The italicized *F*-ratios are those for which the probability is less than 0.10 that the observed differences in group means could be the result of chance; in these cases, the significance levels are shown in parentheses as superscripts to the *F*-ratios.

Source: Kalman J. Cohen and Samuel Richardson Reid, "Effects of Regulation, Branching, and Mergers on Banking Structure and Performance," *Southern Economic Journal*, vol. 34, no. 2, p. 243, October, 1967

TABLE 11.4 Large Banks: Effects of Branching on Growth, Holding Merger Activity Constant

Variable	*No Increase in Branches*	*Small Increase in Branches (1–9)*	*Large Increase in Branches (10-plus)*	F-*ratio**	*No Increase in Branches*	*Small Increase in Branches (1–9)*	*Large Increase in Branches (10-plus)*	F-*ratio**	*Small Increase in Branches (1–9)*	*Large Increase in Branches (10-plus)*	F-*ratio**
Management interest:											
Z^1	15.1	14.1	19.8	1.26	25.0	21.7	26.3	0.96	26.7	33.9	1.45
Z^2	13.5	12.9	19.0	1.41	23.9	21.8	25.3	0.40	24.6	33.7	2.06
Z^3	28.7	31.0	21.0	0.89	39.1	41.7	43.5	0.31	41.3	47.0	0.52
Z^4	13.3	14.5	18.7	0.66	25.8	23.8	28.2	0.34	29.0	33.5	0.55
Stockholder interest:											
Z^5	30.4	21.8	30.4	2.05	23.2	20.3	14.8	1.22	19.0	16.5	0.14
Z^6	44.9	36.9	60.4	*4.54*$^{(0.05)}$	44.8	40.6	34.9	1.53	30.8	40.9	*3.84*$^{(0.10)}$
Public interest:											
Z^7	15.1	14.1	19.8	1.26	12.0	16.2	14.9	0.71	13.6	17.4	1.36
Z^8	13.5	12.9	19.0	1.41	10.8	15.1	14.1	0.71	13.0	16.1	0.87
Z^9	28.7	31.0	21.0	0.89	27.0	35.5	30.8	1.71	28.5	31.1	0.30
Number of banks	25	18	6		13	31	21		11	40	

* The *F*-ratios shown for each variable are based on one-way analysis-of-variance tests of the significance of the observed differences in group means for that variable. The italicized *F*-ratios are those for which the probability is less than 0.10 that the observed differences in group means could be the result of chance; in these cases, the significance levels are shown in parentheses as superscripts to the *F*-ratios.

Source: Kalman J. Cohen and Samuel Richardson Reid, "Effects of Regulation, Branching, and Mergers on Banking Structure and Performance," *Southern Economic Journal*, vol. 34, no. 2, p. 244, October, 1967.

TABLE 11.5 New York Banks: Effects of Branching on Growth, Holding Merger Activity Constant

Variable	*Not Merging*				*Merging*		
	No Increase in Branches	*Small Increase in Branches*	*Large Increase in Branches*	F-*ratio**	*Small Increase in Branches*	*Large Increase in Branches*	F-*ratio**
Management interest:							
Z^1	7.1	8.1	8.8	0.61	10.1	17.4	*3.87*$^{(0.10)}$
Z^2	7.4	8.4	8.5	0.32	9.9	17.0	*3.58*$^{(0.10)}$
Z^3	7.3	7.0	6.4	0.06	12.0	20.8	2.64
Z^4	2.3	2.8	4.4	0.37	4.8	12.9	*4.38*$^{(0.10)}$
Stockholder interest:							
Z^5	5.0	3.2	4.1	0.10	2.2	−1.9	0.61
Z^6	14.6	12.2	13.6	0.33	20.6	10.9	*3.61*$^{(0.10)}$
Public interest:							
Z^7	7.1	8.1	8.8	0.61	7.5	7.0	0.11
Z^8	7.4	8.4	8.5	0.32	7.3	6.7	0.14
Z^9	7.3	7.0	6.4	0.06	8.9	10.1	0.08
Number of banks	20	11	4		5	6	

* The *F*-ratios shown for each variable are based on one-way analysis-of-variance tests of the significance of the observed differences in group means for that variable. The italicized *F*-ratios are those for which the probability is less than 0.10 that the observed differences in group means could be the result of chance; in these cases, the significance levels are shown in parentheses as superscripts to the *F*-ratios.

Source: Kalman J. Cohen and Samuel Richardson Reid, "Effects of Regulation, Branching, and Mergers on Banking Structure and Performance," *Southern Economic Journal*, vol. 34, no. 2, p. 247, October, 1967.

TABLE 11.6 New York Banks: Effects of Merging on Growth, Holding Branching Activity Constant

	No Increase in Branches	*Small Increase in Branches*			*Large Increase in Branches*		
Variable	*Not Merging*	*Not Merging*	*Merging*	F-*ratio**	*Not Merging*	*Merging*	F-*ratio**
Management interest:							
Z^1	7.1	8.1	10.1	0.76	8.8	17.4	*6.47*$^{(0.05)}$
Z^2	7.4	8.4	9.9	0.44	8.5	17.0	*6.50*$^{(0.05)}$
Z^3	7.3	7.0	12.0	2.56	6.4	20.8	*9.26*$^{(0.05)}$
Z^4	2.3	2.8	4.8	0.54	4.4	12.9	*12.47*$^{(0.01)}$
Stockholder interest:							
Z^5	5.0	3.2	2.2	0.08	4.1	–1.9	1.06
Z^6	14.6	12.2	20.6	2.11	13.6	10.9	0.56
Public interest:							
Z^7	7.1	8.1	7.5	0.11	8.8	7.0	1.67
Z^8	7.4	8.4	7.3	0.40	8.5	6.7	1.93
Z^9	7.3	7.0	8.9	0.51	6.4	10.1	1.02
Number of banks	20	11	5		4	6	

* The *F*-ratios shown for each variable are based on one-way analysis-of-variance tests of the significance of the observed differences in group means for that variable. The italicized *F*-ratios are those for which the probability is less than 0.10 that the observed differences in group means could be the result of chance; in these cases, the significance levels are shown in parentheses as superscripts to the *F*-ratios.

Source: Kalman J. Cohen and Samuel Richardson Reid, "Effects of Regulation, Branching, and Mergers on Banking Structure and Performance," *Southern Economic Journal,* vol. 34, no. 2, p. 246, October, 1967.

mergers on bank growth as shown in Table 11.5.[36] Again, one would suspect that interaction effects must be present, although not explicitly isolated, in these one-way analysis-of-variance tests.

Summary

Since the probabilities are high that branch banking laws will be liberalized in the future, the *type* of branching legislation to be considered in a state becomes an extremely important question. It has been demonstrated that the merger alternative of branching not only may have a significant impact upon the performance of banks but also may result in a grossly uneven distribution of benefits to the interested groups. The welfare of special interest groups should naturally be subordinate to the public interest.

A unique opportunity exists for action at the state and local levels which seldom presents itself in a period of growing central government. The role that a state can play in determining its future banking structure has not been sufficiently recognized.

Ideally, the citizens of a state should have a more direct voice in the type of banking laws that are passed in that state. The chances that they will have such a direct voice, however, are slim, since the various bank trade associations undertake extensive lobbying activities. In the absence of the direct voting privilege, state legislators who are concerned about the optimum banking structure in their state should give serious consideration to the various feasible alternatives. These subjects will be discussed in more detail in Chapter 13.

The empirical tests reported in the last four chapters are the most extensive statistical tests ever undertaken on the relative performance of merging and nonmerging commercial banks and industrial firms. These tests were also the first to utilize statistical significance levels in merger research and are therefore the strongest statistical tests which have been applied to the merger problem. As the data concerning mergers improve in the future, other strong statistical tests can be applied. It is interesting to note that recent (as yet unpublished) research utilizing different time periods continues to confirm the pattern of results reported here.

NOTES

[1] This chapter is based on an article Kalman J. Cohen of Carnegie-Mellon University and I coauthored, entitled "Effects of Regulation, Branching, and Mergers on Banking Structure and Performance," *Southern Economic*

Journal, vol. 34, no. 2, pp. 231–249, October, 1967. This study was supported by funds provided by the National Science Foundation, the Ford Foundation, and Carnegie's Graduate School of Industrial Administration.

[2] The number of banking offices is not shown in Table 11.1 since the concern is with independent decision-making units rather than banking offices. The number of banking offices increased in the branching states during this period, as would be expected. It should be recognized that there is a difference between growth in the number of independent decision-making units and in the number of banking offices.

[3] This situation continued in subsequent years, as reported by the Comptroller of the Currency in 1964 in his annual report: "The volume of new chartering was strongly influenced by the prevailing branch laws. Of the 826 banks chartered in 1962–1964, 59 percent were in the 16 unit banking states, 22 percent in the 17 limited branching states, and 19 percent in the 17 statewide branching states and the District of Columbia." The largest population gains during this period were recorded in the branching states, since many of these states are in the western portion of the country. One important barrier to new entry in these states has to do with the location problem. Existing banks can open branches in new market areas and subsidize them (if necessary) until the area chosen reaches the scale that would be necessary to justify a new banking entrant.

[4] As stated previously, the concern is with independent decision-making units. When one bank acquires another bank in a branching state, the acquired bank is usually retained as a branch of the acquiring bank. The loss is not in the number of banking offices but in the number of independent banks.

[5] This was recognized by A. Dale Tussing in his article "Stimulating Bank Competition: Comment," *Journal of Finance*, vol. 20, no. 4, p. 691, December, 1965: commented: "It is worth noting that, within any given state, there is likely to be conflict among bankers themselves over banking law, particularly with respect to branching. Large metropolitan-based banks are likely to favor fewer restrictions on branching, i.e., on their own entry into presently protected markets; for obvious reasons, small-city, town, and rural bankers are likely to oppose active branching, or any other change which would permit entry into 'their' markets."

[6] It is interesting to note that only one state, Missouri, has ever had a direct vote by its citizens on matters affecting bank structure. Some of the largest banks in St. Louis and Kansas City that wanted to expand through branching (which had been prohibited in Missouri since 1899) decided that putting the branch bank question on the ballot in the November, 1958, election was worth the time, trouble, and expense involved. In the election campaign, both sides used all possible means of disseminating information and persuading the public. The result of the referendum was that 677,539 Missourians voted against branch banking, while only 287,931 voted for it. Every city (including St. Louis and Kansas City, where, according to the branch banking advocates, there was such a great demand for branching) and county in the state voted against the referendum. See Committee on Banking and Currency, *Conflict of Federal and State Banking Laws*, 88th Cong., 1st Sess., 1963, p. 78.

[7] After this chapter was initially written, the *Chicago Tribune* reported that a bill is to be introduced in the Illinois State Legislature which would permit

Illinois voters to decide whether or not to permit branch banking on a countywide basis. If approved by the Legislature, the issue will be decided at the next general election in November, 1968. Spearheading the drive for passage of the bill is the Illinois Council for Branch Banking, which represents 103 banks—mainly large-city banks—with about 48 percent of total deposits in the state. The main opposition is coming from the Illinois Bankers Association, which lists 1,050 banks as members. A spokesman for this group stated that only about 8 percent of the membership favor branch banking, a small percentage is neutral, and "the overwhelming majority are strongly opposed." See "Branch Banking Pro, Con Aired," *Chicago Tribune,* Apr. 8, 1967, p. 11.

[8] For example, see Advisory Committee on Banking to the Comptroller of the Currency, *National Bank and the Future,* 1963; Committee on Financial Institutions, *Report to the President of the United States,* 1963; Comptroller of the Currency, *Studies in Banking Competition and the Banking Structure,* 1966; and Board of Governors of the Federal Reserve System, "Research into Banking Structure and Competition," *Federal Reserve Bulletin,* November, 1964, pp. 1383–1399.

[9] In fact, the only major legislation to pass Congress since the initiation of the various studies is designed primarily to decrease the impact of applying the antitrust laws to bank mergers. Public Law 89-356, amending the Bank Merger Act of 1960, was signed by President Johnson on Feb. 21, 1966. This new legislation permits the responsible agency to approve a proposed merger "whose effect in any section of the country may be to substantially lessen competition, or to tend to create a monopoly, or which in any other manner would be in restraint of trade," but only where it finds that the "anticompetitive effects of the proposed transaction are clearly outweighed in the public interest by the probable effect of the transaction in meeting the convenience and needs of the community to be served." The Attorney General now has only thirty days after the approval of a merger in which to institute an action under the antitrust laws.

[10] Under present regulatory procedures, there is no provision for postmerger audits concerning the resulting performance and effects of approved mergers.

[11] Phillips recognized this when he observed: "Commercial banking, as other industries, has its trade associations—local, regional, state and nationwide bankers associations. These associations undoubtedly perform valuable information and educational services. They also provide a forum for communication among bankers and an opportunity for those high in the organizational hierarchy—the leaders of the industry—to make known their views on sundry subjects. . . . When problems arise, established channels of communication are available. And communication, especially when it comes from those at the top of a power hierarchy, tends to facilitate conflict resolution. Perhaps a great deal should not be made of this, but competition is a form of conflict, and in the present context, conflict resolution is a form of restraint on competition. If nothing more, the communication makes it easier to know what is expected of a 'good' banker; easier to conform to 'sound' banking practice." See Almarin Phillips, "Competition, Confusion, and Commerical Banking," *Journal of Finance,* vol. 19, no. 1, p. 42, March, 1964.

[12] It is also widely recognized that the public does not have this type of direct influence, particularly on specialized matters such as banking.

[13] Perhaps this is an inevitable cost in a regulated industry which possesses some of the characteristics of public utilities. Phillips (*op. cit.*, p. 43) has observed: "Good banking practices are equated with 'quiet' non-price forms of rivalry in the view of both bankers and the regulatory agencies."

The following statement appeared in a booklet distributed by the American Bankers Association designed to help promote the legislation recently passed by Congress: "The antitrust laws were passed to make sure that competition in business and industry would not be eliminated by a few giant concerns in any particular field. These laws have helped the United States develop the most competitive economy in the world. But highly regulated industries *are* different." See *Bank Mergers: A Chaotic Situation*, New York: American Bankers Association, April, 1965.

[14] Phillips (*op. cit.*, p. 33) has observed: "Bankers, as is true of other businessmen, will not be persuaded by the academic scribbler who charges that competition does not prevail. For to them—understandably—competition appears primarily as rivalry with other banks and financial institutions and in concern over profits, market shares, and growth. The relationship between competition and efficient resource allocation is not their concern."

[15] The output is actually less than zero, being negative if we include the 1966 bank merger bill. This bill is designed to curb the power of the Antitrust Division to challenge bank mergers. Since the passage of the last major banking legislation by Congress, the Bank Merger Act of 1960, the majority of the mergers approved by the bank regulatory agencies have been opposed (although not necessarily challenged in court actions) by the Antitrust Division. The regulatory agencies' approvals have been binding except in the relatively few cases taken to court by the Department of Justice. The 1966 bill exempted some of these mergers from the antitrust laws, despite the fact that the courts have held them to be in violation of these laws.

[16] For example, branching was forbidden in New Hampshire by regulation until October, 1963. Since that date, branching has been allowed in New Hampshire generally within a specified radius of the head office—fifteen miles for new branches and thirty miles for mergers. Since New Hampshire has few urbanized areas, the law has not as yet resulted in any significant structural changes.

[17] The branching question was not included in the November, 1966, election in Illinois; however, a provision to change the regulatory process did pass by a narrow margin. This provision (which was widely misunderstood by the voters) in effect allows the state banks partially to regulate themselves. The regulatory process will be turned over to an eleven-member commission consisting of seven bankers and four representatives of the public.

[18] Harmon H. Haymes and Charles F. Phillips, Jr., "Banking in Virginia: The 1962 Legislation," *Washington and Lee Review*, vol. 21, no. 1, p. 55, Spring, 1964.

[19] *Ibid.* These authors also point out (p. 57) that despite restrictions, ". . . Virginia's banking structure underwent changes in the 1953–62 period. There were 17 banks organized in the state and 40 mergers and absorptions, resulting in a net decrease of 23 banks."

[20] See *The Virginia Banking Act and Related Statutes*, Charlottesville, Va.: The Michin Co., 1964, p. 13.

[21] Paul M. Horvitz, "Stimulating Bank Competition through Regulatory Action," *Journal of Finance*, vol. 20, no. 1, p. 5, March, 1965.

[22] George W. Mitchell, "Protecting the Public Interest in Bank Mergers,"

unpublished remarks at the annual convention of the Pennsylvania Bankers Association, Atlantic City, N.J., May 24, 1965.

[23] David C. Motter and Deane E. Carson, "Bank Entry and the Public Interest: A Case Study," *National Banking Review,* vol. 1, no. 4, pp. 469–512, June, 1964. In discussing the change in the New York State laws, Motter and Carson (p. 469) stated: "In effect, the act created a unique laboratory in which to examine the effects on banks and bank customers of a major facility expansion occurring in a relatively short period of time."

[24] *Ibid.,* p. 490.

[25] Phillips, *op. cit.,* p. 36.

[26] This was discussed in more detail in the previous chapter.

[27] While bank regulation is not designed primarily to create local bank monopolies, it is unfortunately true that they have developed in some communities. The relevant considerations will be discussed in greater detail below.

[28] Kalman J. Cohen and Samuel Richardson Reid, "The Benefits and Costs of Bank Mergers," *Journal of Financial Quantitative Analysis,* vol. 1, no. 4, pp. 27–28, December, 1966.

[29] *Moody's Bank and Finance Manual* was the primary data source. Some additional data regarding Virginia banks were supplied by the Research Department of the Federal Reserve Bank of Richmond.

[30] One could argue that a single triennium is a very short period of time for the effects of a merger to work themselves out in the market since banking markets contain varieties of imperfections and customers may not shift from bank to bank easily. However, acquiring firms usually have the *time* advantage; that is, they can take over a "going concern" and achieve accelerated market penetration. The timing of returns is also important to bank stockholders since money has a time value.

[31] For a *normative* prescription of one form that such cost-benefit analysis might take, see Eugene E. Carter and Kalman J. Cohen, "The Use of Simulation in Selecting Branch Banks," *Industrial Management Review,* vol. 8, no. 2, pp. 55–69, Spring, 1967.

[32] One must remember that the *only* unique service that banks offer is demand deposits (checking accounts). It is hoped that in the future, the legislative and regulatory agencies will give this fact more recognition in their decision-making functions.

[33] That is, each dependent variable in Table 11.3, Z^i, is defined as $Z^i = \log (1 Y^i)$, where the corresponding variable Y^i was defined in the section headed "Impact of Mergers on Bank Performance in New York and Virginia." The statistical reasons for considering this logarithmic form of the dependent variable were referred to in the previous chapter.

[34] The only minor exception is that the association between growth in the number of employees (Z^4) and merger activity, while positive, is not quite statistically significant at the 0.1 percent level.

[35] Because the sample of banks from Virginia on which adequate data could be obtained was already small, no attempt was made to subdivide Virginia banks into groups reflecting intensity of branching activity.

[36] In order to make the strongest possible case for the significance of branching activity as an explanatory variable for bank growth patterns, the logarithmic form, rather than the percentage change form, of the dependent variable was employed in the tests summarized in Tables 11.5 and 11.6.

Part Three

Public Policy Considerations

12

Industrial Structure and Performance and Public Policies

Public policy recommendations related to merger activity are naturally based upon certain assumptions. The main assumption underlying the recommendations presented and discussed in this chapter is that the United States wishes to encourage and promote a capitalist, competitive, private enterprise system. The validity of this assumption may be questioned in light of economic developments in this country during the past century. One must admit that it certainly would be most interesting to witness an *actual* application of a competitive, private enterprise system in this country instead of reading about it in textbooks and/or hearing about it from businessmen and bureaucrats at chamber of commerce luncheons or trade association meetings.

It is obvious from an examination of the current merger movement in the United States that there is a need for a refurbished public policy concerning these economic events. The growing evidence emanating from various research studies also suggests that certain forms of reform or renewal in the business and government establishments would be a refreshing development in capitalism. Other large institutions and organizations in the world have discovered that renewal is a necessary condition for vitality and relevance in modern times. Big business and big government are subject to the same sort of fundamental bureaucratic hang-ups and these are not going to be solved by new technological innovations. Changes which affect the economic and legal environments are more fundamental to a renewal in the capitalist system, and the public policy recommendations presented here are designed for this purpose.

The Economic Environment

A fundamental aspect of any program which is designed to renew capitalism is that related to the merger problem. A nation that adheres to democratic principles and regularly affirms its belief in a private enterprise economic system should be particularly interested in the merger phenomenon. The reason for this should be obvious—these economic events influence the structure and performance of American industry. It is becoming increasingly apparent that we can no longer cling to an outdated "security blanket" known as the antitrust laws as the sole answer to the merger problem. Nor can we turn our heads and hope the problem will disappear, or take solace in outdated research results which minimized the problem in the past. Times and conditions have changed, which calls for an awareness of fundamental changes that have occurred in the economy. Let us begin by discussing one of these changes.

Mergers and Prosperity

Advancements in economic theory and implementations in monetary and fiscal policy have given added stature and increased confidence to both the so-called new economics school and the more traditional "monetary" school of economists. Both of these groups have made important contributions toward helping this country minimize problems related to business cycle developments. However, they have also omitted a significant variable in the construction of their various models—*mergers* and the resulting impact these economic events have upon the structure of the economy.

If we accept the proposition that government-promoted prosperity (aided by the utilization of monetary and fiscal policy) can continue, with minor readjustments, into the foreseeable future, the linkage of merger activity with prosperity assumes greater importance.[1] Economists and government officials are helping to create the basic economic environment necessary for increased merger activity without being aware of the ramifications of their policy recommendations in terms of the structure of the economy. Recognition of this fact by economists and government officials would be a healthy beginning in any program designed to lead to an eventual deconcentration of business power centers and an improved market structure in this capitalist economy.

Immediate Structure Changes

There are two separate proposals which could contribute toward a goal of deconcentrated industry in a minimum of time and (in my opinion) with a minimum of cost. Perhaps at this point it would be well to caution the reader that many circles will consider these proposals radical and extreme. Much depends upon one's value judgments concerning the urgency of a return toward a private enterprise economic system. In my opinion, it is more fruitful to devote efforts to promoting deconcentration of industry than to debating about whether concentration per se (no matter how it is measured) is increasing slightly, decreasing slightly, or remaining unchanged over time.

The time has come for the burden of proof to be shifted to the proponents of concentration and of mergers: They should begin to demonstrate empirically the benefits which they "assume" to exist. Case studies and subjective opinions should be replaced by insights gained from significant statistical studies. If all segments of the public (rather than special interest groups) are to benefit increasingly from government-encouraged and government-promoted prosperity, bold and imaginative steps will have to be taken. Two proposals which merit consideration because they could speed the deconcentration process are concerned with corporate investment activity.

Corporate Divestiture Several years ago, special interest groups and congressional power blocs successfully teamed to prevent the FTC from conducting its proposed "1,000-firm" study. One of the purposes of that proposed study was to reveal the extent of ownership by this group of large firms in other business enterprises. A proposal should be introduced in Congress which would authorize this study, and the results should be made known to the public.

Coupled with the above proposal, a pragmatic approach should be taken to the problem of firms buying into other firms and obtaining various degrees of control. Legislation should be designed to curb this type of spending behavior by large firms. The demonstrated benefit of this type of behavior is lacking, and the costs to the public appear high. It would be relatively easy to curb this nonessential business practice and at the same time require firms with stock ownership in other firms to dispose of their holdings within a specified period of time. The method of disposition could be chosen by the stockholders of the firm owning the stock. Perhaps the best method of divestiture would be to have these firms distribute the stock to their owners in the form of a special stock dividend.

The General Motors–du Pont case affords a prime example of the corporate ties which can result from corporate ownership of this type. The Supreme Court exposed the anticompetitive potential of this type of relationship. It was discovered that du Pont attained its position as a supplier of finishes and fabrics to GM only after it had accumulated a substantial amount of GM stock and one of its directors had become a member of the GM board. In addition, a former du Pont sales manager was appointed as a GM vice-president. Practices of this type (which promote interlocking directorates and management intercourse) are difficult to justify in an economy and a society in which collusive practices are supposedly looked at askance and in which, at least in principle, there is a belief in a competitive economy. The Court concluded in the du Pont–GM case that the acquisition had made it difficult, if not impossible, for other companies to sell substantial quantities of automotive finishes or fabrics to GM and that therefore, over the years, the acquisition had resulted in a substantial lessening of competitive opportunities for such firms. Consequently, the Court ordered du Pont to dispose of its GM stock holdings, which it did with a minimum of disruption in the stock market, if any at all.

The principle here is clear: Whenever one firm acquires a portion of ownership in another firm, it gains an element of control (or the threat of potential control is created) which can influence the behavior of the management groups concerned. It is difficult to ascertain any potential or realized benefits to the public of investment practices of this type.

Corporate Celibacy Easily the most severe, and yet the most fundamental, recommendation which can be made regarding mergers by large publicly held firms is that they be eliminated, except in the infrequent "failing firm" case. In advocating large-firm corporate celibacy, one must be aware of the importance of the problem as well as the severity of the proposal. Regarding the problem, it is rather obvious that large industrial firms play a significant role in the reported merger activity. A glance at the data presented in Table 12.1 should convince

TABLE 12.1 Acquisitions by 500 Largest Industrial Firms— Distribution by Size of Group Ranked by Sales Size, 1951–1961

Industrial Firms			
Groups of 50		*Groups of 100*	
Rank	*Number*	*Rank*	*Number*
Total	3,404	Total	3,404
Largest 50	471		
		Largest 100	884
Next 50	413		
Next 50	746		
		Next 100	1,059
Next 50	313		
Next 50	320		
		Next 100	577
Next 50	257		
Next 50	250		
		Next 100	453
Next 50	203		
Next 50	237		
		Next 100	431
Next 50	194		

Source: Select Committee on Small Business, House of Representatives, *Mergers and Superconcentration: Acquisitions of 500 Largest Industrial and 50 Largest Merchandising Firms,* 87th Cong., 2d Sess., 1962.

even the most skeptical person that large firms play a dominant role in merger waves.

Continued prosperity will add to the dominance of this group since these large publicly held firms become the major component on the demand side in the market for capital assets. A proposal for large-firm corporate celibacy must include methods for substitution (as well as improvement) in the market for capital assets.

The major cost of a corporate celibacy policy would arise from the curtailment of a growth and investment alternative for large firms. Certainly the elimination of any alternative must be considered a cost and must be examined extremely carefully in relation to the expected benefits. Perhaps the cost is not so high; certainly the numerous empirical tests reported in this book suggest that the internal growth alternative may well be of more benefit to the firm, and especially to the stockholders. Investment expenditures for pure internal growth add new productive capacity to the firm, to the industry (where the investment is made), and to our aggregate productive capacity. The productivity advantages of new technological developments would be promoted, and ultimately it is this productivity increase (per man-hour of labor) which plays such an important role in the economy.

If large firms do not wish to add or replace productive capacity (in either their basic line of activity or other areas), they are free to follow other alternatives such as increasing dividends, retiring debt, or purchasing their *own* securities in the market. After a careful evaluation of the projected impact of a policy of corporate celibacy, I have concluded that the benefits to the economy from such a policy would justify the relatively minor cost of the curtailment of one of several investment alternatives available to a few hundred large firms. The thinking should be in terms of gains of varying magnitude to over two hundred million people, rather than in terms of the personal gains to a group of top professional managers (a group which could be accommodated in most hotel ballrooms). If it is demonstrated that an antimerger law of this type is too restrictive, it can easily be amended. It seems ironic that we have never had an *effective* pro-competitive (or antimerger) law and so have not been able to determine its effectiveness in a capitalist economy. A lesson can be learned from the economies which have admitted some weaknesses in their system and have demonstrated a willingness to experiment. A renewed and progressive American capitalism would be an outstanding example to the capitalist economies as well as to those nations which have not as yet decided which system is superior.

Improved Market for Capital Assets

The major component of demand in the capital assets market is the large firms. If large-firm corporate celibacy regarding mergers and acquisitions is advocated, methods should be found to improve the market for "firms" wishing to sell. One necessary step is to identify and cultivate groups of owner-managers (entrepreneurs), as well as groups of potential owners or managers who could become an effective element of demand in the purchase of firms. Discussion related to each of these possibilities follows.

Increased Entrepreneurialship One important aspect of a corporate renewal program would be the encouragement and development of new entrepreneurs in our society. The younger generation has exhibited a strong desire for, and belief in, independence. Opportunities should be found for young people, particularly those who are willing to be innovators and risk takers. In addition, there are numerous experienced executives wasting away in the middle and upper ranks of management in large bureaucratic industrial firms. The point is that a potential pool of prospective entrepreneurs exists and should be recognized. The recognition should take the form of special educational and financial assistance.

The vast majority of our graduate schools of business are educating and training young men in programs designed to produce future corporate bureaucrats. There are no institutions designed specifically to meet the need for entrepreneurs, and consideration should be given to establishing such schools. Criteria for judging potential entrepreneurial talent should be determined and selections made on the basis of these criteria, which may well be quite different from standard entrance requirements in graduate schools of business. Entrepreneurial training could be conducted on the undergraduate level also; the important point is not so much at what level it should be offered, but that it should be made available.

Perhaps the most important aspect of this problem of increasing entrepreneurial opportunity involves the creation and development of a private or government insurance program to aid in the purchase of capital assets. This program would be an integral part of a program designed to improve the market for capital assets. The objective is to accomplish in the business community what the FHA has accomplished in the housing area. When a firm is up for sale, executives desiring to own and manage a firm of their own could apply for low-cost, federally backed loans made by private financial institutions.

As an aid to these independent entrepreneurs, a pool of seasoned and mature retired executives could be enlisted to serve as board members and consultants—particularly during the early, critical years of entrepreneurship. Government contracts for a variety of goods and services could be awarded to these firms on a priority basis. When appraising a proposal of this nature, it must be remembered that it will involve some costs; however, if this nation sincerely wishes to create a vigorous and more competitive environment with increased opportunity for the individual, the benefits to be derived should more than justify the expenditures.

A program of federally insured loans for the purchase of businesses is just one step toward an eventually deconcentrated industry. It is a humble beginning—but it would be a beginning. Many small and medium-size firms are swallowed up by large firms simply because of the lack of buyers for these firms. In addition, the tax laws are a stimulant to an exchange of shares, which gives an advantage in many cases to the larger firms. In this important area of fiscal policy, Congress should alter the tax laws to stimulate and encourage the development of entrepreneurs and alter or close many of the loopholes which favor the corporate bureaucrats in large publicly held firms.

Ownership Groups Institutions and individuals who do not desire a managerial role but who can provide equity capital could be enlisted and encouraged by a variety of methods. Tax laws can be made that would encourage investments of this type by individuals and institutions, and new proposals toward this end will be suggested below.

Management Talent Another vital and important part of a plan to improve the market for capital assets and eventually to lead to a deconcentration of industry involves the need to increase executive mobility. Action in this area is long overdue, and it is surprising that academic economists have been so silent on this aspect of the manpower market, particularly since many of them are personally familiar with the advantages of full vesting and full funding of their retirement benefits. One major factor the fact that executives lose retirement and other benefits when they change jobs operates strongly against increased executive mobility. While it may not be an important consideration among younger men, experienced executives, in the prime years of their life, are hampered in their personal decision making by this tangible loss of benefits.

Most large firms specially design their benefit programs to *prevent* the movement of managerial talent, "movement" meaning the changing of firms and not the upheaval of the executives' households, since many management men are regularly on the move to places assigned by the firm (a situation similar to that in the military in many respects).

The recommendation concerning full vesting and full funding of executive pensions is not new. In a recent report, President Johnson's Cabinet-level Committee on Public Policy and Private Pensions made the same recommendation; however, no action has been forthcoming. The benefits of such a plan to the individual executive and to the economy should be obvious. Plans of this type have worked in the academic community quite well for a number of years. Since many professors have the reserve fund fully vested in themselves, they have full freedom to change jobs at any stage of their career without forfeiting the contributions made by the academic institution to the pension fund. Application of these same principles to executive retirement plans would most likely have to originate at the national level through new legislation designed to ensure full vesting.

The need for a plan of this type is highlighted constantly. A large percentage of bank mergers are approved by the regulatory agencies on the grounds that the bank to be merged has management problems. The assumption is that this basic difficulty could not be overcome by hiring a new manager or group of managers. It is difficult for me to believe that this assumed (or real) problem in banking—or in industry—could not be solved by increasing the opportunities for managerial mobility and/or ownership. There is little doubt in my mind that a rather large, untapped supply of potential top management talent exists in the ranks of many large firms. Prime consideration should be given to the problem of providing these men with the opportunity to live up to their potential. As long as large firms are permitted to erect barriers to exit of management talent, as well as barriers to entry by other firms, the nation is missing an opportunity to improve its resource allocation mechanism. If the big business establishment does not voluntarily take the lead in increasing the potential freedom of movement of executive talent, it will be passing up an opportunity to improve its image with the younger generation.

Fiscal Policies Related to Growth

Fiscal policy in the United States is allegedly designed to aid in the accomplishment of the national economic goals of full employment, growth, and reasonable price stability. In addition, another very important national economic goal should receive priority—the preservation and promotion of a private enterprise, *competitive* economy. In testimony before a Senate subcommittee, I advocated the use of fiscal measures (as well as the increased enforcement of the antitrust laws) to curb merger activity and promote *internal* corporate growth. This proposal included the increased use of tax credits and accelerated depreciation allowances for investment in *new* plant and equipment. In addition, it was proposed that tax debits be applied to mergers as a "control" tax to raise the price of increased economic power.

The basic purpose of these proposals is to encourage more corporate investment in modern equipment and plants. It is precisely this type of investment which gives a firm and the economy the fruits of increased productivity. Investments of this type add new capacity not only to the firm making the investment but also to the industry and the nation as well. Contrast this situation with that of an acquisition of one firm by another. The acquiring firm invests by buying an existing firm and receives in return a bundle of assets and liabilities in various stages of obsolescence. The acquiring firm has instantly increased its capacity to produce, but the capacity of the industry has not been increased. The result is the transfer of *existing* industrial capacity (as well as patents, brand names, personnel, etc.) from one firm to another. Viewed from a macroeconomic level, the nation has not increased its capacity to produce. It must be remembered that the ultimate strength of any society or nation is its productive capacity. Viewed from a microeconomic level, the acquiring firm has increased its control over the assets in an industry, but only a part of the assets are new, modern facilities capable of productivity gains.

Serious consideration should also be given to changes in the tax laws that could affect the direction increased cash flows will take during periods of prolonged prosperity. Certainly the tax laws influence management and stockholder preferences concerning the dividend–retained earnings option. A number of firms have used retained earnings to purchase partial ownership in other firms (in addition to outright purchase, as has been discussed), thus performing part of the investment function for the shareholders. Existing tax laws encourage manager-investors to substitute their judgment for that of the owner-investors. In many cases, premiums above market price are paid by these manager-investors. Practices of this type should be abolished by law or corrected by new tax policies. The elimination of the capital gains tax, or a tax on retained earnings, or a sales tax to be paid by the acquiring firm based upon the value of the acquisition are other options which could be part of a new tax program.

Corporate Disclosure

One other factor which is not directly related to fiscal policy but which could help the functioning of the market is the need for improved corporate disclosure policies. Corporations should be required to file their financial statements in a deconsolidated manner. The costs of making such a change would be small, and the benefits would be many. Consolidated statements lump together the operating results of numerous divisions and/or subsidiaries, which results in a considerable amount of clouding of the firm's financial and operating picture. An outside, independent observer does not know what products, divisions, or subsidiaries are adding to dilution or contributing to earnings in these multiproduct and/or multidivisional firms.

Public Recognition: Relevant Performance Yardsticks

In order to aid in the proper alignment of objectives the development of relevant performance yardsticks should receive attention.[2] Emphasis on profitability to stockholders should receive special priority, and earnings indicators should be given renewed emphasis. Rather than devoting widespread attention to size indicators, as promulgated by *Fortune*, profit and price performance should be given special attention.[3] The development of performance measures relating quality, price, and cost reductions would help to shift the emphasis to profitability which has the widest public and private benefit. Some private source (such as the Academy of Management or some foundation) could make an important contribution through appropriate recognition of outstanding performance related to profit increases accompanied by relatively stable prices.

The Legal Environment: Policies to Improve Antitrust Effectiveness

Improvement in the legal environment should take the form of framing new and improved ground rules for the business game.[4]

As stated previously, the antitrust laws have not effectively prevented merger waves from occurring in this country. A major merger wave has followed the passage of each law designed to curb such activity. This is not to imply that the antitrust laws have not acted as a deterrent to merger activity. No doubt the United States is relatively better off for having the antitrust laws; however, their limitations and shortcomings should be recognized.

There is a belief in this country that the antitrust laws have caused considerable economic injury to certain firms—those which have been found guilty of violations and, to a lesser extent, those which have entered a plea of *nolo contendere* in a suit. It has yet to be proved whether this is true or not.[5] Damage to a firm or individual could result from fines imposed by the court or the adverse publicity generated by the legal action, as well as from the forced cessation and abandonment of the activity. If none of these sanctions is an effective deterrent, then better ones should be found.

The present system of fines is an economic relic of the past; the fines are not adequate to deter the large corporate giants of the modern industrial world from committing violations of the antitrust laws. Penalties for violations should be more severe, such as payment of one-third of corporate profits since the time of the violation or $100,000, whichever is higher. The stiffening of the economic penalties for antitrust violations should provide the public and the business community with an increased deterrent to the exercise and abuse of the considerable power possessed by many corporate giants.

In addition to stiffer penalties for the firms involved, the individual executives should be fined from one to three years' salary, depending upon the gravity of the crime, and no corporate reimbursement of an executive's fine should be permitted. If prison terms are suggested by the court, the "white-collar" convicts should not be kept on the corporate payroll while serving their time. Equal treatment should be considered for the executive superiors of a convicted subordinate if it can be proved that they had knowledge of his behavior. Consideration should also be given to extending the treble-damage provision to firms that plead *nolo contendere* in an antitrust case.

Strengthening the existing antitrust laws should be accompanied by new laws designed to curb abuses arising out of the newer conglomerate type of merger. Antireciprocity laws would be a valuable addition in the legal arsenal. Interlocking directorate provisions should be expanded to ban interlocking management practices among business firms as well as other abuses which result from modern mergers.

In summary, the public policy recommendations concerning merger activity are based upon the assumption that this nation desires a renewed and vigorous competitive, private enterprise system. Environmental changes in both the economic and legal spheres are necessary. Recognition of the impact of mergers upon the industrial structure as well as the *investment* aspects of these economic events is a vital component in designing adequate safeguards for the various publics affected. The growing preoccupation of professional managers with the "portfolio" type of conglomerate merger suggests that the SEC should assume a more vital role in future merger regulation. Perhaps this regulatory agency could improve upon the rather apathetic record made by the other government agencies traditionally associated with the merger problem.

The so-called synergy syndrome should be replaced by a more pragmatic and relevant measure of performance.[6] Since profit synergy appears to be serendipitous at best, stockholders should be protected from the natural desire of some professional managers to attempt to achieve the more certain sales synergy resulting from merger activity.[7]

NOTES

1 There is abundant evidence that merger waves occur during periods of prosperity. The best authority on the question of the relationship between business activity and mergers is Ralph L. Nelson. He examined the period 1895–1956 and found that "of the twelve clear cycles found in merger activity, eleven showed a definite timing relationship to fluctuations in

general business activity (reference cycles)." See his *Merger Movements in American Industry: 1895–1956,* Princeton, N.J.: Princeton University Press, 1959, p. 7.

[2] A leading investment advisory service examined 1,500 stocks for the period 1957–1967 and designated sixteen (or about 1 percent) as "Premier" Growth Stocks. The sixteen were firms that *(a)* increased their earnings per share every year since 1957 (or longer), *(b)* doubled their earnings (or better) between 1957 and 1962, and *(c)* doubled their earnings (or better) between 1962 and 1967. An examination of the data reveals that four of these firms (or 25 percent) were pure internal growth firms. Seven other firms did *not* engage in mergers in the first period, 1957–1962, and all had higher earnings in this period than during 1962–1967, when they did have one or more mergers. Thus, the earnings of these firms increased at a decreasing rate when they mixed merger with internal growth. Only one conglomerate firm was on the list. The outstanding performance of the pure internal growth firms is noteworthy. See "Will the Real Growth Stocks Please Stand Up?" *Value Line,* part 2, vol. 23, no. 14, p. 148*f.*, Jan. 19, 1968.

[3] A contributing factor to the preoccupation of large United States business firms with sales maximization is the emphasis given this factor by *Fortune* magazine. Their annual ranking has been based upon *sales* growth. Obviously, a more relevant factor should be utilized in a so-called capitalist economy.

[4] The unusual pattern of enforcement by government agencies has resulted in a considerable amount of confusion and uncertainty. Some actions are instituted against small firms, while other abuses go unchallenged. The enforcement pattern appears random and prompted by the desire to lull the public into the belief that their interests are being served by the laws and the agencies responsible for their enforcement.

[5] The preliminary results of a research project currently being conducted by Professor John W. Houck and me concerning the economic impact of antitrust cases upon the performance of firms indicates little (if any) economic damage to the firms involved.

[6] Doubt about the existence and realization of synergy is raised by a businessman who conducted a research project involving merging firms. See John Kitching, "Why Do Mergers Miscarry?" *Harvard Business Review,* vol. 45, no. 6, pp. 84–101, November–December, 1967.

[7] While this book was in press, an article entitled "Learning the Ways of Matchmaking" appeared in *Business Week*, Apr. 13, 1968, p. 127–132. The following statement appeared on p. 132: ". . . George Scharffenberger, former vice-president of Litton Industries and now president of City Investing Co., said some mergers are not made for economic reasons but to satisfy the ego of individual managers—or even to help an incompetent manager keep his job by confusing the stockholders." These candid remarks tend to support the "conspicuous investment" hypothesis discussed earlier. In the same article an officer of a large New York bank termed the current merger movement as "irrational." It may well be that decision making would be improved if stockholders were allowed to express their individual preferences related to policies concerning dividends and retained earnings.

13

Banking Regulation, Structure, and Performance and Public Policy

Public policy recommendations concerning the banking industry are obviously important and should be given serious consideration by legislators, regulatory authorities, and other interested individuals and groups. The subject is particularly important relative to banking since this industry contains highly organized and powerful trade associations at all levels, from the international scene to local areas. The lobbying activities of these groups are formidable, and the public does not have equal representation or protection in the various legislative halls and regulatory agencies. The need for the formulation and implementation of clearly defined *public* policies regarding bank mergers and branching activity is apparent. The recommendations advanced and discussed in this chapter are designed to provide a framework for improving the structure and performance of this quasi-competitive, quasi–public utility-type industry.

The Role of the Regulatory Agencies

Previously it was stated that commercial banking is a partially regulated industry; since there is an element of regulation, presumably commercial banking is conducted to promote and protect the public interest. This subject was treated in Chapters 10 and 11, and there is no need to be repetitive here; however, the basic forms of public control (as exercised by the various regulatory agencies) are related to entry, branching controls, bank merger activity, and deposit safety.

The regulatory agencies have approved the vast majority of merger applications submitted to them since the end of World War II. Nearly three thousand independent decision-making units in banking have been absorbed into the remaining approximately fourteen thousand commercial banks. The regulatory agencies have followed this obviously lenient policy toward bank mergers in the absence of any clear-cut evidence that these mergers have resulted in added benefits to the various publics interested in them. There is a noticeable lack of any type of consistent follow-up to determine whether benefits have accrued from approved mergers. No provision has been made for postmerger audits that would make this information available to the public and the regulators. These agencies have emphasized the alleged advantages to the public resulting from the creation of larger banking units, and they have given the competition factor little consideration. This has happened despite the recommendations of the various commissions which have studied banking and the rulings of the Supreme Court (which appears to favor a more competitive structure in banking).

Perhaps it is a natural, although not necessarily inevitable, development that regulators tend to associate themselves more with the problems of the regulatees than with those of other interested groups since they are in closer contact with these banking groups. The public is not as real to them as the bank managers or the representatives of their powerful trade associations. This fact should be recognized, and it is my opinion that the regulatory agencies should take steps to align themselves more with the public and less with bank management groups.

Protecting the public involves providing not only adequate safeguards for deposits but also safeguards on the various bank service charges, principally by making available adequate alternatives rather than by exercising price controls per se. In addition, the regulatory agencies should set forth clearly defined ground rules for competition so that bank managers will know the constraints imposed upon them as a quasi-public utility and thus be able to compete as vigorously as is practical and lawful within these constraints. These ground rules should include strict and severe penalties for individuals and institutions involved in any type of collusive practices which undermine what competition does exist in commercial banking.

Bank Mergers and Banking Alternatives

Each time a regulatory agency approves a bank merger, the number of alternatives (that is, the number of independent bank decision-making units) declines. Alternatives are important in banking, just as they are important in most spheres of economic activity, since they are a necessary component in providing the benefits of a marketplace. The preservation and expansion of banking alternatives would increase the likelihood of improved market performance in this basically oligopolistic industry. The most desirable type of competition, which would provide the most benefit to the public, is increased price competition for the various services offered by banks, particularly checking accounts (demand deposits) and loans.

Competition of this type (price) would benefit the public more than nonprice competition waged between a few large banks in terms, of advertising expenditures, marketing gimmicks, credit card plans, and so on. It appears reasonable to believe that many segments of the public (given the choice) would prefer lower or no service charges to fancy banking establishments, elaborate advertisements, esoteric dining facilities (available in some large banks), or a deluge of bank credit cards.[1] The opportunity for this trade-off seldom presents itself in concentrated markets.

It appears paradoxical that the regulatory agencies practically "rubber-stamp" every merger application and, at the same time, control entry into banking. Studies have shown that there is less entry into banking than there would be in the absence of regulation. Peltzman recognized this basic fact in his interesting study of bank entry; he said:

> The legal restrictions on entry into banking enacted into the Banking Act of 1935 have significantly reduced the entry rate into banking compared to what it would have been without these restrictions. In the period since 1935 the number of new banks formed each year has averaged .6 per cent of the existing number of banks. Had the legal restrictions been absent, we estimate that this annual average would have been twice as high—about 1.2 per cent of the existing number of banks. At a minimum, it would have been .9 per cent, still 50 per cent higher than the rate we have observed. Put simply in terms of the number of new banks, a total of 2,272 new banks have formed in the years 1936 through 1962—an average of 84 new banks per year. Had there been no legal restrictions on entry in this period, we estimate that about twice that number—approximately 4500 new banks—would have been formed. Regulation has thus caused there to be 2200 fewer banks than there would otherwise have been.[2]

During the same period used in Peltzman's study (1936–1962), there were 3,344 bank mergers—an annual average of 124 mergers—or about 48 percent more mergers than *new entry* with regulation. Using Peltzman's figures, the existence of regulation has resulted in an estimated 2,200 fewer banks than there otherwise would have been, and the rubber-stamp philosophy of the regulators concerning mergers has contributed another 3,344 casualties to the list of potential competitors in the banking industry. It is easy to see that if the bank regulatory agencies had a less stringent entry policy coupled with a strong no-merger policy, there would be many more banking alternatives in existence today. Even if the same entry restrictions were present, curtailment of bank mergers (except in the infrequent failing bank case) would have preserved well over three thousand additional alternatives. The loss of acquired banks as independent decision-making units is particularly severe since an established bank is generally in a stronger competitive position than a newly organized bank.

If we agree that the public will be better served by an increase in the competitiveness of banking markets, a two-pronged program is necessary to provide both facilities and a reasonable degree of competitiveness. First, the merger activity of those large banks which absorb the smaller banks constituting the "competitive fringe" in some markets should be curtailed. Second, new entry into highly concentrated markets, particularly the entry of independent decision-making units, should be promoted. This subject is discussed in more detail below.

Bank Structure and Service Charges

Most commercial banks provide a variety of services for their customers; however, the only major service which banks provide that is relatively unique is demand deposits (checking accounts). Hundred of millions of dollars a year are received by commercial banks in the form of revenues for providing this important service. Contrast this receipt of revenue for *demand* deposits with a relatively large expense item of banks related to the other type of deposit—the *time* deposit. Competition from other financial institutions has contributed to generally increasing rates paid by commercial bankers to their time depositors. At the same time, the prices charged by banks for demand deposits have also generally increased. This is a paradoxical situation, resulting from the fact that commercial banks have a monopoly on the provision of checking accounts and are in competition with other financial institutions for time deposits.

The regulatory agencies have generally neglected this important aspect of the *public* interest, that is, the pricing policies of commercial banks concerning checking accounts. As suggested earlier, the regulatory agencies can protect and promote the interest of demand depositors principally by providing adequate alternatives rather than by exercising price controls per se. By promoting new banking entry or the entry of other financial institutions into the demand deposit service area, alternatives can be increased in concentrated markets where there is evidence of high concentration and/or collusive pricing practices. Consideration should be given to allowing savings banks and savings and loan associations to enter this service area in highly concentrated banking markets or in other banking markets where there is some evidence of collusive pricing policies.

The regulatory agencies should think in terms of the public interest in the broad context regarding demand deposits. Since the check is such a standard form of payment, almost every family and many individuals are affected by policies related to demand deposits. The regulatory agencies have centered their activities upon reserve requirements and bank examination in order to increase the degree of *safety* of these deposits. There has been virtually no concern over the service charges on checking accounts which are paid by millions of families and individuals. Safety of deposits has been of paramount importance to the regulatory agencies, yet it is only one dimension of the problem. The legislative branch of government should also reconsider the ban on the payment of interest on demand deposits.

Another bit of evidence that the policies of the regulatory agencies are aligned more with the interests of the banking community than with the interests of the general public has to do with the *time* deposit problem. The regulators have responded to the commercial bankers' demands during the last few years that they be permitted to raise the rates paid on time deposits in order to improve their competitive position vis-à-vis the savings and loan associations and other financial institutions. The chief benefactors among the saving public have not been the majority of households and individuals in this country, but rather the few large depositors. Ready substitutes for time deposits at commercial banks are available to all segments of the savings public in the form of other savings institutions and instruments. However, the commercial banks have a monopoly on demand deposits, and there has been little evidence of a desire for price competition concerning these deposits, which are important to most households, individuals, and firms. The bank regulatory agencies should give attention and weight to this area of bank pricing in the absence of legislative approval for the payment of interest on this type of deposit.

An analysis of data presented in a research study by Frederick W. Bell and Neil B. Murphy (of the Federal Reserve Bank of Boston and the FDIC, respectively) indicates to me that it would be reasonable for bankers to eliminate service charges on demand deposits as long as they do not have to pay interest on them.[3] The Bell-Murphy study of bank costs and service charges related to checking accounts reveals that the average demand deposit balance for the ninety-two New England banks in the sample was $2,528 and the average marginal direct cost per account was $36.50, both on an annual basis. The study indicates that service charges approximately cover the costs and an additional net earnings per account of $90 is realized.

Bell and Murphy did not make a similar analysis of average marginal direct costs and net revenue for time deposits. However, if an equivalent deposit of $2,528 in a *time* deposit is assumed, the cost to the bank at 4 percent interest would be over $100, or slightly below the net earnings (adjusted for lower reserve requirements and eliminating the float) of about $110.[4] Thus, the net earnings per demand deposit account would be about $90, or about nine times higher than on an equivalent time deposit. Marginal costs on time deposits have also increased faster in recent years than on demand deposits, where new technology has helped to reduce costs. If interest had been paid on demand deposits, it is easy to demonstrate that the public would have benefited considerably since the interest received by the depositor would have been substantially higher than the marginal direct cost of serving the checking account.

Bank Mergers and Bank Management

Many bank mergers are approved by the regulatory agencies on the grounds that the management of the acquired bank is relatively weak or that there is a management succession problem. If the regulatory agencies were concerned about the "alternatives" problem, they could overcome this rather shallow rationalization in a number of pragmatic ways. Admittedly, some imaginative solutions and some ingenuity would be required in the process, but it is possible to mitigate the management deficiency problem.

The granting of insured loans to able and experienced banking executives who might wish to pursue the challenge of operating a banking institution of their own would be a first step. Consideration should be given to using the vast reserves of the FDIC for this purpose. In addition, executives in other fields with experience in marketing and finance should be encouraged to enter the banking industry. Since commercial banking is becoming more consumer-oriented and less commercially oriented, these executives should be able to make valuable contributions to the industry as well as to individual banks.

Because of the public service aspects of the industry, banking should also be in an excellent position to attract many young, intelligent, and idealistic people in the "new" generation. Increased recognition of this fact by graduate schools, in the form of a larger number of course offerings in the banking area, could contribute to this development and swell the ranks of potential banking executives and banking entrepreneurs.

Bank Branching and Bank Merger

Since the probabilities are high that branch banking laws will be liberalized in the future, the *type* of branching legislation to be considered in a state becomes an extremely important question. It has been demonstrated (in Chapter 11) that the merger alternative of branching not only may have a significant impact upon the performance of banks, but also may result in a grossly uneven distribution of benefits to the interested groups. The discussion in this section will be centered upon some possible alternatives which should be considered when formulating public policy regarding bank branching.

Liberalize Branching and Encourage Merger Activity

If branching is liberalized and the merger alternative encouraged in a state (as in Virginia), one should expect an accelerated pace toward a concentrated banking structure. In addition, this type of legislation encourages the payment of "premiums" by the acquiring bank, in its desire to penetrate new bank marketing areas. It appears that the major benefits accrue to the owners of the acquired bank since the charter (granted in the public interest) becomes a more valuable franchise.[5] While this may be a pragmatic method of gaining the support of existing charter holders, it appears to favor a small and select group in the state's population.

Liberalize Branching and Promote de Novo Branching instead of Mergers

When branching is liberalized and the *de novo* alternative is encouraged rather than merger (the opposite of the situation in Virginia), the public will gain banking alternatives and independent decision-making units. The importance of alternatives should not be minimized; as Governor Mitchell observed in his testimony before a congressional subcommittee: "Indeed, the most conclusive way of assuring that a community's convenience and needs will be met is by the maintenance of so many banking choices that the resulting competition among them will give customers all the opportunity they could wish to move from one bank to another in order to obtain whatever mix of services they desire."[6]

The promotion of legislation that would provide additional alternatives would be of particular benefit to citizens in the one-bank towns or cities or in any highly concentrated market. Again, Governor Mitchell recognized the advantage of this type of development when he said:

> It is sometimes said or implied that branches of large banks in small communities are unfair competition for local banks. But there are too many instances in which local banks have held their ground in growth and profitability to support a broad generalization along that line. As a practical matter, it may well be that the communities that are most blessed with banking facilities are those that possess a mixture of local banks and branches of larger institutions.[7]

The addition of a new, independent decision-making unit through entry by *de novo* branching may also improve pricing performance in a market. Some studies have implied that the higher the concentration level in a banking market, the higher will be the prices charged for the more important banking services.[8]

Some Legislative Proposals

The relaxing of branching restrictions (provided the citizens of a state demonstrate their approval, preferably through the voting privilege) could help stimulate banking competition if priority is given to *de novo* branching rather than the merger alternative. Information should be provided in branching applications about the expected rate of return (or some alternative measures of profitability, e.g., present value) for each branch.[9] The purpose of this is to reduce the rather natural desire of bank managers when branching to maximize deposits rather than profitability to existing stockholders.[10] Another provision could be the requirement of a public announcement concerning a proposed branch, with priority for that location given to qualified new entrants. This would tend to increase the number of independent decision-making units as well as banking alternatives.

Perhaps the most important phase in the battle to encourage not only more banking competition but also more banking alternatives for the public will be waged at the state level. State branching laws have a significant effect upon the type of banking structure that will evolve in any given state and in the nation as a whole.

Ideally, the citizens of a state should have a more direct voice in the type of banking laws that are passed in that state;[11] however, because of the extensive lobbying activities of the various bank trade associations, there is little chance that they will have such a direct vote. In the absence of the direct voting privilege, it is recommended that those state legislators who are concerned about the optimum banking structure in their state give serious consideration to the various feasible alternatives. The welfare of special interest groups should naturally be subordinate to the public interest. A unique opportunity exists for action at the state and local levels which seldom presents itself in a period of growing central government. The role that a state can play in determining the kind of banking structure it will have in the future has not been sufficiently recognized. Indifference to the problem at the state level can be corrected by Federal legislation; however, this should come only after the states display an unwillingness to cooperate in the formation of a competitive banking structure operating in the public interest.

The public policy recommendations in the last two chapters have been based upon the assumption that this country would actually like to try a deconcentrated, competitive, private enterprise system. We must examine the current economic events and be alert to changes which will improve the allocation of resources during periods of relative prosperity. The growth of economic power centers, the retardation of growth in new productive capacity, the emergence of "portfolio" conglomerates which are purchasing control in addition to other assets, the structure of banking, and the suggested misalignment of interests between many professional managers and stockholders are among the issues needing attention. Mergers contribute to each of these issues since they are multifaceted economic events of considerable dimension and magnitude.[12] Alternatives exist, and the weighting which they receive will, in the final analysis, depend upon the reactions of individuals in management, government, academia, and other spheres of life.

NOTES

[1] Commercial banks are becoming increasingly involved in consumer credit, and the bank credit card phenomenon is growing rapidly. The most interesting local bank credit card battle was waged in Pittsburgh, beginning in the summer of 1965. Rather than compete directly, bankers in the Chicago

area instituted the Midwest Bank Card plan during the fall of 1966. The clearinghouse approach is used, although each bank in the plan retains a separate identifying subtitle. The hurried introduction of this plan caused many problems, including the mailing of cards to children and to persons who were bad credit risks, etc. It also took place during a period of tight money, and its development contributed to the reluctance of Chicago bankers to lower the prime rate during the spring of 1967 since funds were being shifted to this sector of the banks' business. As these bank credit card plans attain regional or national use, they will cause additional problems for the Federal Reserve System since the sales slips will be processed by its already overburdened check-clearing facility.

[2] Sam Peltzman, "Entry in Commerical Banking," *The Journal of Law and Economics,* vol. 8, p. 48, October, 1965.

[3] Frederick W. Bell and Neil B. Murphy, "Bank Service Charges and Costs," *The National Banking Review,* vol. 4, no. 4, pp. 449–457, June, 1967. Unfortunately the authors did not distinguish between business and consumer accounts in their study, which is revealed by the rather high average balance. Business firms generally pay lower service charges and write many more checks than consumers and are consequently partially subsidized by consumer service charges under existing banking arrangements.

[4] *Ibid.* See table 4 on p. 456. It appears that Bell and Murphy made a minor error since they use a balance of $2,538 in this table and $2,528 in the other tables without explaining the difference. The net earnings per account in the table is determined by subtracting the float (8.7 percent) from the average balance ($2,538 — $221), or a collected balance of $2,317. The required reserves (12 percent) and excess reserves (1.9 percent), or a total of $284, were subtracted from the collected balance of $2,317, leaving a loanable balance of $2,033. The portfolio income from the loanable balance was based on earnings of 5.5 percent per year, or $112, less the total cost of processing loans and security investments of $22, resulting in net earnings per demand deposit account of $90. Time deposit earnings would be higher since the loanable balance is calculated without considering the float and with lower reserve requirements, which adds about $20 to total earnings. The *net* earnings for a bank will be higher for a demand deposit account in contrast to an equivalent amount of time deposits since service charges virtually cover all marginal costs while interest paid on time deposits is a major cost and not recovered through service charges.

[5] Since entry is restricted in banking, the holders of bank charters are given a privileged position in the public interest. Firms in regulated industries such as banking, transportation, communications, etc., should not be expected to have the same freedoms prevalent in the unregulated segments of the economy. This fact is overlooked occasionally, as indicated by the following statement by a congressman, which appeared in *Conflict of Federal and State Laws, Hearings of the Committee on Banking and Currency,* 88th Cong., 1st Sess., 1963, p. 44: "Suppose I own a bank, I am an old man and I am going to die and I do not want my family to have bank stock, so I go to you, another bank and say, Will you buy my bank? That is a free seller and a free buyer and I would think that no one could interfere with that."

[6] Board of Governors of the Federal Reserve System, *Federal Reserve Bulletin,* September, 1965, p. 1250. While the Governor admitted that this may not be

practical, the closer we come to this objective (without endangering the safety of deposits), the more we will increase the welfare of the public.

[7] George W. Mitchell, "Protecting the Public Interest in Bank Mergers," unpublished remarks at the annual convention of the Pennsylvania Bankers Association, Atlantic City, N.J., May 24, 1965.

[8] As reported in his article entitled "Bank Market Structure and Performance: The Evidence from Iowa," *Southern Economic Journal,* vol. 32, no. 4, pp. 429–439, April, 1966, George G. Kaufman found poorer performance to be associated with increased concentration in his study of Iowa banks. Franklin R. Edwards found that there is a positive relationship between the degree of banking concentration and interest rates charged on short-term business loans, but that average loan rates are affected very little. They do result in increased costs to some segments of the public. These results were published in Edwards's article "The Banking Competition Controversy," *National Banking Review,* vol. 3, no. 1, pp. 1–34, September, 1965. Theodore G. Flechsig found no significant difference in interest rates charged in his study, *Banking Market Structure and Performance in Metropolitan Areas: A Statistical Study of Factors Affecting Rates on Bank Loans,* Washington, D.C.: Board of Governors of the Federal Reserve System, 1965. To date, no one has discovered lower rates in concentrated markets. The public in concentrated markets has an additional cost in the form of less choice without the benefit of lower prices. George J. Benston found that total demand deposit operations expenses would be higher if five unit banks were to merge to form a bank with four branches: see his article entitled "Branch Banking and Economies of Scale," *Journal of Finance,* vol. 20, no. 2, pp. 312–331, May, 1965.

[9] Expected rate of return for proposed branches is discussed in an article by Eugene E. Carter and Kalman J. Cohen, "The Use of Simulation in Selecting Branch Banks," *Industrial Management Review,* vol. 8, no. 2, pp. 55–69, Spring, 1967.

[10] When submitting merger proposals to the Interstate Commerce Commission, many railroads include detailed statements concerning anticipated benefits due to cost reductions that are expected to result from a proposed merger. Reduced service levels produce much of the savings. The ICC has not made adequate use of the data in examining postmerger results.

[11] After this chapter was written, some legislators in Illinois announced their intention to attempt to put the branching question on the ballot for the November, 1968, election. A similar proposal has been defeated in the Legislature in the past.

[12] While this book was in press *The Wall Street Journal* reported that the record pace of merger activity continued in the first quarter of 1968. See "Record Pace of Mergers Continued in 1st Period, Bids Near 4-year High," Apr. 10, 1968, p. 21. The report concerned a survey by W. T. Grimm & Co. which shows there were 815 mergers in the first quarter of 1968, a 24 percent increase over a similar period in 1967. Cash transactions increased during this period in response to the lower stock prices earlier in the year. The average price-earnings ratio paid during the quarter was 20.5, the highest since 1964. Thus, the current wave rolls on virtually unabated.

Index

Index